Translated Texts for Historians

This series is designed to meet the needs of students of ancient and medieval history and others who wish to broaden their study by reading source material, but whose knowledge of Latin or Greek is not sufficient to allow them to do so in the original languages. Many important Late Imperial and Dark Age texts are currently unavailable in translation and it is hoped that TTH will help to fill this gap and to complement the secondary literature in English which already exists. The series relates principally to the period 300-800 AD and includes Late Imperial, Greek, Byzantine and Syriac texts as well as source books illustrating a particular period or theme. Each volume is a self-contained scholarly translation with an introductory essay on the text and its author and notes on the text indicating major problems of interpretation, including textual difficulties.

Front cover: Detail of the Ezra miniature (Codex Amiatinus, fol. V), drawn by Gail Heather. Book titles after R. L. S. Bruce-Mitford, 'The Art of the Codex Amiatinus', *Journal of the Royal Archaeological Association*, 32 (1969), p. 10.

A complete list of titles in the Translated Texts for Historians series is available on request The most recently published are shown below.

Pseudo-Dionysius of Tel-Mahre: *Chronicle*, Part III
Translated with notes and introduction by WITOLD WITAKOWSKI
Volume 22: 192pp., 1995, ISBN 0-85323-760-3

Venantius Fortunatus: Personal and Political Poems
Translated with notes and introduction by JUDITH GEORGE
Volume 23: 192pp., 1995, ISBN 0-85323-179-6

Donatist Martyr Stories: The Church in Conflict in Roman North Africa
Translated with notes and introduction by MAUREEN A. TILLEY
Volume 24: 144pp., 1996, ISBN 0 85323 931 2

Hilary of Poitiers: Conflicts of Conscience and Law in the Fourth-Century Church
Translated with introduction and notes by LIONEL R. WICKHAM
Volume 25: 176pp., 1997, ISBN 0-85323-572-4

Lives of the Visigothic Fathers
Translated and edited by A. T. FEAR
Volume 26: 208pp., 1997, ISBN 0-85323-582-1

Optatus: Against the Donatists
Translated and edited by MARK EDWARDS
Volume 27: 220pp., 1997, ISBN 0-85323-752-2

Bede: A Biblical Miscellany
Translated with notes and introduction by W. TRENT FOLEY and ARTHUR G. HOLDER
Volume 28: 240pp., 1999, ISBN 0-85323-683-6

Bede: The Reckoning of Time
Translated with introduction, notes and commentary by FAITH WALLIS
Volume 29: 352pp., 1999, ISBN 0-85323-693-3

Ruricius of Limoges and Friends: A Collection of Letters from Visigothic Gaul
Translated with notes and introduction by RALPH W. MATHISEN
Volume 30: 272pp., 1999, ISBN 0-85323-703-4

For full information, please write to the following:
All countries, except the USA and Canada: Liverpool University Press, Senate House, Abercromby Square, Liverpool, L69 3BX, UK (*Tel* +44-[0]151-7942233, *Fax* +44-[0]151-794 2235, *Email* J.M.Smith@ liv.ac.uk, http://www.liverpool-unipress.co.uk).
USA and Canada: University of Pennsylvania Press, 4200 Pine Street, Philadelphia, PA 19104-6097, USA (*Tel* +1-215-898-6264,*Fax* +1-215-898-0404).

Translated Texts for Historians
Volume 28

Bede:
A Biblical Miscellany

Translated with notes and introduction by
W. TRENT FOLEY and ARTHUR G. HOLDER

Liverpool
University
Press

First published 1999 by
LIVERPOOL UNIVERSITY PRESS
Senate House
Abercromby Square
Liverpool
L69 3BX

British Library Cataloguing-in-Publication Data
A British Library CIP Record is available
ISBN 0-85323-683-6

Printed in the European Union by
Page Bros, Norwich, England

CONTENTS

ACKNOWLEDGEMENTS

In a collaborative work, indebtedness to others seems more than merely doubled. Margaret Gibson began as our editor before her death in 1994. She approached her work on this volume with what seemed to be an inexhaustible energy that was matched only by her alacrity. Carlotta Dionisotti ably picked up where Margaret left off, making many helpful suggestions on the translations and seeing our work through to its end. A special thanks goes to Gillian Clark who, through the wonders of e-mail, served tirelessly as our messenger to those in Britain with whom we needed to keep in more immediate touch. Her efforts greatly expedited the completion of this project.

Thanks to the generosity of the Conant Fund of the Board for Theological Education of the Episcopal Church and of Dean Robert C. Williams and the Committee for Study and Research at Davidson College, the two translators were allowed to collaborate together twice during the course of this project, once in Greenville, South Carolina and once in Berkeley, California.

Brepols Publishers kindly granted permission to translate three texts from *Corpus Christianorum Series Latina*. Sister Benedicta Ward, S.L.G., contributed the preface, which is a revised version of the introductory chapter from her own book *The Venerable Bede*. During the late stages of our project, Paul Meyvaert graciously offered us advance copies of two of his articles, helped more generally to put us in touch with both people and sources that were relevant to our project, and expertly advised us on a host of other matters. Michael Gorman helped enormously, both in reading over portions of the *Thirty Questions* translation and in making his new and badly needed edition of Bede's *On Eight Questions* available to us in advance of its publication. Thanks also are due to M. R. Ritley, who ably prepared the camera-ready manuscript.

W. T. F. & A. G. H.

*   *   *   *

I would like to thank the staff of Davidson College's Little Library—especially Sharon Byrd, Joe Gutekanst, Suzy Yoder and Jean Coates—for their untiring assistance. Karl Plank has always proved a steady friend and wonderful counselor in all things scholarly, including this project. Hearty thanks are also due to the Holder family, the staff at the Church Divinity School of the Pacific, and Frank Albinder, who made my week of research and collaboration in Berkeley as pleasurable as it was fruitful. Finally, I would like to thank my wife, Pam Kelley, and my children, Jackson and Emma, whose presence happily distracted and refreshed me throughout the course of this project.

W. T. F.

*   *   *   *

For their assistance with the translation and interpretation of Bede's letter *On What Isaiah Says*, I am grateful to Linda Clader, Jane Menten, Robert Rennicks, Katherine McFadden, and Anthony Davis. My research assistants Thomasin Alyxander and Teresa Vosper helped track down many elusive references. As always, my greatest debt is to Sarah and Charles, who cheerfully continue to make room in our household for the Venerable Bede.

A. G. H.

ABBREVIATIONS

ACW	*Ancient Christian Writers*
CCSL	*Corpus Christianorum, Series Latina*
CSEL	*Corpus Scriptorum Ecclesiasticorum Latinorum*
D-R	Douai-Rheims Bible
FOTC	*Fathers of the Church*
GCS	*Die Griechischen christlichen Schriftsteller*
JB	Jerusalem Bible
KJV	King James Version
LCL	*Loeb Classical Library*
LXX	Greek Old Testament (= the Septuagint)
MGH AA	*Monumenta Germaniae Historica, Auctores Antiquissimi*
MGH SRM	*Monumenta Germaniae Historica, Scriptores Rerum Merovingicarum*
MGH Epp.	*Monumenta Germaniae Historica, Epistolae*
NEB	New English Bible
NOAB	*The New Oxford Annotated Bible with the Apocrypha*
NPNF	*Nicene and Post-Nicene Fathers*
NRSV	New Revised Standard Version
PL	*Patrologia Latina*
REB	Revised English Bible
SC	*Sources Chrétiennes*
TTH	*Translated Texts for Historians*
Vulg.	Latin Vulgate Bible
WHA	*The Westminster Historical Atlas of the Bible*, ed. G. E. Wright

PREFACE

The Venerable Bede, the most learned man of his age, the father of English history, and the only Englishman to be acknowledged as a doctor of the church, can hardly be traced through contemporary records. He left no personal account of himself and no contemporary celebrated him with either a hagiography or a biography; he appears in no chronicles of the times, nor did he take any part in the government of the abbey or the church of which he was a member all his life; in no instance can his mark be detected in official documents of any kind. And yet it is possible to know Bede more intimately than any other man of his time through the impress of his character conveyed in his voluminous writings.

The sparse 'facts' of his life he himself summarized at the end of his *Ecclesiastical History of the English People*, following an example set by Gregory of Tours:[1]

> I, Bede, servant of God and priest of the monastery of St. Peter and St. Paul which is at Wearmouth and Jarrow, have, with the help of God and to the best of my ability, put together this account of the Church of Britain and of the English people in particular, gleaned either from ancient documents or from tradition or from my own knowledge. I was born in the territory of this monastery. When I was seven years of age I was, by the care of my kinsmen, put into the charge of the reverend abbot Benedict and then of Ceolfrith, to be educated. From then on I spent all my life in this monastery, applying myself entirely to the study of the Scriptures; and amid the observance of the discipline of the Rule and the daily task of singing in the church, it has always been my delight to learn or to teach or to write. At the age of nineteen I was ordained deacon and at the age of thirty priest, both times through the ministration of the reverend Bishop John on the direction of Abbot Ceolfrith. From the time I became priest until the fifty-ninth year of my life I have made

1 Gregory of Tours *Hist. franc.* 10, 31 (*MGH SRM* 1: 448-9; transl. Thorpe, 602-4)

> it my business, for my own benefit and that of my brothers, to make brief extracts from the works of the venerable fathers on the holy Scriptures, or to add notes of my own to clarify their sense and interpretation.[1]

This summary of a life is what a monk should write; what else of importance was there to say, apart from the great moments of reception into the monastery, ordination as cleric, the ordinary round of daily life until death? Based on the ideals of monasticism it may be, but that is not to say that it is anything other than a true reflection of Bede's life also. The passage is of a piece with Bede's other writings, and in them all there is a quality of concentrated attention to his life as a monk and unaffected delight in it. There was, however, a different strand of colour woven into the plain cloth of Bede's monastic life: he was a writer and a well-known one at that; he followed his brief summary of his life with a long and carefully exact list of his own writings.

It is possible to fill in some details about the circumstances of Bede's life within the framework that he himself set out. From the date he gave for the completion of *The Ecclesiastical History of the English People* it seems that he was born in 673.[2] His name was an unusual one, though it was also that of a monk at Lindisfarne. He identified himself with the 'English people' (*gens anglorum*) in his treatise *On the Reckoning of Times*, when he gave a description of the names the English gave to the months of the year.

> It does not seem to be appropriate that when giving an account of the way other races arrange the year, I should be silent about the observances of my own race.[3]

Almost certainly his kinsmen had been both English and Christian, since they offered the boy to a monastery, presumably after his parents' death. Bede wanted to be identified as English, but only as an English Christian and he ends his account of the English months with

> Thanks be to you, good Jesus, for turning us from these vanities and granting us to offer you the sacrifice of praise.[4]

1 Bede *Hist. eccl.* 5, 24 (ed. and transl. Colgrave and Mynors, 567-71)

2 For discussion of the dates of Bede's life, see Plummer (1896), 1: xi, n. 1. 'Usque ad annum aetatis meae LVIII' has been understood to mean either 'until' or 'in' the fifty-ninth year of his age, giving either 672 or 673.

3 Bede *De temp. rat.* 15 (*CCSL* 123B: 329, 2-4)

4 Ibid., 332, 50-2

Bede never mentioned his own family elsewhere in his writings, a freedom from ties of kin which, though certainly part of monastic ideology, might also suggest that his birth was not noble, since he was always ready to mention the noble rank of others, even though it was to say, 'noble by birth but more noble by grace'. 'Home' for Bede was his monastery and when at the age of fifty-nine he wrote about his life, he gave as the place of his birth 'the lands of the monastery', although at that time the monastery had not yet been founded.

Bede's love for the abbots of the twin Northumbrian monasteries at Wearmouth and Jarrow is patent on every page of his *History of the Abbots* and it is probable that this affection was based not only on his place as a child of the cloister at Wearmouth under its founder, Benedict Biscop (628-89), but also on his survival in the foundation made from Wearmouth at Jarrow with its first abbot, Ceolfrith (d. 716), through an outbreak of plague. In the anonymous *Life of Ceolfrith* there is an account of the terrible plague of 686 which struck the north of England with particular violence and reduced the number of monks at the new and fragile foundation at Jarrow to the abbot, Ceolfrith, and a boy of the monastic school; others survived but none who were part of the monastic choir:

> In the monastery over which Ceolfrith presided, all who could read or preach or recite the antiphons were swept away, except the abbot himself and one little lad nourished and taught by him, who is now a priest of the same monastery and both by word of mouth and by writing commends to all who wish to know them the abbot's worthy deeds. And the abbot, sad at heart because of this visitation, ordained that, contrary to their former rite, they should, except at vespers and matins, recite their psalms without antiphons. And when this had been done with many tears and lamentations on his part for the space of a week, he could not bear it any longer, but decreed that the psalms with their antiphons should be restored to their order according to the regular course; and by means of himself and the aforesaid boy, he carried out with no little labour that which he had decreed, until he could either train them himself or procure from elsewhere men able to take part in the divine service.[1]

1 *Vit. Ceol.* 14 (ed. Plummer, 1: 393; transl. Boutflower, 65)

This description of a 'little lad nourished and taught by him' as well as 'one who by writing commends to those who wish to know them the abbot's worthy deeds' fits Bede very well. Moreover, if this was not Bede, then what happened to him during the total destruction caused in his monastery by the plague? If this was indeed Bede, such a traumatic event surely accentuated both his isolation and his dependence upon Ceolfrith, as upon a father, the sole surviving plank in a stormy sea. When Ceolfrith later finally left Jarrow to go to Rome to end his days among the saints of the early church, Bede seems to have experienced a crisis in his life. He wrote two accounts of the departure: the official account, in the *History of the Abbots*, is controlled and edifying and entirely impersonal.[1] The second, which was written first, in the days immediately after the event, is in the letter accompanying his *Commentary on Samuel*. It is very revealing, both about Bede's attachment to Ceolfrith, as shown by the emotional impact of this separation on Bede, and also about the absorption in his writing which made him oblivious to this event until it was happening:

> Having completed the third book of the *Commentary on Samuel*, I thought I would rest awhile and, after recovering in that way my delight in study and writing, proceed to take in hand the fourth. But that rest—if sudden anguish of mind can be called rest—has turned out much longer than I had intended, owing to the sudden change of circumstances brought about by the departure of my most reverend abbot, who after long devotion to the care of his monastery, suddenly determined to go to Rome and to breathe his last breath amid the localities sanctified by the bodies of the blessed apostles and martyrs of Christ, thus causing no little consternation to those committed to his charge, the greater because it was unexpected. He removed the ancient Moses, appointed Joshua to the leadership and ordained Eleazer to the priesthood in the place of the father Aaron. So in the place of the aged Ceolfrith who was hastening to the threshold of the apostles, he ordained the young Hwaetberht who by his love and his zeal for purity had long since won for himself the name of Eusebius and after the brethren had elected him, he confirmed the appointment by his blessing brought by your ministry, dearest bishop. And now with the return of quieter times, I have again leisure and delight for

1 Bede *Hist. abb.* 16-17 (ed. Plummer, 1: 380-2)

> searching out the wondrous things of the Scriptures carefully and with my whole soul.[1]

While this passage illustrates Bede's attachment to Ceolfrith, it also provides insight into Bede as a writer and monk. Absorbed in the steady round of his life in the monastery, he found the departure of Ceolfrith 'sudden' and 'unexpected', whereas in the *Life of Ceolfrith* it is clear that the journey was an open secret and had been planned for some time.[2] Above all it underlines Bede's priorities: the limitations of his life were of choice as much as of rule. Other monks travelled widely, besides Ceolfrith. This letter itself, for instance, was addressed to Bishop Acca of Hexham (700-32), another much travelled monastic friend. Bede was shocked by the departure of Ceolfrith but he showed no inclination to follow him; his concern was to regain the freedom of mind necessary for study in the monastery. Nor did he ever travel widely. Benedict Biscop, his first abbot, was renowned for his journeys abroad and Bede must have often heard of the wonders of the Mediterranean world as well as seen the marvels brought back from it, but he never went there himself. With all his interest in the archives of the papacy, it was the priest Nothhelm who checked them for him.[3] His only visits of which there is any record were local and austerely connected with his writing: he went to Lindisfarne once at least in connection with his *Life of St. Cuthbert*;[4] he visited York at the end of his life to talk with his former pupil Egbert about contemporary church affairs;[5] and he visited the monastery of a certain abbot, Wictred, where he discussed some of the intricacies of computation.[6] In a homily on Benedict Biscop, he talked about 'we who remain within the monastery walls', with gratitude that the travels of others made this possible:

> He (Benedict Biscop) worked so zealously that we are freed from the need to labour in this way; he journeyed so many times to places across the sea, that we, abounding in all the resources of spiritual knowledge, can as a result be at peace within the cloisters of the monastery, with secure freedom to serve Christ.[7]

This 'peace' was Bede's choice even though it was not all gain, and at the end of the preface to his commentary on the *Song of Songs* he wrote

1 Bede *In Sam.* 4 (*CCSL* 119: 212, 1-28; transl. Plummer 1: xv-xvi)
2 *Vit. Ceol.* 21-23 (ed. Plummer, 1: 395-6)
3 Bede *Hist. eccl.* praefatio (ed. and transl. Colgrave and Mynors, 4)
4 *Vit. Cuth. pros.* prologus (ed. and transl. Colgrave, 145)
5 *Ep. Ecg.* (ed. Plummer, 1: 405-23)
6 Bede *Ep. Wict.* (*CCSL* 123C: 635-42)
7 *Hom.* 1, 13 (*CCSL* 122: 93, 185 - 94, 190)

about the dangers of misunderstanding for those who, like himself, were not personally in touch with the wider world of Christian culture, isolated in the distant island of Britain.[1] For Bede, unlike many of his Northumbrian contemporaries, the centre of the world of the mind was Rome; but his body remained in his cell, above all among books and parchments. This 'single eye' of the monk-writer, so clearly a child of the cloister, may well have been the reason for his lack of involvement in any of the practical affairs of his monastery.

Bede's concentration on the life of the mind depended upon three things besides his own abilities: his teachers, the books available to him, and contact with others—teachers, colleagues and pupils—with whom he could share his thoughts, whether in word or in writing. His teachers must have included the great men of Wearmouth when he first went there, and he described Ceolfrith and his successor Hwaetbaerht of Wearmouth as, in their different ways, men of deep learning who had earned his respect and gratitude.[2] He must have learned, whether directly or indirectly, about the world outside the cloister from his first abbot, Benedict Biscop, the much travelled ex-thane of king Oswy, who founded the two monasteries and received Bede as a child.[3] Another learned monk of Wearmouth was Sigfrid, who died as abbot when Bede was fifteen, whom he described as 'amply learned in knowledge of the Scriptures'.[4] His affection for Ceolfrith may well have gone along with instruction by him as a child, especially in Latin, the basis of all Bede's scholarship. He said in a letter to Plegwine, a monk of Hexham, that he was instructed early in chronological studies, and perhaps this branch of learning was also given him by Ceolfrith.[5] In 680, the year in which Bede came to the abbey, another great teacher arrived there: John the archchanter of St. Peter's in Rome came with Benedict Biscop in order to teach chant at Wearmouth.[6] He was the teacher whom Bede was eventually to follow as master of the monastic school. Bede referred also to Trumberht, an Irish monk of Lastingham, as one of his teachers:

1 *In Cant.* praefatio (*CCSL* 119B: 180, 508-14)

2 *Hist. abb.* 15 and 18 (ed. Plummer, 1: 379-80, 382-3); *Hist. eccl.* 5.21 (ed. and transl. Colgrave and Mynors, 532)

3 Bede *Hom.* 1, 13 (*CCSL* 122: 91, 93 - 94, 210); *Hist. abb.* 1-7 (ed. Plummer, 1: 364-71)

4 *Hist. abb.* 10 (ed. Plummer, 1: 374; transl. Boutflower, 195)

5 *Ep. Pleg.* (*CCSL* 123C: 617-26)

6 *Hist. abb.* 6 (ed. Plummer, 1: 369) and *Hist. eccl.* 4, 18 (ed. and transl. Colgrave and Mynors, 388)

> one of his (Chad's) brothers named Trumberht, a monk educated in his monastery . . . and one of those who taught me the Scriptures.[1]

Chad, bishop of the Mercians (d. 672), was described by Bede with affection and veneration.[2] He had been trained in the Scriptures in Ireland and had founded the monastery of Lastingham, where Trumberht, who taught Bede the Scriptures, was educated. This fact may have contributed to Bede's admiration for the Irish and his anxiety about their views on the dating of Easter. Lastly, Bede was ordained both deacon and priest by the saintly John of Beverley, whose miracles he recorded;[3] perhaps this bishop, who had been trained both by Theodore of Canterbury (d. 690) and Hilda of Whitby (614-80) exercised some influence also on Bede.

What did they teach him? Latin certainly, and later Bede learned Greek, perhaps under the influence of the Greek Theodore of Tarsus, archbishop of Canterbury (668-90), and his learned companion the African Hadrian, of whom Bede wrote admiringly, 'Both of them were extremely learned in sacred and secular literature'; he added, 'some of their students still survive who know Latin and Greek as well as their native tongue.'[4] Their school in Kent seems to have influenced the education Bede received at Jarrow: indeed, his own writings correspond to the list he gives of subjects taught at Canterbury: 'the books of holy Scripture, the arts of metre, astronomy, and ecclesiastical computation'.[5] Both Albinus, the successor of Hadrian as abbot of the monastery of St. Peter and St. Paul (later known as St. Augustine's), whom Bede knew well, and a certain Tobias are mentioned by Bede as pupils in that school of learning and therefore competent in Greek.[6] One book at least survives which was almost certainly used by Bede: it is a copy of the Acts of the Apostles, written in double columns with the Greek text on one side and a translation into Latin on the other.[7] The curriculum at Wearmouth and Jarrow was perhaps close to that outlined by Bede's contemporary Aldhelm of Malmesbury (639-709), who said that when he studied at Canterbury under Theodore and Hadrian, in addition to excellent instruction in Latin and Greek, he learned Roman law, methods

1 *Hist. eccl.* 4, 3 (ed. and transl. Colgrave and Mynors, 342)
2 Ibid., 336-46
3 Ibid., 5, 2 (ed. and transl. Colgrave and Mynors, 456-72)
4 Ibid., 4, 2 (ed. and transl. Colgrave and Mynors, 334)
5 Ibid. See Lapidge (1995) passim.
6 *Hist. eccl.* 5, 8 and 5, 20 (ed. and transl. Colgrave and Mynors, 474 and 530)
7 Oxford, Bodleian Library, MS Laud graec. 35.

of combining chant and verse and other poetic arts, mathematical calculation, and the zodiac.[1]

The necessary tools for instruction by such masters were books; they were not only the source but also the aim of such learning. The books Bede used came to him at first through Benedict Biscop, whose journeys to the Mediterranean gave his monasteries a library of unique value, filled above all with copies of the text of the Bible and commentaries on many of its books. Bede says Ceolfrith doubled the number of volumes the library contained. There is no library-list surviving from either Wearmouth or Jarrow and the volumes are long since dispersed; it is only possible to discover what books Bede read through his own writings. Most of the books Bede used were in his own monastery, while others he no doubt borrowed from the libraries which were being built up at Canterbury, Hexham and York. He knew a variety of texts of the Bible: the Old Latin versions, Jerome's Vulgate, parts of the Septuagint, and he frequently discussed the textual problems they presented. It is possible, indeed probable, that his knowledge in this area was utilized for the production of three great Bibles, one of which, the *Codex Amiatinus*, still provides one of the best early Latin texts of the Scriptures.[2] Through the Office, he was well acquainted with the old Roman psalter, which had remained in liturgical use long after Jerome's revised version of the other books of the Bible had become popular.

Along with the Bible, Bede read commentaries on the Scriptures. He was the first to name Augustine, Ambrose, Jerome and Gregory as the four great fathers of the church and their commentaries provided his main source for Biblical exegesis. The twin libraries at Wearmouth-Jarrow probably contained also a number of early grammatical works, some books of Isidore's *Etymologies*, at least parts of Pliny's *Natural History* and many works of the early Christian poets, all of whom Bede used in teaching. The histories at his disposal included Eusebius' *Ecclesiastical History* in the version by Rufinus, several chronicles, including Jerome's translation of the *Chronicle* by Eusebius, Jerome's *On Illustrious Men*, and works by Josephus, Orosius, Gildas, Cassiodorus, and Gregory of Tours. For Biblical commentaries, he

1 Aldhelm *Ep.* 1 (*MGH AA* 15: 476-7)

2 MS Amiatinus 1, is in the Biblioteca Laurenziana in Florence. Fragments survive of one of the other two bibles made at Jarrow: a. The Greenwell Leaf, British Library Add. MS 37777; b. The Middleton Fragments, British Library Add. MS 45025, ten folios with fragments from the third and fourth Books of Kings; c. The Bankes Leaf, National Trust, Kingston Lacy, Dorset, on loan to the British Library as Loan MS 81, from Ecclesiasticus. All are written in the fine uncial script perfected at Jarrow which is described in Lowe (1960), 8-13.

had to hand many works by Augustine, Ambrose, Jerome and Gregory the Great, and others by Origen (in the Latin version of Rufinus), Cassiodorus, Hilary, and Cyprian.[1]

For books specifically about monastic affairs, it seems that Bede knew the *Rule of St. Benedict*, though how far the daily conduct of his life was regulated by this text is by no means clear. There are several passages in his works which show a deep appreciation of the *Rule of St. Benedict*, but it would be anachronistic to suppose that the monastery at Jarrow in any sense 'followed' St. Benedict's *Rule*: the life of the brothers was lived in obedience to Christ through the guidance of the abbot, and while Benedict Biscop knew the *Rule of St. Benedict*, he drew upon many other ancient rules as well as personal observation and advice gained during his travels for the organisation of the life in his monasteries, all being modified and adapted to existing conditions in Northumbria and among new Christians. The *Rule of St. Benedict* was for Bede both more and less than has sometimes been claimed: it was not a 'rule' in the sense of exclusive regulations for a code of behaviour, but it was, perhaps, a 'rule' in the sense of a greatly esteemed source of wisdom providing a norm for reference.[2]

As a monk, Bede's life contained another formative influence, that of the daily round of liturgical prayer, which shaped his mind from his first days in the monastery as a child of seven until his death. The scriptures, and especially the psalms, have always formed the basis of the texts of the monastic Office in the Western church, whether in the order given in the *Rule of St. Benedict* or not. Bede met with his brothers seven times in the day and once in the night to recite with them the psalter and to hear read or sung other parts of the Scriptures; it was the focus to which all his learning was directed. He was known for his 'delight to sing' and a story told later by Alcuin illustrates his care for attendance in choir:

> It is said that our master and your patron, the blessed Bede, said, 'I know that angels visit the canonical hours and the meetings of the brethren. What if they should not find me there among them? Will they not say, "Where is Bede? Why does he not come to the devotions prescribed for the brethren?"?'[3]

1 For an analysis of books available to Bede, see Laistner (1935).

2 For discussion of the role of the *Rule of St. Benedict* at Jarrow see Mayr-Harting (1976) and Wormald (1976).

3 Alcuin *Epistola sanctissimis in Sancti Petri ecclesia fratribus* (ed. Haddan and Stubbs, 3: 470-1). There is little direct evidence about the liturgical practices at Jarrow, but see Cabrol and Leclercq (1907-53), 1: 1166 and 11: 2446-7, s. v. '*Ordines romani*'.

The monk Cuthbert, a pupil of Bede, recorded that when Bede was dying the texts that came naturally to his mind were the antiphons from the Office, among them the antiphon for the Magnificat for vespers of the feast of the Ascension, which he could not sing without tears.[1]

As one of the priests of the monastery, Bede exhibited a deep devotion to the Eucharist. In his writings, he constantly urged ordained priests to be better pastors and more devout celebrants, while the laity, he suggested, should come more frequently to communion. A passage from a homily on the Gospel expressed clearly his serious and devout frame of mind:

> Hence we must strive meticulously my brothers, when we come into the church to pay the due service of divine praise or to perform the solemnity of the mass, to be always mindful of the angelic presence, and to fulfill our heavenly duty with fear and fitting veneration, following the example of the women devoted to God who were afraid when the angels appeared to them at the tomb, and who, we are told, bowed their faces to the earth.[2]

The framework of Bede's life was liturgical, and it was a liturgy both respected and loved, having a profound influence on his thought and writing. Such an influence came to him through books as well as by word of mouth from his teachers. As a natural part of life, Bede had therefore an example of Latin style always before him, forming not only his mind but also his Latinity.

Bibles, commentaries and liturgical books had first reached Jarrow from Europe and especially from Rome, but by Bede's time the books from abroad were not the only volumes in the libraries of the Anglo-Saxons. The Mediterranean books had begun to be copied in England in a hand that was both legible and distinctive. Bede himself took part in the copying of manuscripts, at times acting as his own amanuensis, as well as urging his pupils and fellow-monks to accuracy in copying texts. The great books of Wearmouth-Jarrow came from a scriptorium where books were not ornaments but tools.[3] Elsewhere, books such as the Lindisfarne Gospels and the Book of Kells presented vivid and lively images on their pages, continuing a means of communication already familiar in carvings and jewelry to a nation without a written language; but at Jarrow they were scholars and

1 Cuthbert *Ep. de obitu Bedae* (ed. and transl. Colgrave and Mynors, 582)
2 Cf. *Hom.* 2, 10 (*CCSL* 122: 249, 108-14; transl. Martin and Hurst, 2: 92)
3 Cf. Parkes (1982)

Roman scholars at that. Apart from the Codex Amiatinus,[1] such books as survive from that scriptorium have no pictures or ornamentation; their beauty lies in a clear, well-formed hand. Like Bede's works, they were meant to be used rather than wondered at.

Bede's interests may have been concentrated on learning and writing, but he was not a solitary, alone in his cell with his books. He was a member of a vigorous young community, with teachers, friends and pupils. The *Book on Times* was written for his own pupils at Jarrow and its sequel *On the Reckoning of Times* was addressed to Hwaetberht, the able and energetic monk of Jarrow who visited Rome and succeeded Ceolfrith in 716 as Bede's 'most beloved abbot'.[2] He offered to his 'dearest son and fellow Levite, Cuthbert' his *On the Art of Metrics*.[3] In his *Life of St. Cuthbert* there are references to other monks of Jarrow whom Bede knew well: Sigfrid, who had been a young monk at Melrose in the time of St. Cuthbert, ended his days at Jarrow; a priest, Ingwald, who told Bede about a miracle of Cuthbert, was a monk of Wearmouth;[4] and a priest-monk of Jarrow told Bede about another miracle in which the hermit Felgild had been cured by touching a relic of Cuthbert.[5] In the *Ecclesiastical History* Bede mentioned the names of other monks of his monastery as men with whom he had discussed the past. Cynimund, for instance, told him about a miracle of Aidan which he in turn had heard about from Bishop Utta.[6] There was also Eadgils the monk who told Bede about a judgement which befell the abbey of Coldingham, and it was from another monk of Jarrow that Bede heard about the Irish visionary, Fursey.[7] With all the names he mentioned, Bede was always careful to add, if appropriate, their status as 'priest' as well as monk, often in the phrase, 'my fellow priest-monk', a small indication of the pride and pleasure he felt in belonging to the ranks of the clergy.

Outside Jarrow, Bede had many monastic friends with whom he corresponded about subjects of mutual interest in the world of learning and letters. There was, for instance, 'most beloved brother' Plegwine of Hexham, who wrote to tell Bede that he had been accused of heresy by the priest David in the presence of Bishop Wilfrid.[8] Bede wrote also to his 'dearest

1 Bruce-Mitford (1967)
2 *De temp. rat.* praefatio (*CCSL* 123B: 263, 3-6 and 264, 35 - 265, 44)
3 *De arte metr.* 1, 25 (*CCSL* 123A: 141, 26)
4 *Vit. Cuth. pros.* 5-6 (ed. Colgrave, 170-2)
5 Ibid., 46 (ed. Colgrave, 304)
6 *Hist. eccl.* 3, 15 (ed. and transl. Colgrave and Mynors, 260)
7 Ibid., 4, 25 and 3, 19 (ed. and transl. Colgrave and Mynors, 426 and 274)
8 *Ep. Pleg.* 17 (*CCSL* 123C: 626, 309-15)

brother in Christ', the monk Helmwald, to wish him well as he set out on a pilgrimage.[1] He knew and trusted Albinus, who succeeded Hadrian as abbot of St. Augustine's in Canterbury, claiming that he was 'the principal authority' and 'helper' of his last great historical work.[2]

Twice at least Bede visited friends in other monasteries. Wictred, a priest and perhaps an abbot, had welcomed Bede to his abbey to discuss chronology and Bede wrote to thank him and to reply to his request for further elucidation of topics discussed.[3] Bede visited Lindisfarne and knew the abbot Eadfrid, the creator of the *Lindisfarne Gospels*.[4] He talked at length with the old monk Herefrid who had known Cuthbert intimately and was prepared to tell Bede in detail about Cuthbert's death, information he seems to have withheld from the monk of his own house who had previously written an account of the saint.[5] At Lindisfarne, Bede knew also Baldhelm, Cynemund and Guthfrid the sacrist, who all supplied him readily with intimate and personal reminiscences of Cuthbert, a fact which suggests a man easy to talk to and trust.[6] At the end of his life, he also visited his former pupil, Egbert, in York, and was planning to do so again, when prevented by his last illness.[7]

The *Ecclesiastical History* contains much information about nuns, but Bede himself seems to have had little personal contact with any. He may have corresponded with the abbesses of Ely and of Whitby about the information he included in the *Ecclesiastical History* concerning their houses, and he made a *Commentary on the Canticle of Habakkuk*, another text used in the Office, for his 'dearest sister in Christ', a nun and perhaps an abbess, possibly at one of the convents he praised for their learning, such as Whitby or Ely.[8]

Among the clergy in general Bede had many friends and correspondents. He wrote often to Acca, bishop of Hexham, a man of wide learning with an excellent library, who shared Bede's love of biblical exegesis, was the recipient of many of his commentaries, and provided much information for

1 *Ep. Helm.* (*CCSL* 123C: 629, 1-6)
2 *Hist. eccl.* praefatio (ed. and transl. Colgrave and Mynors, 2)
3 *Ep. Wict.* (*CCSL* 123C: 635-42)
4 *Vit. Cuth. pros.* praefatio (ed. Colgrave, 142)
5 Ibid., 37-40 (ed. Colgrave, 270-88)
6 Ibid., 25; 36; and praefatio (ed. Colgrave, 240, 270, and 146)
7 *Ep. Ecg.* (ed. Plummer, 1: 405)
8 *Hist. eccl.* 4, 19; 4, 23 (ed. and transl. Colgrave and Mynors, 392-6 and 406-8); *In Hab.* (*CCSL* 119B: 381, 1-3)

Bede's historical writings.[1] Bede called him 'the lord most beloved in Christ', 'the most dear and beloved of all the bishops who dwell in these lands', 'the lord most blessed and ever to be revered with deepest love'.[2] Acca is mentioned in connection with nine of Bede's commentaries as well as his *Retractation* on Acts and a poem on the Final Judgement. There was also 'my most beloved lord in Christ', John, a priest to whom Bede sent his metrical *Life of St. Cuthbert* as light reading for his journey to Rome.[3] There was an anonymous 'friend from Britain', presumably a cleric, who questioned the future Pope Gregory II in Rome some time before 716 and sent back to Bede information which he mentioned in the *Retractation* on Acts.[4]

Another man of learning whose interests overlapped with Bede's was Nothhelm, a priest of the church of London, a friend of Albinus and later archbishop of Canterbury. He put thirty questions to Bede about certain points in the Book of Kings which he thought required elucidation and it was Nothhelm who was chosen by Albinus to convey information about Kent to Bede in Northumbria; Bede later trusted his scholarship so far as to accept his transcriptions of the Roman archives about the mission of Augustine to Kent.[5] In the Preface to the *Ecclesiastical History* Bede mentioned also Daniel Bishop of Winchester and Cynebert bishop of Lindsey as well as the abbot Esi as correspondents providing information for his work.[6] Wilfrid of York met Bede at least once and they were on good enough terms for Bede to question him about a most intimate matter concerning the virginity of Queen Aethelthryth through two marriages in which Wilfrid had been her spiritual adviser.[7] Other correspondents may have sent Bede information from coastal districts about the tides, which he used in his book *On the Nature of Things*.[8]

A man devoted to learning through books and letters, Bede also culled much information from visitors to his monastery. Jarrow was by no means an out of the way place; it was a rich, well-endowed abbey, international in its contacts, lying between the highly cultured kingdom of Dalriada to the

1 For an admirable summary of Bede's relationship with Acca and others, see Whitelock (1976), 19-40.

2 *Exp. Act. Apost.* praefatio (*CCSL* 121: 3, 1-2); *In Sam.* prologus (*CCSL* 119: 9, 34-6); *De eo quod ait Isaias* (*PL* 94: 702B)

3 *Vit. Cuth. metr.* praefatio (ed. Jaager, 56-7)

4 *Retr. in Act. Apost.* 19, 12 (*CCSL* 121: 155, 13-17)

5 *XXX quaest.* prologus (*CCSL* 119: 293, 1-6); *Hist. eccl.* praefatio (ed. and transl. Colgrave and Mynors, 4)

6 *Hist. eccl.* praefatio (ed. and transl. Colgrave and Mynors, 4-6)

7 *Hist. eccl.* 4, 19 (ed. and transl. Colgrave and Mynors, 390-2)

8 *De nat. rerum* 39 (*CCSL* 123A: 224, 1 - 225, 15)

north, the learned though eccentric Irish to the west and the English kingdoms to the south, with good sea contact to Gaul and the Mediterranean. In this flourishing kingdom, the monasteries Bede knew best were closely connected with the royal house. Kings had given money for the foundations of Wearmouth and Jarrow; their first abbot had been a thane of a king; and Bede dedicated his *Ecclesiastical History* to King Ceolwulf, sending him a first draft for his approval.[1] The house at Jarrow was lavishly endowed, and many noblemen visited the monastery with gifts. No doubt some of the noble visitors found their way to the cell of Bede where they were welcomed not for their rank but for their information.

Visitors told Bede much and it may be that he also spoke to them for their benefit. He was deeply and personally concerned always to communicate the richness of the Christian faith to all, literate and unlearned, poor and rich alike. He included among his activities sermons to the brothers, whether in chapter or during the liturgy, and perhaps he also preached to the people who visited the monastery.[2] He was determined to communicate what he knew to every level of society, but his first responsibility was to the men and boys of his own monastery. For them he produced the tools for Christian learning, conveying the skills of the ancient world as far as possible with reference to the Bible, the Fathers and the early Christian poets. Of his pupils few are known by name, and none of them ever equalled their master. The monk Cuthbert who later became abbot of Jarrow wrote an account of Bede's death, which had occurred while he was himself Bede's pupil, and he mentions in it the boy Wilberht who took down the last words of Bede as he translated part of the Gospel of St. John into English.[3] Bede's last visit was to Egbert, a former pupil, with whom he talked about the state of the church in England in 734 when Egbert had become bishop of York.

Bede was a man of wide and international culture, and he was always more than the school-master of a monastery on the edge of the civilised world. But just as his first care was for his own pupils at Jarrow, so he was also concerned for his own people. He was the first to coin the phrase '*gens anglorum*', 'the English nation', and he longed for the English to become a people of God, not by abandoning their identity but by discovering it. This

1 *Hist. abb.* 1 and 7 (ed. Plummer, 1: 364 and 370); *Hist. eccl.* praefatio (ed. and transl. Colgrave and Mynors, 2)

2 In the introduction to the translation of Bede's homilies, Dr. Martin is of the opinion that Bede's sermons may not have been preached, while in the preface of that same work I have taken the view that they were. See Martin (1991), xi-xiv and Ward (1991), vii-viii.

3 Cuthbert *Ep. de obitu Bedae* (ed. and transl. Colgrave and Mynors, 580-6)

was not the ideology of a distant scholar but a practical programme. For instance, in the most fundamental matter of a written language, Bede wanted his countrymen to know Latin and enter the wide world of Latin literature connected with the text of the Bible but he recognised that it might not be possible. He mentioned more than once that he found the English unready to study Latin assiduously and when in the last year of his life he wrote to Egbert, he had admitted that many of them would never learn it at all. He therefore recommended a minimum at least of translation into English and he said that he himself had already prepared such translations of the Lord's Prayer and the Creed.[1] It is significant that his last days were spent translating a gospel into English.[2] Though himself possessed of a great thirst for learning so that he knew Latin perfectly, Greek well and even attempted what Hebrew he could find through Jerome, Bede was no pedant; it was the content of the Gospel he wanted to convey, not the externals, and if others could not share his enthusiasm for the ancient languages, he was prepared to use the new ones. The monk Cuthbert in his letter on Bede's death described him as an expert in Anglo-Saxon poetry and quoted an English song which Bede sang when dying.[3]

Bede and his friends, with their care for learning, prayer and preaching, were perhaps the exception rather than the rule among Anglo-Saxon monks; monasteries were not all filled with the devout, and even at Jarrow Bede's master, Ceolfrith, had experience of these 'mockers': he once left the monastery because of the unruly noblemen in it and in the *History of the Abbots* Bede praised him for being 'remarkably strenuous in restraining evil doers'.[4] A story told about Bede in his old age indicates Bede's reputation both for study of the Sacred Page and for the ready communication of it:

> After Bede had devoted himself for a long time to the study of Holy Scripture, in his old age his eyes became dim and he could not see. Some mockers said to him, 'Bede, behold, the people are gathered together waiting to hear the word of God, arise and preach to them.' And he, thirsting for the salvation of souls, went up and preached, thinking that there were people there, whereas there was no-one but the mockers. And as he concluded his sermon, saying, 'This may God deign to grant us,

1 *Ep. Ecg.* (ed. Plummer, 1: 405-23)
2 Cuthbert *Ep. de obitu Bedae* (ed. and transl. Colgrave and Mynors, 582)
3 Ibid., 580-2
4 *Hist. abb.* 16 (ed. Plummer, 1: 381)

the Father, the Son, and the Holy Ghost,' the blessed angels in the air responded saying. 'Amen, very venerable Bede.'[1]

Benedicta Ward SLG
Oxford

1 Quoted from the Erfurt Chronicle of c. 1250 in Plummer, 1: xlviii. See also Jacobus de Voragine *Legenda aurea* 181 (ed. T. Graesse, 2: 833).

INTRODUCTION

In Bede's famous biographical statement at the close of his *Ecclesiastical History*, he asserts that he has devoted his entire monastic life to the study of Scripture.[1] The truth of this assertion is underscored by the catalogue of his writings which he gives there. Most are works devoted to study of Scripture and the world out of which Scripture grew. Yet despite the fact that Bede was seen both by himself and by his later medieval readers primarily as a student of Scripture, modern scholars have tended to value Bede much less for his biblical scholarship than for his historical writing about his own time. In particular, Bede has won acclaim from modern audiences almost exclusively for his *Ecclesiastical History*. Such myopic concern for Bede's historical writings about early England has not only made full appreciation of his biblical scholarship impossible, it has also obscured much about the character of the historical writings themselves, including the *Ecclesiastical History*.

As a student of Scripture first and foremost, Bede concerned himself with the history of the people Israel above all others. Of course, he construed Israel broadly to include not only Abraham's fleshly descendants, namely the Jews, but also his true spiritual descendants, namely Christians. Indeed, one could argue that for Bede the story of England's conversion to Christ was a comparatively recent event in the long history of Israel and that Bede's telling of that story in his *Ecclesiastical History* was only the latest chapter in the greater story whose beginning is found in Genesis and whose end is foretold in Revelation. Bede's *Ecclesiastical History* is thus in a very real sense bracketed by Scripture's narrative framework. As such, it will be impossible to assess what Bede is doing in his *Ecclesiastical History*, and in his other works which we moderns have categorized as 'historical', without having some attendant appreciation of what Bede himself understood God to be doing in Israel's history, which Scripture narrates.[2]

1 *Hist. eccl.* 5, 24 (ed. and trans. Colgrave and Mynors, 566)
2 Cf. Davidse (1982) and Ward (1990), 111-29

In order to place Bede's historical writings in their proper perspective, one must thus be familiar with the history that Scripture narrates, a history that Bede saw as neatly divided into six ages.[1] More than that, one must understand nearly everything else that Bede thought it important to know about Scripture, including its language, style, tropes, turns of phrase, allusions, allegories, and symbolism.[2]

Indeed, there is evidence to suggest that Bede intended one to read his historical work with the same careful and prayerful eye that one uses to read Scripture.[3] Like Scripture itself, Bede's historical works contain a rich symbolism which Bede's own understanding of Scripture will help one to discern. For example, it has been argued that the division of both of Bede's Cuthbert *Lives* into forty-six chapters is no accident, but derives from Bede's exegesis of John 2:20.[4] In his *Homilies on the Gospels* Bede explains that in this verse the number forty-six denotes not only the number of years that it took to rebuild the temple, but also the number of days that it took to complete or perfect the Lord's body, or 'temple', in the womb of Mary.[5] If forty-six denotes for Bede the perfection or completion of the Lord's body, then his division of both Cuthbert *Lives* into forty-six chapters and the fact that he describes his *Prose Life* of Cuthbert as a 'complete' or 'perfect work' (*perfecto operi*) would suggest that he views Cuthbert's life as one that was perfected in accordance with the model that Christ embodied.[6] While Bede, of course, does not explain the significance of dividing Cuthbert's life into forty-six chapters, he may well have expected his monastic readers, who were so steeped in the language and study of Scripture, to understand it and thus to recognize the typological connections between Christ and Cuthbert. The student of Anglo-Saxon history who is unfamiliar with Bede's interpretation of the number forty-six would probably miss the theological significance of Bede's way of structuring his Cuthbert *Lives*, and in so doing

1 On the doctrine of the six ages as it was taught by the Fathers before Bede, see Augustine *De ciu. Dei* 22, 30 (*CCSL* 48: 865, 124 - 866, 148) and Isidore *Etymol.* 5, 38-9 (ed. Lindsay, vol. 1). On this doctrine in Bede, see *De tempor.* 16-22 (*CCSL* 123C: 600-11), *De temp. rat.* 66-71 (*CCSL* 123B: 463-544), *Ep. Pleg.* (*CCSL* 123C: 617-26). For extended treatments of Bede's understanding of this doctrine, see Jones (1969-70), 191-8, Siniscalco (1978) and Hunter Blair (1970), 265-8.

2 See, for example, *De schem. et trop.* (*CCSL* 123A: 142-71).

3 Bede himself gives evidence in his *Ecclesiastical History* that he saw his historical writing as Scripture-like. In 4, 20 he justifies inserting his metrical hymn on virginity into the history by reminding his readers that in so doing he is 'imitating the manner of holy Scripture' (*imitari morem sacrae scripturae*), where songs are often inserted in the midst of historical narrative.

4 Berschin (1989)

5 *Hom.* 2, 1 (*CCSL* 122: 189, 178 - 190, 210)

6 *Vit. Cuth. pros.* prologus (ed. and transl. Colgrave, 144)

would miss yet more confirming evidence for a very important historical fact, namely, that Bede's so-called historical work is always shot through with the theological meanings that he finds in Scripture. The historian's broad familiarity with Bede's biblical writings becomes an indispensable tool for a nuanced appreciation of the *Ecclesiastical History*, the *Prose Life of Cuthbert*, and Bede's other writings about the England of his day.[1]

The present volume offers students and scholars, in a fairly short compass, a broad sampling of Bede's biblical writings. As such it not only illustrates the various genres and methods that Bede employed in explicating the biblical text, it also gives the reader a sense of the occasions and the concerns that led Bede to write about Scripture.[2]

Bede's claim that Scripture has a fourfold sense should not obscure what is perhaps Bede's more fundamental distinction between Scripture's allegorical or figurative sense and its literal or historical sense. In this volume, his commentary *On Tobias* most fully exhibits his allegorical reading of Scripture. This mode of exegesis dates back to Philo of Alexandria, a first-century Jew who in typical Platonist fashion read the literal people, places, events and other details of Jewish Scripture—in its Greek Septuagint translation—as signifying enduring spiritual realities. In one place, for example, Philo allegorizes Sarah as philosophic wisdom and virtue, Hagar as those school studies that are ancillary to such wisdom (e.g., music, rhetoric, mathematics), and Abraham as the soul that learns by instruction.[3] Influenced by Platonism and by Philo's earlier example, Clement of Alexandria and his disciple Origen began interpreting Christian Scripture with a thoroughgoing allegorism in the first half of the third century.[4] Although Origen would be branded a heretic in the late fourth century, his sullied reputation did little to diminish the status of allegorical interpretation in the eyes of such Latin Fathers as Ambrose, Augustine, and Gregory, from all of whom Bede acquired his own bent for allegorical exegesis.

On Tobias is fairly typical of Bede's allegorical commentary, although it does diverge from the norm somewhat by failing to give a continuous verse-by-verse commentary. In the opening sentence, Bede expresses his

1 For an extended treatment of how Bede's appreciation of Scripture influenced the style of his historical narrative, see Ray (1976).

2 For more extended treatments of Bede's exegetical approach, see Brown (1987), 42-51; Holder (1990); and Robinson (1994). For a full bibliography, see Brown (1987), 111, n. 1.

3 *De congressu eruditionis gratia* 5, 23 and 14, 71-80 (*LCL* 4: 468 and 492-8)

4 Origen, however, claims Scriptural authority for his allegorical method, citing Paul's use of the word 'allegory' in Gal. 5:24 and his allegorical interpretation of Abraham's sons there (*De principiis* 4, 2, 6, in *SC* 268: 319-26).

conviction that the allegorical meaning of Tobias is superior to its literal or historical meaning: 'Yet anyone who knows how to interpret [Tobias] not just historically, but allegorically, sees that just as fruits surpass [their] leaves this book's inner sense surpasses its literal simplicity. For if understood spiritually, it is seen to contain in itself the great mysteries of Christ and the Church.'[1] In this commentary, Bede generally couples the literal sense of a given passage with a single allegorical sense. Elsewhere, however, he allows for the possibility that the literal meaning of a particular passage may have two or even three higher meanings associated with it.[2] Noteworthy examples of Bede's allegorical commentaries include *On the Tabernacle*, *On the First Book of Samuel*, *On the Temple*, *On Ezra and Nehemiah*, *On the Song of Songs*, *On the Song of Habakkuk*, and *On the Apocalypse*.

Bede's fame as an allegorist must never be allowed to obscure his deep appreciation of, and fascination with, Scripture's literal or historical sense—an appreciation which Bede likely acquired from his reading of St. Jerome (ca. 342-420). Although Jerome was no stranger to allegorical exegesis, his masterful knowledge of both Greek and Hebrew, his intimate knowledge of the Holy Land and its place-names, and his greater fascination with historical curiosities than with theological systems, made him the Latin scholar *par excellence* of Scripture's literal sense. Bede draws heavily upon Jerome's etymologies of Hebrew personal and place names to elucidate Scripture's literal as well as its allegorical sense. He also draws upon Isidore of Seville's *Etymologies*, though often without attribution.

In this volume, Bede's interest in the Bible's historical sense can best be seen in *On the Resting-Places*, *Thirty Questions on the Book of Kings*, and the *Eight Questions*. Taken together, these three works address a broad range of Scripture's literary and historical puzzles—puzzles which Bede delighted in solving. They include—to name a few—obscure figures of Hebrew speech, problems of biblical chronology and geography, seemingly absurd narratives, and separate but apparently contradictory accounts of the same event.

More often than not, Bede's exegetical works reveal an interweaving of the literal and figurative readings of Scripture. Although the above-mentioned works of Bede were identified as primarily either historical or allegorical in nature, none is exclusively either. Of the works translated in

1 *CCSL* 119B: 3

2 Three meanings: *De tab.* 2 (*CCSL* 119A: 91, 1957-60), *In Sam.* 2, 10 (*CCSL* 119: 87, 799-824); four: *De tab.* 1 (*CCSL* 119A: 25, 781-4), *In cant.* 4, 11 (*CCSL* 119B: 260)

this volume, *On What Isaiah Says* perhaps best exemplifies how Bede uses both approaches to achieve his broader ends. Bede did not regard history and allegory as ends in themselves, but as ways of explicating Scripture that served to build up the orthodox and catholic faith of the Church. Indeed, the experience of the Church up to Bede's time had shown time and again that when an allegorical reading of Scripture had no guiding purpose, it was as amenable to heretical readings as to orthodox ones, or so it seemed to orthodox eyes.[1] In *On What Isaiah Says*, Bede tries to refute a figurative—and heretical—interpretation of Isaiah 24. This interpretation suggests that the devil and his demons, who are figured by the 'kings of the earth' in Isaiah 24:21, will be granted penance in the end time. In refuting this interpretation, Bede resorts to the literal sense of other passages of Scripture, especially those that deal with the end of history and the Last Judgement, in order to clarify the Isaiah passage's figurative meaning. That meaning, as clarified by Bede, precludes any possibility of salvation for Satan and his angels. The *Isaiah* letter-treatise shows Bede bringing one way of interpreting Scripture to the assistance of the other in order to preserve catholic doctrine. As such, it reveals the various motives and methods that at times worked together to guide Bede's exegesis.

Unlike the other works included in this volume, *On the Holy Places* does not aim directly at explicating a biblical text. It seems rather to function as an exegetical tool. As such, it represents Bede's intense interest in the physical landscape of the Holy Land, an interest that Bede inherited from Jerome and others.[2] No idle pastime, the study of biblical geography and place names was deemed by Bede, as well as by Jerome and Augustine before him, as crucial for a proper interpretation of certain scriptural passages.[3]

The translators have tried to produce an accurate translation while yet rendering Bede's eighth-century insular Latin into modern English. This has occasionally required, among other things, breaking up Bede's long periodic phrases into two or more sentences and translating from the passive voice into the active. While the English language's less flexible rules about

1 By the late fourth century, the allegorizing of Scripture, especially as it had been practiced by Origen and the Alexandrian school, was severely attacked by the school of Antioch in the east and by Jerome in the west. Jerome charged that Origen often changed the meaning of the scriptural narrative by his careless application of the allegorical method and that by so doing he undermined the faith of the simple (*Ep.* 51, 4, 4—*CSEL* 54: 401, 14-15). For more on this debate see Froehlich (1984), 15-23.

2 Jerome *Loc.* (*PL* 23: 859-928). See Kelly (1975), 153-7.

3 Jerome *Loc.* (*PL* 23: 859-928) and *Nom.* (*CCSL* 72: 57-161); Augustine *De doct. chr.* 2, 16, 23 and 2, 29, 45 (ed. and transl. Green, 82 and 106)

word order have made it impossible to render all of the stresses and nuances that Bede's Latin word order indicates, every attempt has been made to preserve Bede's major emphases. Gender inclusive language has been employed wherever we believe that the sense of Bede's text justifies its use.

All of Bede's biblical quotations have been translated afresh into a language that reflects a modern English style, as opposed to an archaizing King James one. Because Bede's biblical text often differs considerably from that used by modern translators, his biblical passages will sometimes bear little resemblance to parallel passages in modern English biblical translations. Moreover, since his citations of Scripture come from the Vulgate edition, anyone who does not read Latin may do well to have the English translation of the Vulgate, the so-called Douai-Rheims Bible, ready to hand. Biblical citations are given according to the NRSV numbering. Where the Vulgate numbering differs, it will be included in parentheses. Bede's citations of sources, including citations in which he modifies his source slightly by, for example, altering a verb tense or a noun case, are designated with italics. Unless otherwise noted, the spelling of biblical names and places generally follows the orthographical conventions of the NRSV.

The introduction to each translation identifies the Latin edition upon which that translation was based. The numbers in the side margins indicate corresponding page numbers in the Latin edition.

ON THE HOLY PLACES: INTRODUCTION

Written between 702 and 703, *On the Holy Places* is among Bede's earliest works of biblical scholarship, and one of his least original. In it he draws upon, to use his own words, 'the records of the ancients' and 'the corroborating writings of newer teachers'. It is not always easy to tell whom he intends by 'the ancients' and whom by the 'newer teachers'.

Among his 'ancient' authorities, we must surely include Scripture itself and Jerome. In addition, he also draws upon the somewhat free Latin translation of Josephus' *On the Jewish War*, attributed to a certain Hegesippus. Dating from the fourth or fifth century, the Hegesippus source condenses Josephus' seven-book work into five. Some also allege that Bede drew from a text entitled *On the Site of Jerusalem*, which is falsely attributed to Eucherius, the famous ascetic bishop of Lyons (d. 450).[1] But others believe this text is late, perhaps even later than Bede's *On the Holy Places*, and that it thus uses Bede as its source rather than vice versa.[2] The case for believing that Bede did in fact use Pseudo-Eucherius rests on several pieces of evidence. First, the manuscript tradition for Bede's *On the Holy Places* includes the name EUCHERIUS in the margins beside those passages where *On the Site of Jerusalem* is quoted. This practice of citing sources in the margins is characteristically Bedan.[3] Secondly, if one presumes that Bede did not have Pseudo-Eucherius before him, then one is left with the problem of determining precisely where Bede obtained the information that his margins ascribe to Eucherius, for virtually none of this information can be traced to any other pre-Bedan source.[4] On the other hand, one cannot make too much of the appearance of Eucherius' name in the margins of the ancient manuscripts. The fact that these same manuscripts never include the name of Hegesippus in the margins and that they mention Jerome only once (and in a place where attribution to Jerome is quite dubious) makes

1 E.g., Fraipont, 'Praefatio' (*CCSL* 175: 247)

2 Furrer (1896), 472-3; Heisenberg (1908), 1:129

3 Laistner (1933)

4 Fraipont, 'Praefatio' (*CCSL* 175: 247)

one wonder whether the marginal attributions in the early manuscript tradition of *On the Holy Places*, or the lack thereof, are always Bede's own.[1]

Among Bede's 'newer teachers', Abbot Adamnan of Iona merits singular mention. Adamnan wrote his own *On the Holy Places* some fifteen to twenty years before Bede wrote his.[2] One could justly say that Bede's *On the Holy Places* is little more than an abridgement of Adamnan's work, as Bede himself candidly acknowledges.[3] Adamnan claims that his *On the Holy Places* was more or less dictated to him by Arculf, a bishop of Gaul who had only recently visited the Holy Land and other sites in the eastern Mediterranean. In the *Ecclesiastical History* Bede describes how Arculf's experiences came to be set down in writing by Adamnan:

> But as Arculf was returning to his native land by sea, he was cast by the violence of the tempest on to the west coasts of Britain. After many adventures he came to the servant of Christ Adamnan who found him to be learned in the Scriptures and well acquainted with the holy places. Adamnan received him very gladly and eagerly listened to his words; he quickly committed to writing everything which Arculf had seen in the holy places which seemed to be worthy of remembrance.[4]

Adamnan's work, in turn, must have reached Bede through the agency of Northumbria's King Aldfrith, to whom Adamnan gave a copy. Aldfrith then passed on the work 'for lesser folk to read'.[5] Bede's nearly complete dependence upon Adamnan should make the reader cautious about overstating the number of sources that Bede used to write his *On the Holy Places*. When one detects the words of Hegesippus, for example, in a passage of Bede's text, one need not assume that Bede had Hegesippus' work open before him. One must always remember that Adamnan also used Hegesippus as a source and that Bede, therefore, may very well have been drawing upon Adamnan's citation of Hegesippus, and not Hegesippus himself.[6]

1 Bede cites Jerome in the margins of *De loc. sanc.* 5, 1, but the reference is obscure, or perhaps erroneous (*CCSL* 175: 261, 9).

2 Meehan (1958), 11

3 *Hist. eccl.* 5, 17 (ed. Colgrave and Mynors, 512)

4 *Hist. eccl.* 5, 15 (ed. and transl. Colgrave and Mynors, 507-9); cf. Adamnan *De loc. sanc.* 3, 6, 4-5 (*CCSL* 175: 234, 13-19).

5 *Hist. eccl.* 5, 15 (ed. and transl. Colgrave and Mynors, 508-9). Adamnan may have brought *De locis sanctis* to Northumbria either when he visited in 686 or 688 (Adamnan *Vita sancti Columbae* 2, 46—ed. Anderson and Anderson [1991], 178).

6 E.g., Bede *De loc. sanc.*10, 3 (*CCSL* 175: 270, 21-3). It has been argued, however, that Bede had his own version of Hegesippus with which, at least on one occasion, he corrected Adamnan's faulty text (Bieler [1976], 210). See also Bieler (1956).

In his famous catalogue of works at the end of the *Ecclesiastical History*, Bede makes no mention of *On the Holy Places*. It has been suggested that he omitted it either because of its largely derivative nature or because he had briefly mentioned it and given long excerpts from it earlier in the *Ecclesiastical History*.[1]

If Bede saw his work chiefly as a revision of Adamnan's original, one wonders why he thought that Adamnan's text was worth bothering with at all. Given Bede's constant concern to elucidate the meaning of Scripture, it seems more likely that he saw Adamnan's work and his own revision of it as a tool for biblical exegesis than as a pilgrim's guide to the Holy Land.[2] In Augustine's *On Christian Doctrine*, a work that Bede knew well, Augustine asserts that in order to elucidate Scripture's figurative sense properly, one must have a knowledge of the meaning and location of biblical place names.[3] Knowledge of these things is crucial, says Augustine, for solving certain enigmas within Scripture. In Augustine's own time, Jerome was already instructing the Latin world in the meaning of Hebrew and Greek place names in Scripture.[4] Anyone who has read even a little of Bede's exegesis knows just how fond he is of drawing upon the meaning of a place name to unlock the mystical sense of a particular verse. Similarly, Bede was also known to use contemporary geographical descriptions of a biblical place in order to illuminate a biblical text in which that place was mentioned.[5] Bede probably saw Adamnan's *On the Holy Places* as a potentially useful exegetical tool for just such purposes.[6] Indeed, Bede would later draw freely from his *On the Holy Places* in composing his index of placenames in the book of Acts.[7] Itself a valuable exegetical tool, this index was probably intended for beginners in exegesis, as Laistner suggests.[8]

1 *Hist. eccl.* 5, 16-17 (ed. and transl. Colgrave and Mynors, 508-12); Brown (1987), 61

2 In this way, both Bede's and Adamnan's works would seem to differ from other early medieval guidebooks to the Holy Land, including Egeria's famous *Itinerarium* (*CCSL* 175: 37-90). On Adamnan's *De locis sanctis* as an exegetical tool, see O'Loughlin (1992).

3 Augustine *De doct. chr.* 2, 16, 23 and 2, 29, 45 (ed. and transl. Green, 82 and 106)

4 *Nom.* and *Loc.*

5 Cf. Bede's description of Tapheth in *XXX Quaest.* 27 (*CCSL* 119: 317, 7 - 318, 16).

6 Leyerle (1996) suggests that *itineraria* have ideologies embedded in them. These ideologies may have little to do with the conscious purposes of their authors. Although she does not explicitly mention either Adamnan's or Bede's *On the Holy Places*, her observations on the *itinerarium* of the Piacenza Pilgrim nevertheless are germane for both. See especially 132-8.

7 *Nomina regionum atque locorum* (*CCSL* 121: 167-78)

8 Laistner (1939), xxxvii

Though potentially useful, Adamnan's work was not readily usable. Its tortuous Hiberno-Latin style would have made it all but inaccessible to the Anglo-Saxon clergy who might have used it, for example, in sermon preparation. The Latinity of Bede's revision would have been far more accessible to such preachers than Adamnan's original. Bede himself twice suggests that such was his motive for revising Adamnan's text. At the end of his *On the Holy Places*, Bede describes Adamnan's style as *lacinioso*, which can mean 'wordy' or 'convoluted' and in this case probably means both; and again, in the *Ecclesiastical History*, Bede quotes his own *On the Holy Places* when describing Adamnan's version, adding that the excerpts from his own work convey the sense of Adamnan's text in a more concise style (*breuioribus strictisque sermonibus*).[1] And so, as Bede himself seemed to think, the chief value of his *On the Holy Places* lay in the clarity with which it rendered a valuable exegetical text to those Anglo-Saxon readers of Latin who could not decipher the complexities of the Hiberno-Latin style.

The present translation is based on J. Fraipont's critical edition in *CCSL* 175. That edition, in turn, is based on seven manuscripts, the oldest of which are from the ninth-century (Bibliothèque publique, Laon, 216, and Staatsbibliothek, Munich, 6389). Bede's *On the Holy Places* was first published in 1563 by John Heerwagen in the Basel edition of Bede's collected works.

1 Bede *De loc. sanc.* 19, 5 (*CCSL* 175: 280, 36-7); *Hist. eccl.* 5, 17. On the complicated quality of Adamnan's style, see Meehan (1958), 5-6, especially 5, n. 2.

ON THE HOLY PLACES

[HERE] BEGINS THE VENERABLE BEDE'S BOOK ON THE HOLY PLACES, WHICH HE COMPOSED BY CONDENSING FROM THE WORKS OF THE ANCIENTS *[251]*

HIS VERSES

Following the records of the ancients and inspecting them
Together with the corroborating writings of newer teachers,
I, Bede, have briefly described the territory and sites of the places
Which Holy Scripture would have us particularly remember.
Grant, O Jesus, that we may always press toward that homeland
Which delights eternally in the highest vision of you.

THE VERSES ARE ENDED. THE CHAPTERS BEGIN.

THE CHAPTERS END. THE BOOK ON THE HOLY PLACES BEGINS.

I. CONCERNING THE SITE OF JERUSALEM

1. *The city* of Jerusalem is built *upon an almost circular site and is enclosed by fairly impressive perimeter walls. With these walls the city also encloses Mount Zion nearby, which looms over the city in the south like a fortress. The greater part of the city lies below the mount on the plateau of a lower hill.*[1] For the city was destroyed after the Lord's passion by the emperor *Titus*, but restored and made much larger *by Aelius Hadrian* Caesar, after whom it is *named Aelia* even today.[2] It is for this reason that although the Lord suffered and was buried outside the city's gates, the places of his passion and resurrection are now to be seen inside its walls.

2. *Inside its huge perimeter walls eighty four towers* and six *gates* can
[253] be seen: *first is the gate of David, west of Mount Zion; second is the gate of the Fuller's house; third is the gate of St. Stephen; fourth is the gate of Benjamin; fifth is the Portula,* or *little gate, from which one descends by steps to the Valley of Jehoshaphat; and sixth is the gate of Tekoa.*[3] *Three* of these *gates are more commonly used as exit points*: that is, *one on the west, another on the north, and a third on the east.*[4] But *the northern summit of Mount Zion looms over the city's southern part* and *one can see that the wall has towers interspersed at intervals but no gates in this section,* that is, *from the aforementioned gate of David to the steep cliff on Mount* Zion's *eastern face.*[5]

1 Cf. Ps.-Eucherius *De sit. Hier.* 2 (*CCSL* 175: 237, 11-15)

2 Cf. ibid. (*CCSL* 175: 237, 7-8). The fall of Jerusalem under Titus occurred in 70 CE The emperor Hadrian built the Gentile city Aelia Capitolina on the site of Jerusalem between about 130 and 135 CE

3 Adamnan *De loc. sanc.* 1, 1 (*CCSL* 175: 185, 7-13)

4 Cf. Ps.-Eucherius *De sit. Hier.* 5 (*CCSL* 175: 237, 22-3) and Adamnan *De loc. sanc.* 1, 1 (*CCSL* 175: 185, 17-19)

5 Adamnan *De loc. sanc.* 1, 1 (*CCSL* 175: 185, 19-24)

3. In fact *the site* of the city itself, *with [its] gentle slope that begins at Mount Zion's northern summit and extends to the lower places at the northern and eastern walls*, is laid out in such a way that falling rain does not stand there at all, *but* flowing out *through the eastern gates like rivers, it swells the torrent of Kidron* in *the valley of Jehoshaphat*, taking *with it* all the street refuse.[1]

II. CONCERNING THE HOLY PLACES IN JERUSALEM *[254]*

1. *When pilgrims enter the city from the north side, the first of the holy places at which they must call, owing to the layout of the streets, is* the church of Constantine, *which is called* the Martyrium.[2] The Emperor Constantine *built* it in a regal and magnificent *style* because it was there that the Lord's cross was discovered by his mother Helena.[3] *West of here,* one can see the church of Golgotha *in which one can also find the rock that once supported the very cross to which the Lord's body was nailed,*[4] but which now supports an enormous *silver cross. A* great *bronze chandelier with lamps hangs* overhead. In fact, *underneath* that very *spot* is the crypt *of the Lord's cross, which has been hewn from the rock.* In this crypt it is customary *to offer a sacrifice on the altar for the honourable* dead *while their bodies rest in the court.*[5] And to the west of this church is *the round church* of the Anastasis (*that is, of the* Lord's *resurrection*[6]*).* It is surrounded *by three walls, supported by twelve columns, and has a wide space between* each *wall for a passageway.* The passageway *in the middle wall* contains *three altars at three places* (that is, the southern, the northern, and *[255]*
the western). *This [church]* has *two fourfold gates*, or *entrances. In both, each of the four gates is aligned with the others through the three walls. Of these gates, four face southeast* and *four face east. In the middle of this church* is the Lord's *round* tomb which was hewn from a rock. A person standing inside can touch [its] ceiling with his or her hand. The tomb's *entrance is on the east* and the great stone has been set down beside it.[7] On the inside one can see even today markings made from iron tools.[8]

1 Adamnan *De loc. sanc.* 1, 1 (*CCSL* 175: 186, 42-52)

2 Cf. Ps.-Eucherius *De sit. Hier.* 6 (*CCSL* 175: 237, 24-6) and Adamnan *De loc. sanc.* 1, 6 (*CCSL* 175: 190, 7-8)

3 Cf. Ps.-Eucherius *De sit. Hier.* 6 (*CCSL* 175: 237, 26-7) and Adamnan *De loc. sanc.* 1, 6 (*CCSL* 175: 190, 5-7)

4 Cf. Ps.-Eucherius *De sit. Hier.* 6 (*CCSL* 175: 237, 27 - 238, 32)

5 Adamnan *De loc. sanc.* 1, 5 (*CCSL* 175: 190, 5-14)

6 Ibid. 1, 4 (*CCSL* 175: 190, 5-6) and Ps.-Eucherius *De sit. Hier.* 6 (*CCSL* 175: 238, 28)

7 Cf. Matt. 27:60 and parallels

8 Presumably tools with which the tomb was hewn.

2. On the *outside* the tomb *is covered* completely *with marble* to the top *of the roof,* but *the roof's ridge is adorned with gold* and supports a great *golden cross. In* this *tomb's northern part, the seven-foot long sepulchre* of the Lord *has been hewn* from that same *rock and* rises *three palms* higher *than the floor.*[1] *Its entrance is on* the south where *twelve lamps burn day* and *night: four* inside the sepulchre and eight above it *on the right-hand side.*[2] *The stone which* had [once] been placed *at the door of the tomb* is now split into two pieces: *the smaller piece* functions *as a square altar in front of the door to the tomb, but the greater piece can be seen beneath some linens in the eastern locale of that same church and functions as another four-cornered altar.*[3] Now *the colour of that tomb and sepulchre appears to be a mixture of white and red.*[4] Next to this church *on the right*
[256] is *the four-cornered church* of the Blessed Mother of God.[5] On the street which joins the Martyrium and Golgotha[6] *there is a chamber in which the Lord's cup is stored in a small chest;* it is the custom to *touch* and *kiss* it through *an opening in the lid.*[7] *Having two handles* on either side, *this silver cup* holds *a Gallic pint. In it* also is *the sponge* that served drink to the Lord.[8] In *that place, which is where Abraham* built *the altar* for *sacrificing his son,* is a *sizeable wooden table* on which *the people* customarily offer *alms for the poor.*[9] But each place that I have mentioned here I have taken pains to depict also for your eyes, that you may know it more fully:

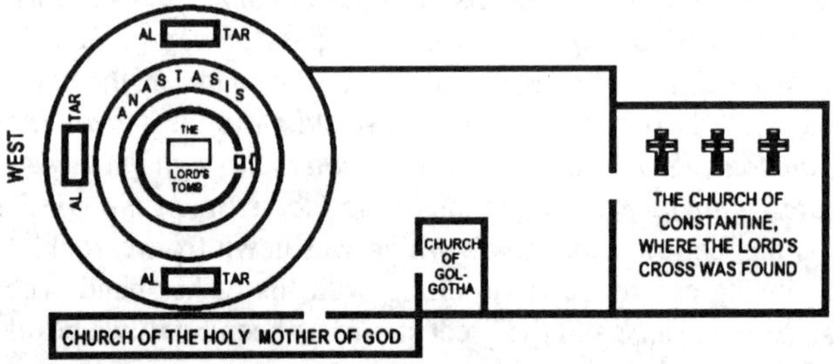

1 Adamnan *De loc. sanc.* 1, 2 (*CCSL* 175: 187, 33-40)

2 Ibid. 1, 2 (*CCSL* 175: 188, 58-65). On Bede's refraining from allegorizing this and other features of the Church of the Holy Sepulchre, see Holder (1989a), 127-31.

3 Adamnan *De loc. sanc.* 1, 3 (*CCSL* 175: 189, 4-14)

4 Ibid. 1, 3 (*CCSL* 175: 189, 23-4). Bede later cites this chapter of his *De loc. sanc.* (i.e., chapter II: Concerning the holy places in Jerusalem) from its beginning up to this point in *Hist. eccl.* 5, 16 (ed. Colgrave and Mynors, 508-10).

5 Adamnan *De loc. sanc.* 1, 4 (*CCSL* 175: 190, 6-7)

6 Ibid. 1, 6 (*CCSL* 175: 191, 18-21)

7 Matt. 26:27 (and parallels)

8 Matt. 27:48 (and parallels); Adamnan *De loc. sanc.* 1, 7 (*CCSL* 175: 191, 5-17)

9 Adamnan *De loc. sanc.* 1, 6 (*CCSL* 175: 191, 12-172)

3. *The soldier's lance, which is lodged in a wooden cross, is kept in the porch* of the Martyrium. *Its shaft having been broken in two, it is venerated by the whole city.*[1] [257]

One can see that all *these* holy places which we have mentioned *are situated beyond Mount Zion, where a little hill to its north falls away from it and levels off. But in the lower part of the city*—where *the temple was situated near the eastern wall*[2] and joined to the city by a bridge that served as a passage between them—*the Saracens now assemble* for prayer. There *they have built a square house of shoddy workmanship with upright planks and great beams over certain remains of the ruins. It* seems *to hold three thousand people.*[3] *One will find there a few cisterns for supplying water.*[4]

4. In the vicinity *of the temple one can see the pool of Bethsaida, which is known for its twin reservoirs. One of them is mostly filled by winter showers, while the other is variegated in colour because of its red water. From the side of Mount Zion that has a steep cliff facing east, the spring of Siloam rushes forth inside the walls and* toward *the foot of the hill. It flows south with a sporadic stream of water:*[5] that is, its water bubbles up not constantly, but [only] on certain hours and days. Usually it comes with a loud roar through the hollows of the earth and cavities of extremely hard rock.

5. On the *plateau* atop Mount *Zion, cells of monks are* crowded *around the* great *church* said to have been *founded there by the apostles. For it was there that they* received the Holy *Spirit*, and there that St. Mary died.[6] On display in the church also is the holy place of the Lord's Supper.[7] But in the middle of the church, the marble column to which the Lord clung when he was whipped is also standing.[8] Accordingly, the outline of this church is said to be like this: [258]

---

1 John 19:34; Adamnan *De loc. sanc.* 1, 8 (*CCSL* 175: 191, 2 - 192, 72)

2 Cf. Ps.-Eucherius *De sit. Hier.* 6-7 (*CCSL* 175: 238, 32-5) and Adamnan *De loc. sanc.* 1, 1 (*CCSL* 175: 186, 60-2)

3 Adamnan *De loc. sanc.* 1, 1 (*CCSL* 175: 186, 60-5)

4 Cf. Ps.-Eucherius *De sit. Hier.* 7 (*CCSL* 175: 238, 37-8)

5 Cf. ibid. 8-9 (*CCSL* 175: 238, 40-6)

6 Cf. ibid. 4 (*CCSL* 175: 237, 16-21)

7 Matt. 26:20-9 and parallels

8 Matt. 27:26 and parallels; Adamnan *De loc. sanc.* 1, 18 (*CCSL* 175: 197, 10)

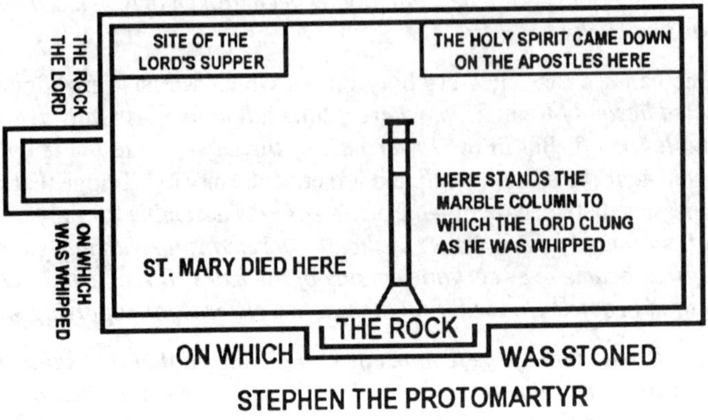

6. *Here one sees the rock on which St. Stephen* the protomartyr was stoned outside the city.[1] Yet in the centre of Jerusalem, where a dead *man was restored to life when the Lord's cross was placed over him,* there stands a tall *column* which *casts no shadow on the summer solstice.* From this they reckon that the centre of the earth is at that spot and that literally true is the saying: *But God our king, before the ages, effected salvation at the centre*
[259] *of the earth.*[2] Influenced by this opinion also, Victor, bishop of the church of Poitiers, begins writing about Golgotha as follows:

> *There is a place that we believe to be centre of the whole world;*
> *The Jews call it by its ancestral cognomen: Golgotha.*[3]

III. CONCERNING AKELDAMA AND THE PLACE WHERE JUDAS WAS HANGED

1. *Those leaving by the Gate of David will see a straight bridge going south through the valley.* It is said that *Judas hung himself in the middle of it, on [its] west side.* A great and very old *fig tree* also stands there, just as Juvencus said:

1 Acts 7:54-60; Adamnan *De loc. sanc.* 1, 18 (*CCSL* 175: 197, 6-7)
2 Ps. 74:12 (73:12); Adamnan *De loc. sanc.* 1, 11 (*CCSL* 175: 194, 2 - 195, 19)
3 Victorinus (Ps. Cyprianus) *De Pascha* 1-2 (*CSEL* 3, pt. 3: 305). Ed. Wilhelm Hartel. Vienna, 1871.

He snatched ugly death from atop a fig tree.[1]

2. Further on at Akeldama, *to the south of Mount Zion*, some corpses of *foreigners* and paupers are buried even today, while others *lie rotting and unburied.*[2]

IV. CONCERNING THE LORD'S HEAD-CLOTH AND ANOTHER GREAT SHROUD MADE BY ST. MARY

1. The Lord's head-cloth was stolen soon after his resurrection by a certain pious Christian Jew. He kept it until his death and riches accrued to him. When he was about to die, he asked his sons which of them wanted to take the Lord's head-cloth and which the father's other riches. The elder chose the earthly treasures, the younger chose the head-cloth. Soon the *[260]* elder's treasures diminished so much that he was on the brink of poverty, but his brother's material wealth increased with his faith.

2. And so up to the fifth generation the faithful held on to the cloth. At this point it fell into the hands of the impious and for a long time increased their wealth as much as it had done for the Christian Jews. At last, after long quarrels in which the Christian Jews were claiming that they should be heirs of what had belonged to Christ, while the infidels were claiming that they should be heirs of what had belonged to their fathers, King Mauvias of the Saracens, who lived during our lifetime, was asked to mediate their quarrel. He lit a large pyre and implored Christ, who had deigned to wear the cloth on his head for the salvation of his own, to serve as judge. As the head-cloth was consigned to the flame it arose with a sudden jerk and soared through the sky almost playfully for a long time. Finally, while everyone on both sides was staring at it, it alighted on the breast of one of the Christians. The next morning, all the people saluted and kissed it with deep veneration. It was eight feet long.[3]

3. *Another* somewhat *bigger shroud* is *also* venerated in a church. *Said to have been woven* by *St. Mary, it contains images of the twelve apostles* and *the Lord.* It is *red* on one side and *green* on the other.[4] *[261]*

---

1 Adamnan *De loc. sanc.* 1, 16-17 (*CCSL* 175: 197); Juvencus *Euang.* 4, 631 (*CSEL* 24: 138)

2 Adamnan *De loc. sanc.* 1, 19 (*CCSL* 175: 198, 3-8); Acts 1:19. Unlike modern English Bibles, the Vulgate version of Matt. 27:8 gives the name of this place as Akeldama.

3 From the beginning of this chapter up to this point, Bede is relying heavily upon Adamnan *De loc. sanc.* 1, 9 (*CCSL* 175: 192, 11 - 194, 81).

4 Adamnan *De loc. sanc.* 1, 10 (*CCSL* 175: 194, 1-9)

V. CONCERNING THE PLACES AROUND JERUSALEM AND THE CHURCH IN THE VALLEY OF JEHOSHAPHAT

1. Around Jerusalem *one can see rough and mountainous* places.[1] *North* of here, *as far as Arimathea, one can* also *see rocky and rough land in places. The valleys which extend up to the region of Thamna*[2] *are also full of thorns.* But *between Aelia and Caesarea of Palestine, there are mostly* level plains *with olive groves here and there, although one may occasionally see short stretches of rough terrain.*[3] Now Aelia and Caesarea are 75 miles apart.[4] In fact, the length of *the promised land from Dan to Beersheba is 165 miles;*[5] *46 miles from Joppa to Bethlehem.*[6]

2. *Just east of the temple wall, and of Jerusalem, lies Gehenna, which* is *the valley of Jehoshaphat. It stretches from north to south and the brook of Kidron runs through it whenever it receives a rain shower.*[7] A level plain that is small, well-watered, wooded, and full of delights, this valley once had a place in it sacred to the Baals. In it is the *tower* of King *Jehoshaphat,*
[262] which houses his *sepulchre; to* its *right a separate house cut from the face of the Mount of Olives* holds *two hollowed-out sepulchres*: one is that of the aged *Simeon*, the other *of Joseph, husband of St. Mary.*[8]

3. In the same valley is *the round church of St. Mary,* divided into storeys *by means of a stone-floor.* Of its *altars, four are on the upper floor,* one *on the lower at the eastern* side; and *to the right of this is an empty* tomb *in which St. Mary* is said *to have lain for some time,* but it is not known by whom or when she was carried away. *Those entering the church see a rock lodged in the wall on the right;* on it *the Lord prayed the night he was betrayed. His knees left an imprint [on it] as though on soft wax.*[9]

---

1 Cf. Ps.-Eucherius *De sit. Hier.* 10 (*CCSL* 175: 238, 50-1)

2 MAP 11, X4 (*NOAB*)

3 Adamnan *De loc. sanc.* 1, 20 (*CCSL* 175: 198, 5-13)

4 At this point in the *CCSL* edition upon which this translation is based, editor includes *Hieronymus* (='Jerome') in the margin, even though the identification is found in only two of the seven manuscripts upon which he bases his edition. It is a matter for conjecture whether this marginal note is original to Bede, who typically indicated his sources in this way, or the work of later copyists. Whichever is the case, no one has yet identified the passage in Jerome's corpus from which this statement is supposedly derived. The term 'mile' in this text always refers to the Roman mile, which is 1618 English yards, or approximately nine-tenths of an English mile.

5 Cf. Ps.-Eucherius *De sit. Hier.* 16 (*CCSL* 175: 239, 88 - 240, 90)

6 Cf. ibid. 18 (*CCSL* 175: 240, 98-9)

7 Cf. ibid. 9 (*CCSL* 175: 238, 46-9)

8 Luke 2:25 and Matt. 2:24; Adamnan *De loc. sanc.* 1, 13-14 (*CCSL* 175: 196)

9 Luke 22:41 (and parallels); Adamnan *De loc. sanc.* 1, 12 (*CCSL* 175: 195, 4 - 196, 22)

VI. CONCERNING THE MOUNT OF OLIVES AND THE HOLY PLACES ON IT

1. *The Mount* of Olives is *a mile* from Jerusalem,[1] being equal in height to Mount Zion, but surpassing it in breadth and length.[2] *Besides vines and olives*, it has the occasional tree and is fertile for corn and barley too. *For* its soil is *not barren, but filled with grass and flowers*.[3] At its summit, where the Lord ascended to the heavens, a large round church *has within its circumference three colonnades with vaulted roofs on top*.[4] The inmost house could not be vaulted and covered because of the upward path of the Lord's body.[5] On the east it has an altar covered with a narrow roof.[6] In its *[263]* centre are seen the last footprints of the Lord which were made as he ascended when the heavens opened from above. *Although* believers *daily* carry away some soil [from this place], it yet remains and *to this day* retains *its same appearance, as though the footprints have been engraved therein.* Around these is a *bronze circular structure* about *neck high*. It has an entrance on the west and a large *lamp hanging on pulleys overhead* which gives light all *day and night*.[7]

2. *On the western side* of the same church eight windows and as many lamps hanging opposite them on ropes cast a glow *through the glass* all the way to Jerusalem. It is said that those who behold the light [of those lamps] are filled with fear and with a certain sense of elation and compunction.[8] Every year on the day of the Lord's ascension, after mass had been celebrated, *a violent blast of wind* used to come from above and dash to the ground all who came to the church.[9] So many lamps burn there on that night

---

1 Cf. Ps.-Eucherius *De sit. Hier.* 13 (*CCSL* 175: 238, 51-2)

2 Adamnan *De loc. sanc.* 1, 22 (*CCSL* 175: 199)

3 Ibid. 1, 21 (*CCSL* 175: 198-9). The word 'barren' here translates *bruc(h)osa*, which is contained in the mss. of both Adamnan and Bede. Although not otherwise attested, *bruc(h)osa* presumably derives from *bruc(h)us* ('locust'), and so would mean 'locust-country'. Meehan here conjectures *bruscosa*, which is attested later as meaning 'scrubland' or 'brushwood-country'. Whatever the word's literal meaning, Bede clearly means here to contrast a *brucosa* landscape with one that is grassy and flowery. Hence the translation of *brucosa* as 'barren'.

4 Ibid. 1, 23 (*CCSL* 175: 199, 5-6)

5 Acts 1:9-12. Adamnan *De loc. sanc.* 1, 23 (*CCSL* 175: 199, 6-14)

6 Adamnan *De loc. sanc.* 1, 23 (*CCSL* 175: 199, 6-7)

7 Ibid. (*CCSL* 175: 200, 26-31 and 42-4)

8 Cf. Ambrose *Exp. Psalm. CXVIII* 8, 17: 'fulgente eius lumine pavefactus est' (*CSEL* 62: 160, 14-5); Adamnan *De loc. sanc.* 1, 23 (*CCSL* 175: 200, 45 - 201, 66)

9 Acts 2:2. Adamnan *De loc. sanc.* 1, 23 (*CCSL* 175: 201, 67-76). Bede later cites this chapter (i.e., chapter six) of *De loc. sanc.* from its beginning up to this point in *Hist. eccl.* 5, 17 (ed. Colgrave and Mynors, 510-12).

that the mountain and the places below it seem *not* only to glow, *but to burn.*[1] It seems a good idea to sketch for the eyes an outline of this basilica as well:

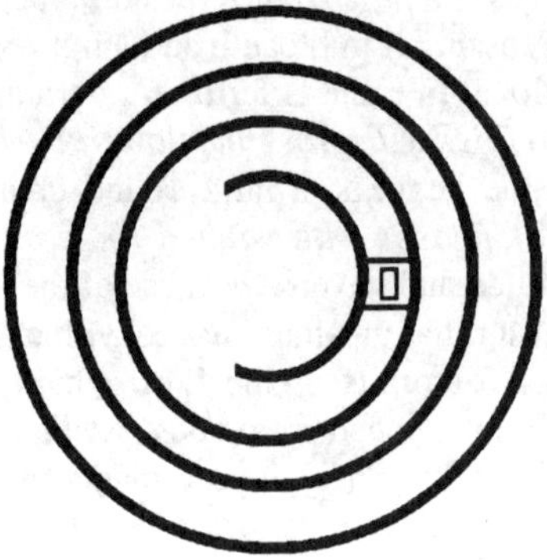

[264] **3.** *A church* built there over the tomb of *Lazarus* also designates *a large monastery* in *a certain field that is surrounded by a great forest of olive trees at Bethany.*[2] Now Bethany is 15 stades from Jerusalem. A third church on the same mountain *is south of Bethany* where before his passion the Lord spoke to his disciples about the day of judgement.[3]

VII. CONCERNING THE SITE OF BETHLEHEM AND THE HOLY PLACES THERE

1. *Bethlehem* is *six miles* south *of Jerusalem, situated on a narrow ridge surrounded on all sides by valleys.*[4] *It is a mile* long *from west to east* and *a low wall without towers has been built* all along the outer edge of its plateau.[5] *On* its *eastern corner,* there is a certain natural half-grotto, *as it*
[265] *were,* the exterior of which *is said to be the place of the Lord's birth; its interior is called the manger of the Lord.* Covered *completely* inside *with precious marble,* this *cave* supports *the great church of St. Mary,* [which is

1 Adamnan *De loc. sanc.* 1, 23 (*CCSL* 175: 201, 93-9)
2 Ibid. 1, 24 (*CCSL* 175: 202)
3 Matt. 24:3 ff.; Adamnan *De loc. sanc.* 1, 25 (*CCSL* 175: 202, 3-6)
4 Cf. Ps.-Eucherius *De sit. Hier.* (*CCSL* 175: 238, 56)
5 Adamnan *De loc. sanc.* 2, 1 (*CCSL* 175: 206, 3-15)

built] over the very spot *where the Lord is said to have been born.*[1] A hollowed-out rock by the wall holds the water from the Lord's first bath which was poured out from the wall into it. If by some chance or for some reason the rock is emptied, it nevertheless fills back up immediately, just as it was before, while you look at it.[2]

2. *In the valley just north* of Bethlehem is *the sepulchre of David,* which is covered *with a low stone in the middle of a church, with a lamp placed overhead.*[3] But *in the valley* just south *in a church is St. Jerome's sepulchre.*[4]

3. *A mile east* of the city in *the tower of Ader* (i.e., 'sheepfold')[5] is *a church holding the tombs of the three shepherds* to whom *the Lord's birth* was revealed.[6] I have said these things following the account of Bishop Arculf of Gaul, although Ezra plainly states that David was buried in Jerusalem.[7]

4. *Bethlehem is on the east side of the royal way leading from Aelia*[8] *to Hebron; on the west side is the tomb* holding *Rachel,* which is marked even to this day *with the inscription of her name.*[9]

VIII. CONCERNING THE SITE OF HEBRON AND THE TOMBS OF THE FATHERS *[266]*

1. Now *Hebron is situated in a broad plain,* 22 miles from Aelia.[10] It has a double cave *one stade* to *its east* in a valley.[11] *A square wall* there encloses

1 Adamnan *De loc. sanc. 2, 2 (CCSL* 175: 206, 2-12). In his short *vita* of Adamnan, Bede attributes this passage, which is his own redaction of Adamnan's work, to Adamnan himself (*Hist. eccl.* 5, 16—ed. Colgrave and Mynors, 508).

2 Ibid. 2, 3 (*CCSL* 175: 207, 4-13)

3 1 Kgs. 2:10; Acts 2:29; Adamnan *De loc. sanc.* 2, 4 (*CCSL* 175: 207, 3-11)

4 Adamnan *De loc. sanc.* 2, 5 (*CCSL* 175: 208, 3-8)

5 Gen. 35:21; Jerome *Nom.* Ios. A (*CCSL* 72: 88, 29) and *Hebr. quaest.* 35, 21 (*CCSL* 72: 43, 21-4). Bede takes the liberty here of altering the *Gader* of his source, Adamnan, to *Ader.* By doing this and giving Jerome's etymology of the name *Ader,* Bede cleverly forges a connection between the name of the place and those who are buried there.

6 Luke 2:8-20; Adamnan *De loc. sanc.* 2, 6 (*CCSL* 175: 208)

7 Neh. 3:16. In the Vulgate, the modern biblical books of Ezra and Nehemiah were grouped into a single bipartite book of Ezra. 1 Ezra is our Ezra and 2 Ezra is our Nehemiah. When Bede here refers to Ezra, he probably means Ezra-Nehemiah as a whole and not either the person of Ezra or our modern biblical book of Ezra. This may explain why Bede attributes this information about the location of David's tomb to Ezra.

8 The name of the Roman city that was built on the site of Jerusalem.

9 Cf. Gen. 35:20; Adamnan *De loc. sanc.* 2, 7 (*CCSL* 175: 208, 5 - 209, 12)

10 Adamnan *De loc. sanc.* 2, 12 (*CCSL* 175: 211, 4)

11 Ibid. 2, 10 (*CCSL* 175: 210, 35-6); cf. Gen. 23:9 (Vulg.)

the sepulchres of the patriarchs. Their heads are oriented northward, and each sepulchre is covered with *a single stone* which has been hewn in the likeness of *a basilica: a white one* for each of the three patriarchs, [but one] *of a paltrier* and *cruder workmanship for Adam* who *rests not far* from them *at the far northern* wall. *Cruder and smaller tombs of their three wives* also are seen [there].[1]

2. *The hill of Mamre is a mile north of* these *tombs. Very grassy and flowery, it has a level plateau* on top. On its *northern slope the oak of Abraham,* which has a trunk as tall as two people, is enclosed in *a church.*[2]

3. *For those who head north from Hebron, a* little *mountain with pines*
[267] *appears* on the *left* side of the road *three miles from Hebron.* From here *pine timbers* are carried on camels *to Jerusalem; for wagons and chariots* are *seldom* found *in any part of Judea.*[3]

IX. CONCERNING JERICHO AND ITS PLACES

1. *Jericho* is *18 miles* east of Aelia.[4] After it was razed to the ground for the third time, *only the house of Rahab remains* as a sign of [her] faith;[5] for its *walls* survive to this day *without a roof. The site of the city [now] sustains cornfields and vineyards. Between* here *and the Jordan,* which is five or six miles, there are *huge palm-groves with clearings interspersed here and there* and *with Canaanites dwelling there.*[6]

1 Adamnan *De loc. sanc.* 2, 9/10 (*CCSL* 175: 209, 4 - 210, 32). Adamnan identifies the three women as Sarah, Rebecca, and Leah. In the Vulgate, Joshua 14:15 says that 'Adam, the greatest among the Enacim' was buried in Hebron. It seems likely that this verse is the source for both Adamnan's and Bede's statements that Adam is buried in Hebron.

2 Gen. 13:18; Adamnan *De loc. sanc.* 2, 11 (*CCSL* 175: 210, 2 - 211, 20). Bede cites this chapter (i.e., 8, on Hebron) from its beginning to this point in his *Ecclesiastical History* (5, 17—ed. Colgrave and Mynors, 512).

3 Adamnan *De loc. sanc.* 2, 12 (*CCSL* 175: 211, 4-9)

4 Cf. Ps.-Eucherius *De sit. Hier.* (*CCSL* 175: 239, 60-1)

5 Cf. Josh. 2:1-6 and Adamnan *De loc. sanc.* 2, 13 (*CCSL* 175: 212, 1-8). According to Adamnan, who is Bede's source here, the three occasions on which Jericho was razed to the ground were as follows: (1) when Joshua destroyed it during the conquest of Canaan (Josh. 6:20-4), (2) when the Romans attacked and besieged Jerusalem (70 CE or 132 CE), and (3) some indeterminate third occasion which occurred 'a considerable interval' after its second destruction. Since Adamnan quotes Jerome's *Liber Locorum* almost verbatim for his history of Jericho up to its third destruction (*PL* 23: 904B), one can conclude that the third destruction of Jericho took place after Jerome, that is, sometime during the fifth through seventh centuries. A West-Syrian chronicle that dates to 664 records that in 659 the greater part of Jericho fell in an earthquake (Palmer [1993], 31). Perhaps this is the third fall of Jericho to which Adamnan and Bede refer, although the source of their information remains unknown.

6 Adamnan *De loc. sanc.* 2, 13 (*CCSL* 175: 212, 7-20)

2. *The twelve stones* that *Joshua commanded to be taken from the Jordan* lie in the church of Gilgal by the wall on either side.[1] Each stone now can scarcely be lifted by two men; *one* of them was broken *(by some accident about which* I *know nothing),* but *has been* r*ejoined by means of iron.*[2]

3. *Near Jericho [is] a spring that abounds in drinking water and that is good for irrigation.* At one time too *sterile for growing plants and not very good for drinking, it was purified by the prophet Elis'ha* when he put a *bowl of salt* in it.[3] *Now around the spring lies a plain 70 stades long and 20 wide. It has gardens of wondrous beauty, various kinds of palm-trees, and the most extraordinary beehives. In that place the opobalsamum tree is grown, whose name has the prefix 'opo' for the following reason: farmers using sharp stones cut narrow channels into the bark and the balsam oozes into them so that the exquisite fluid trickling down through these cavities gradually accumulate in dewy drops. Now a cavity is designated by the Greek* word *'ope'.*[4] *In that place they say that the henna and the ben-nut grow.*[5] *The water, as at other springs, is cold in summer and warm in winter, but there exceptionally so; the climate is so mild that they wear linen robes in the dead of winter.*[6] [268]

4. *The city* itself *is built on the plain. Over it looms a mountain that is spread over a large area and is devoid of plants;*[7] for *the soil is poor and barren and was for this reason abandoned by inhabitants.*[8] *Spread out as it is, the mountain is home to those who live* from *the area around the city of Scythopolis up to the Sodomite region and the Asphalt territory.*[9] *Opposite this, above the Jordan, is a mountain* extending *from* the city *of Julias to Zoar of Arabia, which borders on Petra, where there is also a mountain called Ferreus.*[10] *Between these two mountains lies a plain that the ancients called Magnum in Latin, but Aulon in Hebrew.*[11] Its l*ength is 230 stades, its width 120; beginning at the village of Genvavari, it extends as far as the Lake of Asphalt. The Jordan divides it in the middle, with its banks made* [269]

1 Josh. 4:19-25
2 Adamnan *De loc. sanc.* 2, 14/15 (*CCSL* 175: 212, 8 - 213, 20)
3 2 Kgs. 2:19-22; Hegesippus *Hist.* 4, 17 (*CSEL* 66: 267, 15 - 268, 1)
4 I.e., ὀπή; Hegesippus *Hist.* 1, 15 (*CSEL* 66: 24, 15-17)
5 Ibid. 4, 17 (*CSEL* 66: 269, 9-10)
6 Ibid. 4, 17 (*CSEL* 66: 269, 12-14)
7 Ibid. 4, 16 (*CSEL* 66: 266, 12-13)
8 Ibid. 4, 16 (*CSEL* 66: 266, 17-18)
9 Ibid. 4, 16 (*CSEL* 66: 266, 14-16)
10 Julias: NOAB MAP 11, Y5; Petra, see NOAB MAP 12, G4
11 Jerome *Loc.* (*PL* 23: 866C-867A)

lush and green from the river's alluvial deposits.[1] *For the fruit from the trees on its banks* is *quite plentiful, but much scantier elsewhere;*[2] *for everywhere beyond the river's edge is arid.*[3]

X. CONCERNING THE JORDAN AND THE SEA OF GALILEE

1. Now *the source of the Jordan* is commonly reckoned to be *in the province of Phoenicia at the foot of* Mount *Lebanon, where Paneas* (that is, *Caesarea Philippi*) is situated.[4] *We understand* this to be the same Paneas (that is, a *cave*) *through which the Jordan flows and that* King *Agrippa built up and beautified with exquisite decoration.*[5] *Now in the region of Trachonitis* is a fountain *circular in shape*. For this reason it is *called Fiala*[6].
[270] Fiala is 15 miles from Caesarea and *always filled with waters in such a way that they neither spill over* nor ever diminish.[7]

2. Into this [fountain] *Philip, the tetrarch* of this *district, put some straw which the current spewed out in Paneas. From this it is clear that* the *Jordan's* origin *is* in *Fiala,* but *that* after *passing through subterranean channels it begins as a stream in Paneas.*[8] Next, it enters the lake *and flows right through its marshes.*[9] *From there, pursuing its course for* 15 miles *without intermingling with any other waters, it proceeds to the city named Julias.*[10] *Afterwards, in mid course, it passes through Lake Gennesaret.*[11] From there *it winds through a number of places* before entering *the Asphaltium* (that is, the Dead Sea) where it loses its excellent waters.[12] There it becomes *white in colour,* like *milk,* and because of this *one can discern the long trail* that it leaves in the Dead Sea.[13]

1 Hegesippus *Hist.* 4, 16 (*CSEL* 66: 266,19-267,4)
2 Ibid. 4, 16 (*CSEL* 66: 267, 12-14))
3 Ibid. 4, 16 (*CSEL* 66: 267, 10-11)
4 Adamnan *De loc. sanc.* 2, 19 (*CCSL* 175: 215, 1-6)
5 Hegesippus *Hist.* 3, 26 (*CSEL* 66: 234, 20-3). Paneas seems to derive its name from Pan, the Greek deity who was reputed to choose caves and mountains as his favorite haunts. Caesarea was named by Herod the Great in honor of Augustus and was designated as the capital of Judea from 6 to 66 CE The Agrippa here mentioned may either be Agrippa I (9 BCE - 44 CE) or Agrippa II (28 - 92? CE), to whom Paul allegedly preached in Caesarea (Acts 25:13, 26:1ff.).
6 Derived from the Greek φιάλη, a *fiala* is a broad, flat bowl, dish or saucer.
7 Hegesippus *Hist.* 3, 26 (*CSEL* 66: 234, 11-15)
8 Ibid. (*CSEL* 66: 234, 4-10)
9 The lake here mentioned is presumably Lake Semechonitis.
10 Julias is Bethsaida-Julias.
11 I.e., the Sea of Galilee
12 Hegesippus *Hist.* 3, 26 (*CSEL* 66: 235, 1-5)
13 Adamnan *De loc. sanc.* 2, 17 (*CCSL* 175: 214, 3-6)

3. Now Gennesaret (that is, the Sea of Galilee) is *140 stades long, 40 wide*, and surrounded *by great forests*.[1] *Its water is fresh and suitable for drinking inasmuch as it has nothing slimy or muddy from the marsh in it; for it is surrounded by sandy shore on all sides* and is encircled also by delightful towns: Julias and Hippo on the east, and healthful Tiberias with [271]
its warm waters on the west.[2] *The varieties of fish are also tastier and handsomer than in any other lake.*[3]

XI. CONCERNING THE NATURE OF THE DEAD SEA

1. The Dead Sea *is 580 stades long, extending as far as Zoar of Arabia, and 150 wide, reaching all the way to the neighbourhood of Sodom.*[4] It is also quite certain that it overflowed from the pits that were once filled with salt after the burning of Sodom, Gomorrah, and neighbouring cities.[5] But to those looking *from the distant lookout atop the Mount of Olives*[6] the saltiest salt appears to be stirred up *by the colliding waves* and washed ashore. Once it is dried by the sun, it is procured for the benefit of many nations.

2. *But salt* is said to be made *in a different way on a certain mountain in Sicily*, where *stones torn out of the earth* supply *a salt* that is called *the salt of the earth, which is really very salty* and quite suitable for all kinds of uses.[7] Now the Dead Sea is so named because *it supports no kind of living creature, neither fish nor waterfowl*; bulls and camels float on it.[8] Indeed, if the Jordan, having been swollen with rains, empties fish into it, they die instantly and float on its thick waters. *They say that a lighted lamp floats* [272]
on it without turning over and that it sinks when its light is extinguished; that if a living thing is somehow submerged, it stays on the bottom only with great difficulty;[9] *and that all living things submerged there, even those that have been violently battered, immediately float to the surface.*[10]

---

1 Adamnan *De loc. sanc.* 2, 20 (*CCSL* 175: 215, 4) and Hegesippus *Hist.* 3, 26 (*CSEL* 66: 233, 10-11)

2 Hegesippus *Hist.* 3, 26 (*CSEL* 66: 233, 13-16); Adamnan *De loc. sanc.* 2, 20 (*CCSL* 175: 216, 7-9)

3 Hegesippus *Hist.* 3, 26 (*CSEL* 66: 233, 23 - 234, 1)

4 Ibid. 4, 18 (*CSEL* 66: 271, 8-10)

5 Gen. 19:24-6

6 Adamnan *De loc. sanc.* 2, 20 (*CCSL* 175: 216, 19)

7 Matt. 5:13; Adamnan *De loc. sanc.* 2, 17 (*CCSL* 175: 214, 6-13)

8 Hegesippus *Hist.* 4, 18 (*CSEL* 66: 270, 8-10); Pliny *Nat. Hist.* 5, 15, 72 (*LCL* 2:274)

9 Hegesippus *Hist.* 4, 18 (*CSEL* 66: 270, 10-13)

10 Ibid. (*CSEL* 66: 270, 6-8)

3. *Finally, [they say that] Vespasian commanded men who did not know how to swim to be thrown into a deep part with their hands bound tight, and they all floated instantly.*[1] *The water itself is sterile, bitter, and darker than other waters,*[2] *looking as if it were charred.*[3] *It has been confirmed that lumps of bitumen drift in a jet black liquid on the water's surface, and the natives gather them in skiffs. They say that the bitumen sticks to itself and cannot be broken apart at all with a sword, [that it] dissolves only by a woman's menstrual blood or by urine. But it is useful for luting boats and for healing the human body.*[4]

4. That region retains to this day a mark of the punishment it suffered.[5]
[273] *For the loveliest apples are grown there which arouse in their beholders a desire to eat [them]; if you pick [them], they crack open, disintegrate into cinders and smoke as though still burning.*[6] *It is a fact that on summer days an excessive vapour steams all over the plain. For this reason and because of the combined impact of severe drought and an arid soil, the air is polluted and engenders diseases that plague its inhabitants.*[7]

XII. CONCERNING THE PLACE WHERE THE LORD WAS BAPTIZED

1. Now in *the place where the Lord was baptized* there stands *a wooden cross* that is as high *as a man's neck*. From time to time it is covered by high water. The further bank, that is, the eastern one, is within a sling's shot of that place, while the nearer bank is the site of *a large monastery located on the ridge of a small mountain* and renowned for the church *of blessed John the Baptist*. The monks descend from the monastery to the cross by means of a bridge supported by arches, and there they pray.

2. *At the river's edge a square church* has been erected *on four stone piles*, covered *on top with baked tiles, where* the Lord's *clothes* are said to
[274] have been kept when *he was baptized.*[8] People do not enter this [church], but waves [of water] surround and inundate it. *It takes eight days to go from*

1 Hegesippus *Hist.* 4, 18 (*CSEL* 66: 270, 13-15)
2 Ibid. (*CSEL* 66: 270, 8)
3 Ibid. (*CSEL* 66: 270, 21-2)
4 Ibid. (*CSEL* 66: 270, 24 - 271, 8)
5 Bede here seems to refer to the punishment of Sodom and Gomorrah in Gen. 19:24-8.
6 Hegesippus *Hist.* 4, 18 (*CSEL* 66: 272, 2-5)
7 Ibid. 4, 16 (*CSEL* 66: 267, 7-10)
8 Adamnan *De loc. sanc.* 2, 16 (*CCSL* 175: 213, 3 - 214, 31)

the place where the Jordan leaves *the straits of the Sea of Galilee to where it enters the Dead Sea.*[1]

XIII. CONCERNING THE LOCUSTS, THE WILD HONEY, AND THE SPRING OF JOHN

The smallest species of locusts, the kind that John the Baptist ate, appears even today.[2] *Having slender and short bodies, about the size of a finger, they are easily caught in the grass* and, when *cooked* in *oil, supply meagre nourishment. In that same desert* are *trees* having *broad round leaves of milky colour and a honey taste. Naturally fragile, the leaves are rubbed in the hands* and *eaten. This* is said to be *the wild honey.*[3] At that place also they point out *St. John* the Baptist's spring which has *clear* water and *is covered by a white-washed stone roof.*[4]

XIV. CONCERNING JACOB'S WELL NEAR SICHEM[5] *[275]*

Near the city of Sichem, which is now called Neapolis, there is a *church divided into four parts*, that is, made like *a cross.*[6] *At its* centre is *Jacob's well, which is forty cubits deep* and as wide as the distance *from* one's *side to the tips of one's fingers.*[7] *It was water from this well that the Lord deigned to seek from the Samaritan woman.*[8]

1 Adamnan *De loc. sanc.* 2, 20 (*CCSL* 175: 216, 16-18)

2 Matt. 3:4, Mark 1:6

3 Matt. 3:4, Mark 1:6; Adamnan *De loc. sanc.* 2, 23 (*CCSL* 175: 217, 10-19)

4 Adamnan *De loc. sanc.* 2, 22 (*CCSL* 175: 217, 3-6)

5 According to Adamnan, Sichem is the Hebrew name of this place. Found in the Vulgate, it corresponds to what is given in English Bibles as Sychar (John 4:5). Departing from this volume's standard practice of using the name forms given in most modern English bibles, the present translator here uses Sichem rather than Sychar because Adamanan specifically states that this place is customarily, and wrongly, called Sychar.

6 Neapolis: MAP 11, X4 (NOAB); Adamnan *De loc. sanc.* 2, 21 (*CCSL* 175: 216, 5-9).

7 Bede's Latin is quite problematic here. Adamnan clearly describes this width (*extentus*) as the length of a cubit, and not as the width of the well. Unless Bede was working from a defective copy, it is difficult to see how he could have misunderstood Adamnan so badly. The present translator tried to construe the Latin in a way that is congenial to Adamnan's sense, but finally could not. Nor could Giles, whose translation of Bede here reads: 'In the midst of it is Jacob's well, forty cubits deep, and as wide as from the side to the ends of the fingers.' Perhaps the phrase 'as wide as the distance from one's side to the tips of one's fingers' was present in Bede's autograph as a gloss and then intruded into the text by a later copyist.

8 John 4:7; Adamnan *De loc. sanc.* 2, 21 (*CCSL* 175: 216, 10-21)

XV. CONCERNING TIBERIAS, CAPERNAUM, NAZARETH, AND THE HOLY PLACES THERE

1. *On this side of the Sea of Galilee* to the north *of the city of Tiberias* is that *place* where the Lord blessed *the loaves* and *fishes.*[1] *Its grassy flat plain has not been cultivated* since that time. It has *no buildings,*[2] but only a spring from *which they drank* at that time.[3] *Those who* go from Aelia *to Capernaum* thus take the road that goes *through Tiberias and continues from there along the Sea of Galilee* and by *the place where the* bread was *blessed. Capernaum is not far from there on the border of Zebulun and Naphtali. It has no wall*
[276] *[and] is located between a mountain and the lake on a narrow* site *that stretches* east to west *along the seashore for a long way. The mountain is to the north, the lake to the south.*[4]

2. *Nazareth has no* walls, but huge *buildings* and *two large churches. The one in the centre of the city was built* on *two piles, where once stood the house in which the* infant *Lord* was *nursed.* Now *being built on two mounds, as was just said, with arches in between, this church has the clearest spring beneath it, between the mounds.* The citizens draw water from it *into little vessels by means of pulleys in the church. The other church* is *on the site of the house in which* the angel came *to Mary.*[5]

XVI. CONCERNING MOUNT TABOR

Mount Tabor, which is in the middle of the plain of Galilee in Manasseh, *is three miles from* the Sea *of Chinnereth* towards the north and is round *on every side. Covered with grass and flowers, it is 30 stades high.* Its *summit*
[277] has a most delightful *plateau, 23 stades* wide, where *a large monastery* is encircled by a similarly *large forest.*[6] The monastery has three *churches* in accordance with what *Peter said, 'Let us here make three tents.'*[7] The place is surrounded *by a wall* and has large buildings.[8]

1 Matt. 14:19; Mark 6:41; Luke 9:16: John 6:11

2 Adamnan *De loc. sanc.* 2, 24 (*CCSL* 175: 218, 3-11)

3 Ibid. (*CCSL* 175: 275, 3 - 276, 11)

4 Ibid. 2, 25 (*CCSL* 175: 218, 2-12). Following Adamnan, Bede probably also intends for 'the lake' and 'the Sea of Galilee' to be taken here as different designations for the same body of water. As Adamnan makes clear, the Lake of Chinnereth and the Sea of Galilee are the same (*De loc. sanc.* 2, 25—*CCSL* 175: 218, 3-5).

5 Luke 1:26-8; Adamnan *De loc. sanc.* 2, 26 (*CCSL* 175: 218, 2 - 219, 16)

6 Adamnan *De loc. sanc.* 2, 27 (*CCSL* 175: 219, 2 - 220, 10)

7 Mark 9:5, Luke 9:33

8 Adamnan *De loc. sanc.* 2, 27 (*CCSL* 175: 220, 12-18)

XVII. CONCERNING THE SITE OF DAMASCUS

Damascus is situated *on a broad plain* and *is fortified with a long circle of walls* and *numerous towers. Four great rivers flow through it.* Here Christians frequent the church of St. John the Baptist, while *the king of the Saracens* and his own people have erected and consecrated another church for themselves. *Beyond the walls several olive groves lie* round about.[1] It takes seven days to travel from Tabor to Damascus.

XVIII. CONCERNING THE SITE OF ALEXANDRIA AND THE NILE

1. Alexandria *extends a long way from west to east.*[2] *It is bounded on the south by the mouths of the Nile and on the north by Lake Mareotis.*[3] *Its port is more hazardous than the others. Alike in form to a human body, it is rather wide at the head, or roadstead, but quite narrow at the neck where it takes in the passing sea and boats. By means of these, vital necessities are supplied to the port. Once one arrives through the straits and mouths of the port, the sea's expanse increases far and wide, much like the rest of* *[278]*
a body.[4] *To the right of* this *port is a* small *island on which* is the *colossal* Pharos. Pharos is *a tower* that glows *at nighttime* with *flaming torches in order that* sailors *will not be deceived by darkness and crash onto the rocks, being unable to discern the entrance's outline*[5] which *always shifts* because of *the waves* crashing this way and that.[6]

2. *The port, however, is always calm, and is 30 stades wide.*[7] For those entering the city from *Egypt there is a church* on the right *in which the* blessed *evangelist Mark rests.* His body is interred[8] *in front of the altar in the eastern* part *of that church, with a monument overhead* made of squared *marble.*[9] *In the area around* the Nile *the Egyptians* build thick embankments because of the floodwater. *If* by chance the [embankments] *are*

1 Adamnan *De loc. sanc.* 2, 28 (*CCSL* 175: 220, 2-9)

2 Ibid. (*CCSL* 175: 224, 82)

3 Ibid. (*CCSL* 175: 222, 12-14)

4 Ibid. (*CCSL* 175: 222, 18-23). The *CCSL* edition indicates that Bede here is paraphrasing Hegesippus, whereas he is in fact quoting Adamnan verbatim. By 'the rest of the body', Bede with Adamnan presumably intends that part of the body below the neck (i.e., the trunk).

5 Hegesippus *Hist.* 4, 27 (*CSEL* 66: 284, 21 - 285, 5) and Adamnan *De loc. sanc.* 2, 30 (*CCSL* 175: 222, 23-30)

6 Hegesippus *Hist.* 4, 27 (*CSEL* 66: 285, 19-22). See Bieler (1976), 210.

7 Hegesippus *Hist.* 4, 27 (*CSEL* 66: 285, 23-4)

8 'Interred' translates *humanatum* ('made human') in the text of the CCSL edition. Clearly the Latin text should read *humatum*, as it does in the Giles edition of *De locis sanctis* (4: 438).

9 Adamnan *De loc. sanc.* 2, 30 (*CCSL* 175: 224, 89-94)

ruptured owing to the negligence of its *custodians*, the waters do not irrigate, *but inundate* the lands *lying below*. *Those who inhabit the plains of Egypt* build their houses by placing them upon beams *set crosswise* over canals.[1]

[279] XIX. CONCERNING CONSTANTINOPLE AND THE BASILICA THEREIN WHICH CONTAINS THE CROSS OF THE LORD

1. Constantinople is surrounded on all sides except the north by a sea *which stretches 60 miles from the Great Sea to the city wall,* and 40 *miles from the* city *wall to the mouths of the Danube*. The city is enclosed *by a twelve-mile circuit of walls angled so as to parallel the seacoast.*[2] *Constantine* first determined *to build* it *in Cilicia* next to the sea *that separates Asia and Europe,* but *after all the iron tools* were carried off *one night*, those sent out to look for them found them *on the European side*, where the city is now.[3] For it was understood to be God's will that it be built there.

2. In this city a basilica of *marvelous workmanship*, which is called St. Sophia, has been built up *from its foundations* in a circular shape and domed in, enclosed *by three walls*, and raised high with the support of great columns and arches. *The interior of* this *house in* its *northern part* has *a great and very handsome repository. In it is a wooden chest* covered *with a lid, also of wood*, which holds three pieces of the Lord's *cross*, namely, *the long timber*, cut into two parts, and the *cross* beam of the same holy cross. It is brought out for only *three days* a *year* for the people to adore, *that is, on [the day of] the Lord's supper*,[4] Good Friday, and Holy *Saturday*.

3. On the first of these days, that chest, which is *two cubits* high and *one wide*, is set upon a golden altar with the holy cross open to view. *The emperor is the first to approach*, adore and kiss the holy cross, then all the ranks of laymen in their order. On the next day the empress and all the *married women* and virgins do the same, while on the *third* day, *the bishops* and all the grades of clergy do likewise. Then *the chest* is closed and *carried back to the aforementioned repository*. But as long as it stays open on the altar, *a marvellous odour* permeates the whole church. For *a fragrant fluid* like *oil* flows out of the knots of the holy wood and if even only a little of it touches any disease, it heals all of that person's infirmities.[5]

1 Adamnan *De loc. sanc.* 2, 30 (*CCSL* 175: 225, 100-8)
2 Ibid. 3, 1 (*CCSL* 175: 226, 7-13)
3 Ibid. 3, 2 (*CCSL* 175: 227, 2-10 and 26)
4 I. e., Maundy Thursday
5 Adamnan *De loc. sanc.* 3, 3 (*CCSL* 175: 228, 3 - 229, 53)

4. I have explained these things concerning the holy places as best I could, having followed reliable accounts, especially the Gallic bishop Arculf's dictations which the priest Adamnan, a man most learned in the [280]
Scriptures, recorded in a prolix style, writing them down in three books. Now as a bishop renowned for his longing for the holy places, he forsook his own country and went to the promised land. After he had lingered for some months in Jerusalem and had employed an experienced monk named Peter as his guide and interpreter, he eagerly travelled by a circuitous route to all the places he had longed to see.

5. He also passed through Alexandria, Damascus, Constantinople, and Sicily. But when he wanted to return to his own country, the boat on which he was sailing was carried to our island (that is, Britain) after many diversions caused by a contrary wind. And at last, having faced not a few dangers, he reached the aforementioned venerable man Adamnan. In recounting his journey and describing the places he had seen, he showed Adamnan how to write a charming narrative. Drawing from some of this narrative and comparing it with the writings of the ancients, we pass along to you what should be read, praying that in all respects you take pains to temper your toil in the present age not with the leisure of idle amusement, but with a zeal for reading and prayer.

ON THE RESTING-PLACES: INTRODUCTION

In or around the year 716, while Bede was engaged in writing his commentary on 1 Samuel, he received a letter from his friend Acca, the bishop of Hexham.[1] In response to Acca's inquiries about two specific points of biblical interpretation, Bede composed a pair of letters, both of which he deemed worthy of inclusion in the catalogue of his works at the end of the *Ecclesiastical History*.[2] The first letter, which Bede described as *De mansionibus filiorum Israel* (*On the Resting-Places of the Children of Israel*), deals with the chronology of the Israelites' itinerary from Egypt to Canaan as set forth in Num. 33. The second letter, on Isaiah 24:22, is introduced and translated subsequently in this volume.

For the most part, Bede's treatment of the stages of the Exodus remains on the level of the historical sense; he is particularly concerned to harmonize what he calls the 'catalogue' of resting-places in Num. 33 with relevant dates and locations derived from references to the resting-places elsewhere in Numbers, and also in the books of Exodus and Deuteronomy. At the conclusion of the letter, however, Bede offers a brief but suggestive explication of what he calls the moral sense of Israel's wanderings in the desert, understood as the ascent of the Christian Church (or the individual faithful soul) along the upward path of spiritual virtue.

In adopting this allegorical approach, Bede was following the example of Jerome (whom he explicitly names) in a letter addressed to the Roman matron Fabiola in the year 400.[3] Jerome himself had made use of a homily on the same subject by the great Alexandrian biblical scholar and theologian Origen, but there is no indication that Bede was aware of this, or that he had read Origen's homily for himself—even though it circulated in the West

1 On the dating of Bede's *In primam partem Samuhelis* to the year of Abbot Ceolfrith's departure to Rome, see the prologue to *In Sam.* 4 (*CCSL* 119: 213, 1-28). On Acca, see Plummer (1896), 2: 329-30, and Whitelock (1976), 26-7.

2 Bede *Hist. eccl.* 5, 24 (ed. Colgrave and Mynors, 568)

3 Jerome *Ep.* 78 (*CSEL* 55: 49-87). On Jerome's relationship with Fabiola, who died before he finished this letter to her, see Kelly (1975), 210-12.

in a Latin translation by Rufinus.[1] Whereas both Origen and Jerome had devoted considerable attention to detailed explications of the names of the various resting-places according to their (often fallacious) interpretations of Hebrew etymology, Bede was content simply to explain that the circuitous route of the Exodus is an apt symbol of the Christian journey with its repeated occasions of repentance and renewal.

This letter is extant in two manuscripts: Paris, Bibliothèque Nationale lat. 2840, from the late ninth/early tenth century, and Zurich, Zentralbibliothek C 78 (451) IV 12, from the late ninth century.[2] It was first published by J. A. Giles in 1843, and the present translation is based upon his text as reprinted by Migne in *PL* 94: 699-702.

1 Origen *Hom. in Num.* 27 (*GCS* 30: 255-80), which is extant only in Rufinus's translation. Nor does Bede appear to have used either of the other major patristic treatments of the subject: Ps.-Ambrose *De XLII mansionibus filiorum Israel* (*PL* 17: 9-40); and Isidore *Quaestiones in Numeros* (*PL* 83: 339-60).

2 Laistner and King (1943), 119

ON THE RESTING-PLACES OF THE CHILDREN OF ISRAEL

To the Lord Bishop Acca, most beloved in Christ and always to be named with every honour, from your faithful servant Bede. [699]

By sending me at the same time, most beloved Bishop, certain questions to be solved (not, however, of one and the same difficulty), you compel me to turn somewhat aside for a short while from the unfinished exposition of the blessed prophet Samuel[1] to the examination of Moses and Isaiah. The first of these [questions], which has reference to the history of a bygone time, may well become clear easily, or else it will remain obscure without any great danger. But since the second pertains to faith regarding things to come, we must take care not to run into the pit of a most impious heresy should it be considered otherwise than is proper.

Well then, you inquire how the resting-places of the children of Israel, which in the last part of the Book of Numbers are reckoned to be forty-two all together,[2] relate to the number of years of that long journey which was made from Egypt to the land of promise,[3] and are meant to correspond to them. For although it is evident to all readers that the years of that same journey and the resting-places were very nearly the same in number, nevertheless it is by no means clear that they stayed[4] one year in each encampment. On this question, as is my custom in all things, I am ready to tell Your Beatitude what I believe, which is that the same encampments or resting-places correspond to the courses of only three of the years of the departure from Egypt, namely, the first, the second, and the fortieth.

1 The reference is to Bede's *In primam partem Samuhelis* (*CCSL* 119: 1-287), the first three books of which were completed by June, 716, with the fourth book written soon thereafter.

2 Num. 33:1-49; Jerome *Ep.* 78, 2, 2 (*CSEL* 55: 52, 2-4)

3 I.e., forty years; see Num. 32:13

4 'stayed' = *commoratos*, an emendation for the *PL* reading *commemoratos*

Of these, the first year contained twelve resting-places clearly distinguished.[1] The first [place] was entered on the twelfth day of the first month;[2] the last was reached in the wilderness of Sinai on the first day of the third month,[3] and through eleven successive months, for the purpose of building the tabernacle and teaching the law, it was not left at all.[4] Only nine of these twelve resting-places are expressly named in the Book of Exodus; three others it passed over indistinctly under the name of 'the desert of Sin', which is said to be between Elim and Sinai.[5]

The second year encompasses twenty-one resting-places,[6] which in the course of the narrative are all comprehended without distinction under the name of 'the wilderness of Paran'; only the first, second, and last (that is, the Graves of Lust, Hazeroth, and Kadesh) are distinguished by their proper names.[7] But in the catalogue of the resting-places[8] it is diligently shown how many there were all together, and by what names they were called. The first of these resting-places (that is, the Graves of Lust) was entered on the second month of the same second year, on the twenty-second day of the month. For as Scripture says, *In the second year, in the second month, on the twentieth day of the month,*[9] they set forth from the encampment in the
[700] desert of Sinai, and (it says) *a cloud rested over the wilderness of Paran,*[10] and they proceeded on their way from the mountain of the Lord for three days,[11] until they came to the site of the resting-place which rightly received the name of 'Graves of Lust' because the people were longing for the

1 Bede is calculating the number twelve from his reading of Num. 33:3-15.

2 The dating of the arrival at Rameses (which Bede takes as the first resting-place rather than the Israelites' residence in Egypt) is derived not from Scripture but from a reference in the Church's baptismal liturgy, as Bede indicates in his commentary *In Ezr.* 2 (*CCSL* 119A: 323, 1408-14).

3 Exod. 19:1; cf. Num. 33:15

4 According to Num. 10:11-12, the Israelites set out from the wilderness of Sinai on the second day of the second month of the Hebrew calendar, precisely eleven months after they had entered that place.

5 Exod. 12:37-19:2. The encampment of the Israelites in the wilderness of Sin is narrated in Exod. 16:1, but the locations of the camps by the Red Sea, at Dophkah, and at Alush (Num. 33:10-13) are not mentioned at all in Exodus, as noted by Jerome in *Ep.* 78, 9, 3; 10, 1; 12, 1 (*CSEL* 55: 59, 9-10 and 18-20; 61, 1-5).

6 Each of these places is named in Num. 33:16-36.

7 Num. 11:34-5; 13:26 (27); 'Graves of Lust' = *sepulcra concupiscentiae*, which the Vulgate uses to translate the Hebrew place-name Kibroth-hattaavah.

8 I.e., Num. 33

9 Num. 10:11

10 Num. 10:12

11 Num. 10:33

fleshmeats of Egypt.[1] Now it is not said on what day or in which month they entered the last of these resting-places (that is, Kadesh[2]), but nevertheless it is no secret that it also was in the wilderness of Paran, because it was reached in the same year. For it is written: *And the people did not move from that place until Miriam had been recalled. Then they marched from Hazeroth, and pitched their tents in the desert of Paran. There the Lord spoke to Moses, saying, 'Send men to view the land of Canaan.'*[3] And so that it should not be thought that this order and action took place in the resting-place of Hazeroth, but should rather be understood to have been carried out in the last of those described as 'in the wilderness of Paran',[4] let us consider what is written below: *And when those who had gone to spy out the land returned after forty days, having gone around the entire country, they came to Moses and Aaron and to all the company of the children of Israel in the desert of Paran, which is in Kadesh.*[5] But in Deuteronomy Moses himself also says to the people: *And when you had come into Kadesh-barnea, I said to you, 'You have come to the mountain of the Amorites, which the Lord our God will give us. See the land which the Lord your God gives you, go up [and possess] it.' And all of you came to me and said, 'Send men to view the land,'* and so forth.[6] Now in the second year of the exodus from Egypt they arrived at that resting-place, but owing to their sin of murmuring they were turned back from it again and were condemned to wander aimlessly through the desert for a long time and to fall here and there, as Moses bears witness in what follows, saying: *Therefore you stayed in Kadesh-barnea for a long time, and departing from there we came into the wilderness that leads to the Red Sea, as the Lord had told me, and we circled around Mount Seir for a long time.*[7] And below: *Now the time that we traveled from Kadesh-barnea until we passed over the brook Zered was thirty-eight years, until the entire generation of warriors had perished from the camp, as the Lord had sworn.*[8] Now Zered is not the name of a resting-place (of which there are, as I say, forty-two) but the name of the brook to which, as we read

1 Num. 11:33-4 (cf. Num. 33:16); Jerome *Ep.* 78, 15, 2 (*CSEL* 55: 64, 17)

2 Num. 33:36

3 Num. 12:15-13:2 (12:15-13:3)

4 Jerome *Ep.* 78, 17, 2 (*CSEL* 55: 66, 7-11)

5 Num. 13:25-6 (13:26-7)

6 Deut. 1:19-22; Vulgate reads 'Let us send men', but Bede has conformed to the verb form in Num. 13:3, quoted above.

7 Deut. 1:46-2:1

8 Deut. 2:14. Because they had continually tested God with their unfaithfulness in the wilderness, none of the Israelites who had been adults at the time of the Exodus (excepting Caleb and Joshua) were permitted to enter the land of Canaan; see Num. 14:20-35.

in the Book of Numbers, they came after having passed over the thirty-eighth resting-place, which was named Iye-abarim.[1] *Which they left,* it says, *and encamped on the other side of the Arnon, which is in the desert and extends into the territory of the Amorites;*[2] that this happened in the fortieth year is not revealed to us.

The resting-places of the very long journey through the desert which are contained in this same year (namely, the fortieth and last) are ten in number. The first of them was attained only with great effort; this was the same Kadesh in the desert of Zin,[3] to which, as we have said, they returned after having been turned back thirty-eight years before by a crime of transgression. Thus is it written concerning it: *And the children of Israel and the whole multitude came into the desert of Zin in the first month, and the people stayed in Kadesh. And Miriam died there, and was buried in the same place. And when the people were in need of water they gathered together against Moses and Aaron,*[4] and so forth, up to that which is written, *This is the Water of Contradiction, where the children of Israel quarreled with the Lord, and*
[701] *he was sanctified in them.*[5] And we should note that Scripture relates that the same Kadesh was located in the desert of Paran and in the desert of Zin; hence it is permissible, in accordance with the customary usage of place-names, to construe that part of the desert of Paran within which Kadesh is [located] as being particularly designated by the name of Zin.[6] Now this Zin is not the one between Elim and Sinai that they passed through soon after crossing the Red Sea, but another one altogether, and among the Hebrews they are written with different letters.[7] But the second resting-place in the same fortieth year is Mount Hor, upon which Aaron died on the first day of the fifth month;[8] the last one is the encampment in Moab across the Jordan opposite Jericho where they stayed while meditating on

1 Num. 21:11-12; cf. Num. 33:44

2 Num. 21:13

3 The Vulgate refers to this as the desert of *Sin*, which is the same name used of the wilderness mentioned in Exod. 16:1. As Bede explains later on, in Hebrew the two names are actually written with different initial letters.

4 Num. 20:1-2

5 Num. 20:13; 'Water of Contradiction' = *aqua contradictionis*, used in the Vulgate to refer to the place known in the Hebrew Bible and most modern translations as 'Meribah', which means 'Quarrel'.

6 Confronted with the fact that Numbers locates Kadesh in both the wilderness of Paran and the wilderness of Zin, Bede concluded that the latter was a particular portion of the former. Modern scholars, however, surmise that Kadesh may have been on the border between the two areas; see Seely (1992).

7 Jerome *Ep.* 78, 35, 1 (*CSEL* 55: 76, 3-6)

8 Num. 20:23-9 (22-30); 33:38

Deuteronomy, until the time after the death of Moses when, with Joshua as [their] leader, they crossed the dry depths of the River Jordan on the first day of the tenth month.[1]

Thus in the first year there were twelve resting-places in all; in the second [year], twenty-one; in the last [year], the same twenty-first (which is Kadesh) again and also nine others, which is forty-two all together. Here we ought to consider more carefully why the lawgiver [Moses] who had so diligently composed a catalogue of three of the years preferred to pass over the rest in silence, in such a way that he fashioned the distinct locations of the resting-places of such great periods of time (or rather ages) into the form of a continuous narrative, as though they were following in turn, one right after another: *And departing from Abronah they encamped at Ezion-geber. Going on from there, they came into the desert of Zin (that is, Kadesh). Departing from Kadesh, they encamped at Mount Hor.*[2] When the preceding investigations explain more thoroughly that they came away from Ezion-geber in the second year of the journey and after thirty-eight years of long meanderings finally left the same Kadesh and came to Mount Hor, this is by no means without purpose, but ought to be understood as having been done and written down in such a way for the sake of a great mystery, wherein I believe there is a lesson that ought to be perceived in the moral sense, while still preserving the plainer meaning.

As blessed Jerome explains quite plainly in the book he composed about these things,[3] the successive upward movements of the same resting-places, which advance from their being freed from slavery in Egypt to the land of promise, are the ascent of spiritual virtues seeking the sublime, to which the Church of Christ (and indeed, every faithful soul) hurries to climb in hope of being set free from this vale of tears to go up to the place laid out for it above (that is, to see *the God of gods in Zion*[4]). As long as we are advancing *from virtue to virtue*[5] as if to certain camps and resting-places, throughout the desert of [this] arid world let us do whatever things are right and proper in the sight of God, secure in the progress of our good work and with God as our leader. And whenever through any sort of vices that snatch us away we turn aside from the path of truth [which we have] undertaken, we are not able to ascend at once to the higher ranks of virtues, but are obliged to do penance for a while in order to turn back again little by little

1 Num. 22:1; 33:48; Deut. 1:1-5; Josh. 4:19
2 Num. 33:35-7
3 Jerome *Ep.* 78 (*CSEL* 55: 49-87)
4 Ps. 84:7 (83:8)
5 Ps. 84:7 (83:8)

from the lowest failings of a wretched mind toward the higher things, until through deeds worthy of the fruits of repentance[1] we are brought back to that way from which we have fallen and attain the summit. This is what it means to follow the way of virtues for a while by putting off the old self with its deeds and being clothed with a new [self] *which was created according to [the likeness of] God in righteousness and holiness;*[2] this is what is meant by the death and burial of the fathers who had sinned in the desert and the ardour of the youth which had grown to adulthood there and which, having overcome the river of death, was worthy to enter into the kingdom of the heavenly promise. For since the youth of our good conduct
[702] has been renewed like that of an eagle,[3] we are now able to fortify the camps of [our] heavenly advances against evil spirits with so much and such kinds of spiritual grace that we thereby attain rest. [Camps] such as these are not only pleasing in the sight of God but also most worthy of praise and of the writings of the spiritual fathers.

Most Beloved, I have taken the trouble to write these things in response to your first question as soon as I read Your Beatitude's letter, because they are plain to those who consider [them] and can be dealt with in a historical way. But concerning the testimony of the prophet [Isaiah] which you sent to be expounded at the same time, if God grants us the ability to find anything worth writing down, that too as quickly as possible we shall take care not to conceal from you. May the Holy and Undivided Trinity keep Your Holy Beatitude safe as you are praying for his church.[4]

1 Matt. 3:8; Luke 3:8; Acts 26:20

2 Eph. 4:22-4

3 Ps. 103:5 (102:5)

4 While there is no reason to suspect that this benediction is anything more than a conventional formula, in later years the Bishop of Hexham was to face an onslaught of ecclesiastical troubles. Sometime between 729 and 731, Bede referred to Acca's trials and persecutions in his preface to *De templo* (*CCSL* 119A: 144, 30 - 145, 74), and according to the Moore MS's continuation of Bede's *Historia ecclesiastica* (ed. Colgrave and Mynors, 572) Acca was driven from his see in 731.

ON WHAT ISAIAH SAYS: INTRODUCTION

Scholars have frequently had occasion to remark upon Bede's pragmatic cast of mind.[1] As Bernard Capelle put it, 'Bede was not a speculative thinker. He was more at home with facts than with ideas, better at the exposition of the truth than at its discovery, more teacher, in short, than thinker.'[2] It may come as something of a surprise, then, to find that Bede wrote a rather extensive treatise on the eternal nature of punishment for the damned. This work, the second of a pair of letters that Bede addressed to his friend and bishop, Acca of Hexham, around the year 716, takes the form of an interpretation of Isa. 24:22. In the catalogue of his writings Bede described it as a letter *de eo quod ait Isaias 'Et claudentur ibi in carcerem et post multos dies uisitabunter'* (*on what Isaiah says: 'And they will be shut up there in prison, and after many days they will be visited'*).[3] The point at issue in this letter, though certainly doctrinal in character, was for Bede not a matter for aimless speculation. Whenever he suspected that heresy might be afoot, Bede's intellectual passion was unrelenting.[4]

Acca's first question, which Bede tackled in *On the Resting-Places*, had been relatively easy for him to answer. 'But', he explained to Acca, 'since the second pertains to faith regarding things to come, we must take care not to run into the pit of a most impious heresy should it be considered otherwise than is proper.'[5] It appears that Acca was confused and troubled by something Bede had written in his commentary on 1 Samuel. With reference to the stone from David's sling that killed the giant Goliath, which he interpreted as the everlasting punishment of the devil and his fallen angels, Bede had observed:[6]

1 Mayr-Harting (1972), 219; Bonner (1973), 87-9; Davidse (1982), 672; Holder (1990), 406-7

2 Capelle (1936), 16

3 Bede *Hist. eccl.* 5, 24 (ed. Colgrave and Mynors, 568)

4 On Bede's abhorrence of heresy and schism, see Plummer (1896), 1: lxii-lxiii; and Bonner (1973), 73-4.

5 Bede *De mans.* (*PL* 94: 699B)

6 Bede *In Sam.* 3 (*CCSL* 119: 160, 998 - 161, 1013)

> This is similar to what Isaiah testifies concerning [the devil's] irrevocable condemnation, when he says, *And the passage of the rod which the Lord God will make to fall upon him will be confirmed.*[1] That is: he will never be saved so as to be delivered from his torments, nor will he alternate at various times between punishments and repose, as we do when we are scourging someone and we repeatedly take the rod or whip off the back of the one being flogged just for an instant as we raise it up so that we can strike the person again, but that one, subjected to constant punishment, will continue to groan without any alternation of rest. This is contrary to those who—on the basis of the testimony of Isaiah in which he says when writing about the impious, *And they will be shut up there in prison, and after many days they will be visited*[2]—give the devil and his angels and all the reprobate reason to hope that, after however long and innumerable successions of ages, they will receive remission of such great crimes, and eternal life with the Lord—which is contrary to the sentence of the Lord and Judge who foretells that at the critical moment of the Last Judgement he will say: *Depart from me, you accursed, into everlasting fire.*[3]

The obsequious tone of Bede's second letter to Acca, which is even more deferential than usual, is understandable in light of his rather delicate task, which was to expose his own bishop as having so misconstrued his words as to have attributed to Bede himself the heretical notion that he was in fact attempting to refute. With elaborate protestations of humility, then, but very firmly, Bede strove to prevent Acca from believing and preaching a doctrine that might encourage the faithful to be less than diligent about confessing those sins which they had already committed and avoiding those sins that may tempt them in the future. After all (Bede seems to have reasoned), if hell be anything less than eternal, how can the preacher still invoke the fear of hell in order to persuade people to do what is right?

Bede appeals to a passage in Jerome's commentary on Isaiah to support his argument that the 'visitation' of the souls in hell will not bring them any lasting relief from torment; indeed, Bede is skeptical even of Jerome's suggestion that the visitation of the Lord may bring some alteration of their

1 Isa. 30:32
2 Isa. 24:22
3 Matt. 25:41

condition, however slight.[1] To counter any such idea, Bede proceeds to examine a number of biblical verses that seem to promise either an increase in suffering or a temporary respite, concluding in every case that they pertain to those here on earth who still have time to repent, rather than to those in hell for whom repentance is no longer possible. This leads him to distinguish between prophecies that speak of the final judgement, and those that speak of the days just before the judgement; this requires careful discrimination, as the two are often mingled together in one biblical passage, or even in a single verse.

Continuing his painstaking investigation, Bede next examines the words of Isaiah that precede the verse in question, and those that immediately follow. Both are explicated with reference to other scriptural passages containing similar expressions, and in relation to church history, which abounds with examples of saints who were vindicated and persecutors who suffered the untimely and painful deaths which in Bede's estimation they so obviously deserved. Since Bede believed that several of the passages in question refer to the defeat of Antichrist, he deems it necessary to describe the days of tribulation preceding the end of time, the final conflict between the forces of good and evil, and God's ultimate victory over Antichrist and his minions.

As Bede rehearses the traditional apocalyptic scenario he has inherited from Augustine and Jerome, it is clear that he has no sympathy with any attempt to calculate the precise time of the end of the world; nor does he express any chiliastic expectations of a thousand year reign of the saints with Christ in some earthly kingdom, whether before or after the day of judgement.[2] However, he does quote approvingly Jerome's suggestion that the peaceful period of forty-five days which Dan. 12:11-12 was thought to imply between the defeat of Antichrist and the Last Judgement might be explained as 'a trial of patience for the saints'—thereby calling attention to an interpretation destined to play an important role (contrary to the intentions of Jerome and Bede) in the reintroduction of the notion of a thousand-year sabbath into medieval Western Christian thought.[3]

1 Bede *De eo quod ait Isaias* (*PL* 94: 702D-703A), quoting Jerome *In Es.* 8 (*CCSL* 73: 323, 49 - 324, 60)

2 On Bede's anti-millennialism and its patristic background, see Bonner (1966); Landes (1988), 174-8; Matter (1992), 47; and McCready (1994), 89-99.

3 On the history of interpretation of the discrepancy of forty-five days in Dan. 12:11-12 and its implications for medieval millennial expectations, see Lerner (1988) and (1992).

This letter is extant in only one manuscript: Paris, Bibliothèque Nationale lat. 2840, from the late ninth/early tenth century.[1] It was first published by J. A. Giles in 1843, and the present translation is based upon his text as reprinted by Migne in *PL* 94: 702-10.

1 Laistner and King (1943), 119

ON WHAT ISAIAH SAYS: *AND THEY WILL BE SHUT UP THERE IN PRISON, AND AFTER MANY DAYS THEY WILL BE VISITED.* [702]

To the most blessed lord who is always to be venerated with profoundest charity, the holy Bishop Acca, I Bede, the humblest of Christ's servants, send greetings.

While responding promptly to your first question, I deemed it more fitting to consider the second (which appeared to me to be more obscure) at a more opportune time. So it is only now that I shall expound what can be both said and understood about it without any faltering of the catholic faith, in so far as it is within my small understanding. For you ask something that is certainly worthy of investigation (although I do not know whether it should be asked of the likes of me), namely, how we ought to understand what Isaiah says concerning the day of judgement when he writes, among other things: **And on that day it shall come to pass that the Lord will visit upon the host of heaven on high, and upon the kings of the earth who are upon the earth, and they will be gathered together into a gathering of one bundle into the pit, and they will be shut up there in prison, and after many days they will be visited, and the moon will blush, and the sun will be confounded, when the Lord of hosts will reign on Mount Zion, and in Jerusalem, and will be glorified in the sight of his elders.**[1]

Now you claim that you were prompted to inquire about this from the reading of my third little book on Samuel, where we made mention of this same verse when we interpreted the stone lodged in the head of Goliath as the punishments of the devil and his fellow angels, which are more than everlasting and never entirely to be shaken off.[2] However, that is not how

1 Isa. 24:21-3. Here and throughout the translation that follows 'will visit upon' renders *uisitabit...super*, an ambiguous Latin phrase which Bede seems to understand as meaning 'will punish'.

2 Bede *In Sam.* 3 (*CCSL* 119: 161, 1006-13)

this [verse] ought to be understood, but we were rather explaining how it ought not to be understood, that is, that they can never be set free after many days, those to whom it is said at the Last Judgement, *Depart from me, you accursed, into everlasting fire.*[1] For the same prophet cannot be contrary to himself, who says elsewhere: *And they shall see the corpses of the men who transgressed against me; their worm shall not die, and their fire shall not be quenched.*[2] But if it is asked how this should be understood, most beloved lord in Christ, I declare openly before Your Holiness that I have never ventured to say that I have understood what the prophet Isaiah perceived, and what he wanted to be perceived in this verse. Nevertheless, I am not unwilling to explain to you, as you ask me to, what I believe myself to have perceived plainly and in a catholic manner.

First, let us examine very diligently what blessed Jerome said about this [verse] in that most pleasing work of his on the same prophet: *Now what*
[703] *follows* (he says), *'And after many days they will be visited,' seems to agree with my friends who grant penance to the devil and to demons, because after much time they are to be visited by the Lord. But let them consider that Divine Scripture does not say openly, 'They will be visited by the Lord,' or 'They will be visited by angels,' but simply 'They will be visited.' From the ambiguity of the word, it is possible to understand either 'relief' or 'reproach' since, after the righteous have received their rewards, those are to be visited in eternal punishment. Nevertheless, we must understand that human fragility is unable to know God's judgement, or to pass judgement on the magnitude and the measure of punishments, which is reserved to the decision of the Lord.*[3] With these words, the most learned man surely refuted the error of those who affirm that the devil, along with reprobate angels and humans, is permitted to be released from torments a long time after the Last Judgement is completed.[4] He also shows how it can be understood from the words of the prophet that—since the rewards given to the righteous at the judgement are eternal—when the reprobate are damned they are visited

1 Matt. 25:41

2 Isa. 66:24

3 Jerome *In Es.* 8 (*CCSL* 73: 323, 49 - 324, 60)

4 Jerome is here refuting the teaching of Origen and his followers that even the devil will eventually be saved. On Jerome's anti-Origenism (which intensified with the passage of time and was virulent by the time he wrote his commentary on Isaiah), see Clark (1992), 121-51. Elsewhere, Bede condemns Origen by name in the course of a defense of eternal punishment; see *In. Prou.* 2 (*CCSL* 119B: 70, 19-28). He would also have been familiar with Augustine's arguments in favor of the eternity of punishment for the damned, as expressed in *Enchir.* 29, 109-13 (*CCSL* 46: 108, 1 - 110, 77), and *De ciu. Dei* 21, 17-27 (*CCSL* 48: 783, 1 - 805, 228); on which see Bernstein (1993), 322-32.

in perpetual punishment in a manner unknown to us; that they may obtain a little relief (surely not, however, being released from all torments), or perhaps be punished with a still more grievous reproach; and that, in any case, we must consign whatever and however and whenever it may be to the eternal knowledge of the only Judge. But in truth, nowhere else in the Scriptures have we read any idea of this sort, namely about the increasing or diminishing of the torments of the reprobate after the day of judgement.

To be sure, there are some who, as if in support of this kind of understanding, take up an ambiguous saying from Habakkuk, along with that of the prophet [Isaiah]: *In wrath, you will remember mercy.*[1] But it is as clear as day that this means something different, namely, that God, angry on account of the breach of virtuous conduct by human beings, expelled them from the joys of Paradise into this vale of tears; nevertheless, from them he did not take away the hope of recovering their senses,[2] as [he did] from the angels who fell from heaven, but more than that, he summoned the throng of listeners to the [hope of] regaining salvation. To each of us sinners, the renowned *Spirit that goes forth and does not return*,[3] which in himself is always tranquil, may appear to be wrathful while he is inflicting punishment. And yet, soon afterwards he will remember to be suitably merciful to the penitent. Accordingly, the prophet said this to [that same Spirit] in a prayer *for those who are ignorant*,[4] that if for an hour he grows wrathful at the ignorance of the sinner, he will at once be merciful to the one who prays; similar to this is that [saying] of the Psalmist: *Will God forget to be merciful, or will he in his wrath shut up his mercy?*[5] Surely it is certain that this and all other sayings of this sort (such as also that one, *I will visit their iniquities with the rod*, as well as *I will increase your stripes sevenfold*,[6] and other such things) are appropriate to the circumstances of this age, in which the saints sing to the Lord of mercy and judgement. But it is doubtful if [such sayings also refer to the age] to come, in which there takes place what is said to God in another psalm: *For you render to all of them*

1 Hab. 3:2, Old Latin

2 *resipiscendi*; cf. 2 Tim. 2:26

3 Ps. 78:39 (77:39). In its original context this phrase refers not to the Divine Spirit but to the children of Israel who are like the wind (Lat.: *spiritus*) in their inconstancy; however, vs. 38 does refer to the mercy of God and the restraint of his wrath. Bede's thought (though not his language) is actually much closer to Isa. 55:11, in which the word of the Lord goes forth from his mouth and does not return to him empty.

4 Hab. 3:1; 'for those who are ignorant' = *pro ignorantibus* (Old Latin); cf. Vulg. *pro ignorantiis*

5 Ps. 77:9 (76:10); 'his mercy' = *misericordiam suam* (Old Latin); cf. Vulg. *misericordias suas* = 'his mercies'

6 Ps. 89:32 (88:33); Lev. 26:21

according to their works,[1] because, I say, clearly Scripture does not say anything about an alteration of this sort which is to come after the universal judgement.

As for that little verse of the prophet in which he asserts that the kings of the earth who have been shut up in the prison of the pit will be visited after many days, there are those who think that this is not going to be fulfilled a long time after the last examination is accomplished, but in the examination itself. For it is evident that the people who are answerable for greater offenses, having been gathered together in the pit of misery for many
[704] days before the judgement, must be called forth temporarily by resurrection at the very time of judgement; then, when the judgement has been accomplished, after receiving their bodies they must be shut up in that same pit.

At the time of this visitation which is to come after many days, that is, [at the time of] the coming resurrection and judgement, there will also be fulfilled[2] the following little verses in which it is said: **And the moon will blush and the sun will be confounded, when the Lord of hosts will reign on Mount Zion,**[3] and so forth. For these things shall come to pass on the day of judgement, when Christ is going to show forth to all people the glory of his kingdom, and to the saints the blessedness of the vision of himself. [Of these things] the company of prophets speaks often, and the gospel Scripture more openly, as the Lord says: *But in those days, after that tribulation, the sun will be darkened, and the moon will not give its light, and the stars of heaven will be falling down, and the powers that are in the heavens will be shaken, and then they will see the Son of Man coming in the clouds, with great power and glory.*[4] Let no one think it contrary to this assertion that it is said, **And on that day it shall come to pass that the Lord will visit,** as if it cannot be said that on that day there will come to pass what must obviously be completed in a great many days before the judgement. For surely Scripture, when it speaks of the day of judgement, is accustomed to designate the times that immediately precede the judgement, calling them not only 'that day' but also 'that hour'. Accordingly, John the Apostle also, writing such a long time before the day of judgement, says: *Little children, it is the last hour, and as you have heard that Antichrist is coming, even now many antichrists have arisen, whereby we know that*

1 Ps. 28:4 (27:4). Bede's rendition of this verse does not conform to the Vulgate; it is probably based on an unidentified Old Latin version.

2 literally, 'fill out'

3 Isa. 24:23

4 Mark 13:24-6

it is the last hour.[1] And after the Lord himself had said in the gospel, *And on the day that Lot went out from Sodom, it rained fire and brimstone from heaven and destroyed them all—it will be like this on the day when the Son of Man shall be revealed,*[2] he immediately continued and said, *In that hour, anyone on the housetop whose goods are in the house must not go down to take them away, and likewise anyone in the field must not turn back.*[3] For it appeared as though, having first mentioned the day of revelation, he immediately added 'that hour'—not that any hour ought to be understood other than that in which the revelation itself would occur.

Nevertheless, by naming the hour, the Lord was not designating those things which are to take place on the day when judgement is revealed, but those things which must occur prior to the day on which judgement is to be revealed. For when the Lord was raining fire and brimstone from heaven, no one in Sodom had any time to run back and do penance for offenses, or to run ahead and add to them, and when the Son of Man will be revealed no one will possess either the capacity or the will to revisit the pleasures that were left behind in the course of ascending to the world above, or to forsake the fruits of the spiritual virtues which were practiced with devotion for so long. For this is what it means to be going down to take away the goods left in the house, and to be going back too late to work in the field: when the unexpected advent of the Judge will catch people in the act [of their sin], compelling them all to fear, and to think only of the recompense for their own works. Therefore the Apostle [John] testified even at the very beginnings of the New Testament that the last hour had already come. And even if the Lord, speaking of the day of judgement and the revelation of his own advent, unexpectedly added what should be guarded against in that hour, and what should be done by the faithful, nevertheless, by the very fact that they were being admonished it is evident that [the hour] was being shown not to pertain to the very moment of the judgement that is coming, [705]
but rather to the times just prior to the judgement which is at hand, concerning which the promise had been: *The days will come when you will long to see one of the days of the Son of Man, and you will not see it; and they will say to you, 'Look here,'*[4] and a little later: *And just as it happened*

1 1 John 2:18
2 Luke 17:29-30
3 Luke 17:30-1
4 Luke 17:22-3

in the days of Noah, so too it will be on the day of the Son of Man: they were eating and drinking, they were taking wives and being given in marriage.[1] Consider, then, how much more the prophet, who preceded the times of the New Testament by the succession of so many ages and was thus stretching forth the eye of prophecy far ahead to the things to be expected at the end of time, was able when speaking of the consummation of the age to interpose at the same time those things which he was perceiving were not already present, but were still imminent at the very consummation to come.

Hence it is pleasing to examine more diligently the things a little further above this prophetic passage concerning which there is a question, and to explain how they were pertaining partly to the day of judgement, partly to the times close to the judgement: **The prevaricators have prevaricated, and with the prevarication of transgressors have they prevaricated.**[2] Is there anyone who does not see that these things are to take place before the day of judgement, when (as the Lord has foretold) *many will be caused to stumble; and they will betray one another and hate one another. And many false prophets will arise and lead many astray. And because iniquity will abound, the love of many will grow cold*?[3] Then he adds: **Fear and the pit and the snare are upon you, O inhabitant of the earth. And it will come to pass that the one who flees from the noise of the fear shall fall into the pit; and the one who climbs out of the pit shall be caught in the snare.**[4] Now it is clear that these things will come to pass when the judgement is drawing near but has not yet appeared, that is, in the times of Antichrist. For is there anyone [who does not see] that it is only in this life that it is possible to flee empty from place to place when the Lord comes from heaven and all are revived in the blink of an eye, or to change one's mind by diverse strategies of evasion? Therefore, as I have said, these words (**Fear**, and so forth...) apply more aptly to the times of the final persecution. For because he says that an inhabitant of the earth must be caught in the act, [God] himself is the whirlwind of the aforesaid persecution, concerning which the Lord said to blessed Job when explaining the deeds of Antichrist: *Fear is all around the circle of his teeth;*[5] and to the disciples in the gospel:

1 Luke 17:26-7

2 Isa. 24:16

3 Matt. 24:10-12; 'because...will abound' = *cum abundabit* (Old Latin); cf. Vulg. *quoniam abundauit* = 'because...has abounded'

4 Isa. 24:17-18

5 Job 41:14 (41:5)

For there will be then a great tribulation, such as there has not been since the beginning of the world until now, nor will there be,[1] and it was from this kind of fear that the prophet was desiring to be freed when he says: *From the fear of the enemy preserve my soul.*[2] For it ought to be noted that he does not say 'from the sword of the enemy,' but he says *From the fear of the enemy preserve my soul,* because, as a brave martyr, he does not pray that the enemy should not kill him bodily, but rather that he should not fear the one who kills the body but is not able to kill the soul, lest by chance in fearing that one he might offend *him who can destroy both soul and body in Gehenna,*[3] which is well known to have happened to those placed in the midst of battle—those who, in not bearing the adversities of penalties, deny eternal life. Concerning things of this sort it is said here: **And it will come to pass that the one who flees from the noise of the fear shall fall into the pit.**[4] Thus, one who flees from the noise of the fear falls into the pit when, because of the threats or torments of persecution, that person deserts the constancy of faith and does not fear to lose Christ.

Now there have been some who were compelled by the violence of tortures to deny Christ with the voice but not with the mind, and for that *[706]*
reason, when they escaped from the hands of the torturers and were aided by fraternal compassion, they turned back to Christ again and bravely stood fast once more in the confession of him whom they had previously denied timidly, and obliterated the blame of their apostasy most perfectly, either by the lengthy remedy of penitence or even by renewing the struggle of the martyrs. And surely in martyrdom the lapsed, lest they should have time to rededicate themselves to the penitence which they had intended and to return to pardon, were instantly slain by the enemy who was ardent to cut the throat of their souls, not their bodies. So it is appropriate that the prophet adds here: **And the one who climbs out of the pit shall be caught in the snare.** For when we have learned that this sort of slaughter of souls was inflicted upon Christians by the ancient persecutors of the Church (that is, by the members of the devil), who can doubt that the same thing must be inflicted many times over when Satan himself, the leader and source of all evil, will raise his own head up out of the abyss in order to persecute the Church?

1 Matt. 24:21
2 Ps. 64:1 (63:2)
3 Matt. 10:28
4 Isa. 24:18

Now to these things predicted concerning a time just before the day of judgement the prophet later adds some things which, if I am not deceived, can be understood quite properly in two ways: **The flood gates from on high are opened, and the foundations of the earth shall be shaken; with breaking shall the earth be broken, with crushing shall the earth be crushed, with jarring shall the earth be jarred, with agitation shall the earth be agitated like a drunkard.**[1] For this saying can be taken with reference to the very substance of the earth, which at the end time must be shaken to the core from its original condition. Or, maybe the word 'earth' indicates human beings, because they live on earth, and that shaking, breaking, crushing, jarring, and agitation like a drunkard can also be understood of that same rational earth concerning which the Lord, when he had said in the gospel, *And there will be signs in the sun and moon and stars,* added saying, *And on the earth distress among the nations;*[2] or perhaps that concerning which he immediately added, saying: *by reason of the confusion of the roaring of the sea and the waves, people withering away from fear and expectation of what is coming upon the whole world.*[3]

Moreover, what the prophet adds, **And it shall be carried off like the tent of one night, and its iniquity shall lie heavy upon it, and it shall fall, and will not rise up again,**[4] pertains especially to the day of judgement, when *the form of this world shall perish,*[5] and that way of human life which is in it now shall pass away. After the interposition of this sentence concerning the last day, he turns his discourse back to the terrible things which precede the last day, that is, to predicting the destruction of Antichrist, saying, **And on that day it shall come to pass that the Lord will visit upon the host of heaven on high, and upon the kings of the earth who are upon the earth, and they will be gathered together into a gathering of one bundle into the pit, and they will be shut up there in prison.**[6] For surely God will visit upon the host of heaven on high when, after Antichrist has been killed, he will for the most part have crushed the power of the unclean spirits, which are rightly called the host of heaven, either because in the beginning they fell from the heavens to the depths below, or because they abide in the air, which in the Scriptures is often called 'heaven', obstinate in their zeal for waging war with the human race.

1 Isa. 24:18-20
2 Luke 21:25
3 Luke 21:25-6
4 Isa. 24:20
5 1 Cor. 7:31
6 Isa. 24:21-2

Hence the Apostle says that our struggle is not *against flesh, but against principalities and powers, against the rulers of the world of this darkness, against the spirits of wickedness in the heavens.*[1]

And through the prophet the Lord, describing the future perdition of those, says: *My sword was drunk in heaven.*[2] Therefore on that day—that is, in the time in which the fear and the pit and the snare of that greatest final tribulation will seize the inhabitant of the earth—when with nation rising up against nation and kingdom against kingdom[3] the foundations of the earth will be shaken, and [the earth] itself with its residents fighting against one another will be shaken, broken, crushed, jarred, and agitated like a drunkard, as its own destruction and ruin approaches and is already imminent, the Lord visits upon the host of heaven on high by sending an angel from heaven to slay by divine power that *Man of Sin, the Son of Perdition, who is raised up and extolled above every so-called god or object of worship, so that he takes his seat in the temple of God.*[4] Blessed Pope Gregory understands that this must be accomplished by Michael the archangel,[5] on the basis of the Apocalypse of John in which it is written: *And there was a battle in heaven; Michael and his angels battled with the dragon, and the dragon and his angels were fighting, and did not prevail, and there was no longer any place for them in heaven.*[6] [707]

Therefore, it will be visited upon the host of heaven when Antichrist will be slain, both because when he is killed the power of the evil spirits who have assisted him in the showing of false signs will be annulled by being made void, and because it is not unreasonable to reckon him among the host of heaven, since he presumes to exalt himself not only over all the angels, but even above all the grandeur of divine majesty. It will be visited also upon the kings of the earth who are [upon the earth], namely, the servants of Antichrist and those who have advanced and cooperated with his deeds and deceits, who with base and earthly minds rule by evil domination; they will doubtless perish when the fury of their own tribulation is accomplished.

1 Eph. 6:12

2 Isa. 34:5; quoted with reference to Isa. 24:21 in Jerome *In Es.* 8 (*CCSL* 73: 323, 35-6)

3 Matt. 24:7

4 2 Thess. 2:3-4; 'is raised up' = *eleuatur*; cf. Vulg. *aduersatur* = 'opposes'; *homo* and *filius* are in the nominative in the Vulgate, but in the accusative here. On the teaching of 2 Thessalonians about the Final Enemy, see McGinn (1994), 41-5.

5 Gregory the Great *Hom. euang.* 2, 34, 9 (*PL* 76: 1251B); but cf. *Moral.* 32, 15, 27 (*CCSL* 143B: 1650, 135-47), in which Gregory follows 2 Thess. 2:8 in saying that Christ himself will destroy Antichrist. On the confusion resulting from Gregory's apparent approbation of these conflicting traditions, see McGinn (1994), 82.

6 Rev. 12:7-8

As the histories report, this is precisely what happened to all the instigators of wars who fought against the Church.[1] For it should be noted that it does not say openly 'Upon all the kings of the earth', just as it does not say 'Upon every host of heaven', but it simply says that God has visited **upon the host of heaven on high, and upon the kings of the earth who are upon the earth.** Hence it is permissible to understand these things which are said not of the general casting down of all things, but of the particular casting down of those same evil persons and angels. **And they will be gathered together into a gathering of one bundle into the pit, and they will be shut up there in prison:** this is said concerning the souls of those whose bodies will be given to death when the Lord visits, which although they did not leave their bodies at the same time will nevertheless all of them in their order be gathered together into the same bundle and shut up in a prison of unceasing penalties. Surely it accords with the decree of the strict Judge that those who have fought against the Church with a like mind should undergo a like penalty for their contending against God. The doctors of the Church also teach this concerning the rest of the reprobate, namely, that those who are alike in sins must be damned alike in punishments, and that the Lord says this concerning the weeds: *Bind them into a bundle to be burned,*[2] the avaricious with the avaricious, the wanton with the wanton, the perjurers with the perjurers, and the other sinners also with those who have been joined together in similar crimes, to be thrust together into eternal flames.

[708] Therefore, when Antichrist has perished, the ministers of his deceptions will be gathered together into a prison of hellish punishments, and after many days they will be visited: namely, at the time of the resurrection of all people, when for a short time their souls will be called forth for a little while out of the infernal regions so that, having received their bodies, they may sink back into the same punishments along with the rest of the sinners as soon as the judgement has been completed. Nor should anyone think to oppose to this assertion of ours, in which we say that Antichrist must be killed many days before the universal judgement which is coming, that in speaking of the same thing the Apostle says: *Whom the Lord Jesus will kill with the breath of his mouth and will destroy with the manifestation of his*

1 Bede seems not to have known Lactantius' *De mortibus persecutorum*, which details the unseemly and violent ends of the Roman emperors who persecuted the Church, but he certainly knew Rufinus' Latin translation of the *Historia ecclesiastica* of Eusebius of Caesarea, with its vivid descriptions of the deaths of the persecutors Galerius and Maximin (with his confederates) in 8, 16 and 9, 10-11 (*GCS* 9.2: 789-91, 839-53).

2 Matt. 13:30

coming.[1] For surely by saying this the Apostle signifies that the power of that devil[2] must be crushed and terminated with such a great and so terrible a blow that it is doubted by no one that the presence of the Lord's coming will have appeared to destroy pride, in accordance with what Scripture relates as having happened to Herod, who killed James and sent Peter into prison,[3] and also with what the ecclesiastical histories likewise record as having been done to the rest of the persecutors of Christians.[4] Or perhaps [the Apostle] says that [Antichrist] will be killed by the breath of the Lord's mouth and destroyed by the manifestation of his coming because doubtless when [the Lord] comes for judgement *the last enemy to be destroyed is death,*[5] and everyone who together with him holds *the power of death*[6] (that is, every one of the devil's accomplices), will perish by [the Lord's] power.

For surely Daniel the prophet testifies that the universal judgement will not come immediately after the annihilation of that *Man of Sin, the Son of Perdition.*[7] In the final vision of his prophecy when he describes the deeds of that reign, after he has described that same [Antichrist] with the times of the reign being a thousand two hundred and ninety days (that is, three and a half years), he immediately adds: *Blessed is the one who waits and comes to a thousand three hundred and thirty days.*[8] The blessed presbyter Jerome explains this little verse with these words: *Blessed (he says) is the one who, after Antichrist has been killed, stands ready for forty-five days beyond the completed number, in which the Lord and Saviour will come in his majesty. Now the reason why there will be a silence of forty-five days after the killing of Antichrist is reserved to divine knowledge, unless perhaps we should say the delay of the reign is a trial of patience for the saints.*[9] But it should also be noted in this regard that it is written, *And after many days* they will be

1 2 Thess. 2:8

2 Bede's language implies that he understands Antichrist as the devil incarnate; cf. his comment on the number of the Beast of Rev. 13:17-18 in *In Apoc.* 2, 13 (*PL* 93: 172B): 'For it is the number of a man, that we may not suppose him, according to the opinion of some, to be either devil or demon, but one from among men, in whom Satan is to dwell altogether bodily.' Here Bede was following the teaching on Antichrist of his master Gregory the Great, on which see Savon (1986), and McGinn (1994), 80-2.

3 Acts 12:2-3. For the death of Herod, see Acts 12:20-3.

4 Again, see Rufinus' translation of Eusebius *Hist. eccl.* 8, 16 and 9, 10-11 (*GCS* 9.2: 789-91, 839-53).

5 1 Cor. 15:26

6 Heb. 2:14

7 2 Thess. 2:3; *homo* and *filius* are in the nominative in the Vulgate, but in the ablative here.

8 Dan. 12:12

9 Jerome *In Dan.* 4, 12, 12 (CCSL 75A: 943, 671 - 944, 677); quoted also in Bede *In Apoc.* 1 (PL 93: 154C), and *De temp. rat.* 69 (CCSL 123B: 539, 53-8). On the role that Jerome's comment as transmitted by Bede would play in later medieval millennial speculation, see Lerner (1988) and (1992).

visited, because the very designation of many days is more fittingly assigned to the times of this age, which are multiplied by the interchanging alternations of days and nights, rather than [to the age] to come, where once the runnings-to-and-fro of the hours have ceased, the Lord will be with the saints in eternal light, and the impious, with their hands and feet bound, will be sent into outer darkness.[1] And therefore it is rightly to be understood that those who are now kept in a prison of infernal shadows will be visited after many days of this passing age, surely in that hour in which *all who are in the graves will hear the voice of the Lord and will come out—those who have done good things, to the resurrection of life, and those who have done evil things, to the resurrection of judgement.*[2] At the time of his visitation there shall also take place that which follows: **And the moon will blush, and the sun will be confounded**[3]—to which very event the Lord testifies in the gospel, when he says, *And immediately after the tribulation*
[709] *of those days, the sun will be darkened, and the moon will not give its light;*[4]
and a little later: *And then all the tribes of the earth will mourn, and they will see the Son of Man coming on the clouds of heaven with power and great majesty, and he will send out his angels with a trumpet and with a great voice, and they will gather his elect from the four winds.*[5]

But what the prophet adds in conclusion, as it were, immediately after that same text, when he says, **When the Lord of hosts will reign on Mount Zion and in Jerusalem, and will be glorified in the sight of his elders,**[6] will be fulfilled precisely at the moment of judgement, for when the impious have been carried away in order that they should not see the glory of God, all the saints shall enter into the dwelling place of the heavenly city to contemplate their Creator's face forever. Here we should note that just as in this passage events which reason[7] declares will be manifested separately are related as though they will occur at the same time, so, further above, things which are well known to be fulfilled partly when that very day of judgement is imminent and partly when it is already appearing are woven together at the same time, as though at the instant of a single day of

1 Matt. 22:13
2 John 5:28-9
3 Isa. 24:23
4 Matt. 24:29. A portion of this passage is quoted in reference to Isa. 24:23 in Jerome *In Es.* 8 (*CCSL* 73: 324, 67-71), but Bede's quotation is more extensive, which suggests that while he may have been influenced by his reading of Jerome he was not directly dependent upon him at this point.
5 Matt. 24:30-1
6 Isa. 24:23
7 following *PL*'s emendation of *quae ratio* for *quaeratis*

judgement. For what reader cannot see that the blush of the moon and the confusion of the sun are to come before the day of judgement, or on the day itself, whereas the glorification of the Lord—not the one in which he will appear in judgement for all, both the just and the unjust, but the one in which he will be revealed **in the sight of his elders** (that is, the elect)—will then be manifested rather to those [saints] at the time when the impious will go to eternal punishment, and they to eternal life? At this time—if it is even permitted to say that something eternal is in time—neither the blushing of the moon nor the confounding of the sun will obscure [its] radiance, but, as the same prophet says in another place: *The light [of the moon] will be like the light of the sun, and the light of the sun will be sevenfold, like the light of seven days, on the day when the Lord binds up the wounds of his people, and heals the affliction of his blows.*[1]

Having expounded these things concerning this most hazardous question according to our measure, Holy Bishop, I repeat at the end what I said in the beginning: I have not presumed to say[2] that I have understood what the prophet wanted to perceive in these things. But I hope, with the assistance of heavenly grace, that the things which I have written in discussing these matters are not incompatible with the text of the prophet or the principles of the catholic faith. Indeed, I do not believe that I shall be fruitless to my reader in these things which I have written. Even if I have not known how to usher him into the sanctuary of the prophetic sense, I have nevertheless taken him a long way from the plough of heretical deception[3] by forewarning him in order that he might not come to believe, through wrongly interpreting the words of the prophet, that each of those sinners condemned for their crimes once and for all to the prison below should at some other time be called back to mercy by divine visitation. But let him rather be diligent and take care for himself and for his own, so that, once they have been purified from faults and adorned with good works, they may await the last day, as there is no doubt that both the prophet here and all the teachers *[710]* of the Church have taught. May [the Lord] deign to help Your Beatitude always with heavenly grace as you are interceding for us!

1 Isa. 30:26
2 following *PL*'s emendation of *non sum ausus* for *non summe ausus*
3 Cf. Jerome's reference to believers who are victorious *aratro fidei* ('with the plough of faith') in his commentary *In Es.* 17 (*CCSL* 73A: 709, 38).

ON TOBIAS: INTRODUCTION

What Bede called the Book of Tobias, moderns call the Book of Tobit. Included in modern Protestant Bibles as part of the Old Testament Apocrypha, this book was regarded by Bede and his contemporaries as canonical. The discrepancy between Bede's name for this book and modern designations can be traced to the peculiar nomenclature of Jerome's Vulgate translation. Bede used a version of the Vulgate Tobias as the basis for his commentary. The two chief characters in the work are a father and his son. Ancient versions and modern translations of the story give the characters different, but similar-sounding names. For example, while all versions agree that the son's name is Tobias, they variously name the father Tobeit, Tobeith, and T(h)obis.[1] By contrast, Jerome saw fit to give the same name, Tobias, to both characters. Although this identity of names can at times be confusing, it is a fact to which Bede attaches important allegorical significance.[2] For this reason the present translation retains the same name for both characters, the potential confusion notwithstanding.

Another potential source of confusion for the reader of Bede's *On Tobias* lies in the multiple—and very different—versions of the Tobias/Tobit story, each of which serves as the basis for a different English translation. Although most authorities would agree that the Book of Tobias/Tobit was originally composed in a Semitic language—either Hebrew or Aramaic—all modern English translations are largely based on one of two Greek manuscripts. One, the R^S, is a recension from the Codex Sinaiticus; while the other, the R^V, is a recension composed from several codices, the chief of which is the Codex Vaticanus. Sometimes called the 'shorter text,' the R^V has about 1,700 fewer words than the R^S. The versions of Tobit found in the Jerusalem Bible, the New English Bible, and the New American Bible are based largely on R^S; while the versions in the King James or Authorized Version and the Revised Standard Version are based on R^V.

1 The Greek versions in the Codex Vaticanus and the Codex Sinaiticus give Τωβειτ (Tobeit) and Τωβειθ (Tobeith), respectively. The Old Latin gives T(h)obis.

2 *In Tob.* 1, 9 (*CCSL* 119B: 3, 34 - 4, 40)

When writing *On Tobias* Bede had before him a copy of Tobias that was the product of certain emendations made at Wearmouth-Jarrow, perhaps by Bede himself, to an earlier Vulgate version of Tobias that had become corrupt in many places.[1] Jerome's Vulgate translation of Tobias, upon which Bede's copy was largely based, derives largely from the Old Latin version which in turn is based on a Greek text that looks something like Codex Sinaiticus.[2] Besides the Old Latin, Jerome also relied on some Aramaic texts of the Book of Tobias/Tobit. Unable to read Aramaic well himself, he employed the services of an Aramaic interpreter and completed his version in a single day.[3] Because Jerome's translation is based on such an idiosyncratic and hybrid text of Tobias/Tobit, readers of Bede's commentary may find that the content as well as the versification of some of Bede's Tobias citations do not square with a version of Tobit in a modern study Bible. For this reason, one who wishes to follow closely an English version of the biblical text while reading Bede's commentary should have ready to hand the Douay-Rheims Bible, a fairly literal English translation of Jerome's Vulgate.

In his *Ecclesiastical History* Bede claims that he devoted much of his life's energies to summarizing and compiling the works of the Fathers for both his own use and that of his ecclesiastical brethren.[4] This claim notwithstanding, his commentary on Tobias is thoroughly original, being in fact the first sustained commentary on this traditionally overlooked work of Scripture.[5]

When and for whom Bede composed his *On Tobias* remain matters for speculation. Since Bede lists it among his works in his *Ecclesiastical History*, it can have been composed no later than 731. It is difficult to say anything more certain about the date. Dom David Hurst estimates that it was composed sometime between 720 and 730, but gives no reason for this judgment.[6] Because Bede stresses the importance of allegorical interpretation in his opening descriptions of both *On Tobias* and *On the Temple*, M. L. W. Laistner suggests that both were written at about the same time

1 Cf. Marsden (1994) 2, esp. n. 5 and 6, and (1995) 171-9; Fischer (1985) 31.

2 Moore (1992), 591-2. Brooke et al. (1940) provides a critical edition for the Codex Vaticanus, the Codex Sinaiticus, and the Old Latin versions of Tobit (85-110; 111-22; 123-44).

3 Jerome *Prologus Tobias* (*Biblia Sacra iuxta vulgatam versionem*, 676)

4 *Hist. eccl.* 5, 24 (ed. and transl. Colgrave and Mynors, 566)

5 St. Ambrose wrote a *De Tobia* (ed. L. M. Zucker), but his work is deceptively titled. A moral rather than an exegetical treatise, it only briefly mentions the figure of Tobit in order to frame a larger denunciation of the practice of usury.

6 *Praefatio* (CCSL 119B: v)

and that since *On the Temple* is dated between 729 and 731, *On Tobias* is probably closer to 730 than 720. Laistner hastens to add, however, that his suggestion is based on no hard internal evidence from the text.[1] Lacking a dedicatory Preface or the mention of any person or group of persons contemporary with Bede, *On Tobias* gives the modern reader no clue about either its intended audience or what prompted its composition.

According to Bede, the Book of Tobias is understood best when it is interpreted not as a history, but as an allegory of the mysteries of Christ and the Church.[2] In keeping with his conviction, Bede proceeds to give a full though not a verse-by-verse commentary on Tobias in which he explains the allegorical significance of the main characters, their actions, and their relations to each other. In the midst of forging a multitude of allegorical links between elements of the Tobias story and the mysteries of Christ and the Church, Bede yet manages to stamp this commentary with at least one continuous theme, namely, the progression of salvation history toward its end during this the world's sixth and final age, which lasts from the Incarnation of Christ to the end of the world. Of special interest to Bede in that history are the salvation of the Jews and Jewish-Gentile relations.

Following the apostle Paul, Bede subdivided the sixth age of salvation history into three stages, each of which is characterized by those who are saved during that stage. God's mercy is extended during the first stage to a small remnant of Christ-believing Jews among whom are included Paul and the apostles; during the second stage, that mercy is extended to the full number of Gentiles; and during the third, to the full number of Jews (Rom. 11:7-26). The end of the third stage brings with it the end of the sixth age and the end of world history.[3]

For Bede, the elder Tobias (=Tobit) represents the Jews in a double aspect: one good, one bad. Insofar as Tobias is portrayed as a man of good works in Tob. 1:1-2:9, Bede sees him favorably as an allegory either for the people Israel, which once distinguished itself from the Gentiles by serving God faithfully and avoiding idolatry, or for Israel's teachers of old.[4] On the other hand, when Tobias is blinded by swallows' dung in Tob. 2:10, Bede views him more unfavorably as an allegory for the great majority of Jews

1 Laistner and King (1943), 78

2 *In Tob.* (*CCSL* 119B: 3, 5-7)

3 For more on Bede's sense of salvation history, see Davidse (1982), 656-71.

4 *In Tob.* (*CCSL* 119B: 3, 7-9 and 23-6)

who now, during the second stage of the sixth age, are so blinded by pride that they refuse to receive God's revelation in Christ.[1]

By contrast, the younger Tobias represents Christ's humanity, while the angel Raphael, who journeys with and counsels the young Tobias, represents Christ's divinity.[2] In the same way that Christ first comes to save the Gentiles and then at the last to save the Jews, so too do Tobias and Raphael go first to exorcise the demons from Sarah—who represents the Gentiles—and then to restore sight to the elder Tobias—who represents the Jews.[3] Moreover, Bede expresses the kinship between Jews and Gentiles in salvation history in the peculiar way that he allegorizes the relation between the elder Tobias and Gabael, to whom the elder Tobias loaned some money and from whom he now seeks it back.[4] Bede understands the money that Tobias loans to Gabael as an allegory of Scripture in its literal aspect: it was the literal sense of Scripture which the Jews 'loaned', as it were, to the Gentiles when the Hebrew Bible was made available to Gentiles in the Greek translation now known as the Septuagint. By contrast, Bede understands the money that Gabael pays back to Tobias as the spiritual understanding of Scripture which Christ has made possible. It is this spiritual understanding of Scripture that will be 'returned' to the Jews by the Gentiles when the Jews at last are gathered into Christ's church at the end of the age.[5] As charming as the Tobias story itself, Bede's commentary upon it is an excellent brief example of Bede's allegorical reading of Scripture and it exhibits Bede's logical and creative talents to their fullest extent.

The present translation is based on the critical edition prepared by David Hurst for *CCSL* 119B. That edition is based on one late-eighth century Continental manuscript (Mons, Bibliothèque publique, 6307), four ninth-century Continental manuscripts, and one eleventh-century English manuscript (Oxford, Bodleian, Hatton 23). Bede's *On Tobias* was first published in 1563 by John Heerwagen in the Basel edition of Bede's collected works.

1 *In Tob.* 2, 10 (*CCSL* 119B: 5, 1-21)

2 Ibid. 3, 7-8 (*CCSL* 119B: 6, 7-19)

3 On the exorcism of the demons from Sarah, see Tob. 7-8 and *In Tob.* 8, 2-3 (*CCSL* 119B: 11-12); on the curing of the elder Tobias' blindness, see Tob. 11 and *In Tob.* 11, 13-15 (*CCSL* 119B: 16, 36 - 17, 66).

4 Tob. 1:17, 4:21-2, 9:1-12

5 *In Tob.* 1, 9 (*CCSL* 119B: 4, 44-55) and 9, 3 (*CCSL* 119B: 13, 1-17)

ON TOBIAS

The book of the holy father Tobias is accessible to readers certainly on the beneficial level of the letter, as it abounds in the greatest examples and lessons of the moral life. Yet anyone who knows how to interpret it not just historically, but also allegorically, sees that just as fruits surpass [their] leaves this book's inner sense surpasses its literal simplicity. For if understood spiritually, it is seen to contain in itself the great mysteries of Christ and the Church. Because Tobias represents the people Israel, which typically served God with upright faith and righteous works while all Gentiles were given over to idolatry, it is said of him that **when all went after the golden calves that Jeroboam king of Israel had made, he alone fled the company of all these, and went on to Jerusalem, and there adored the Lord, the Lord God of Israel.**[1] Now inasmuch as Jeroboam fabricated golden calves to deceive those subject to him, he represents the authors of idolatry. *[3]*

(1:2) Tobias was taken prisoner **in the days of Shalmaneser, king of the Assyrians,** but **did not desert the way of truth in captivity.**[2] This captivity imposed by the king of the Assyrians represents the human race's captivity by which the king of all the wicked, namely the devil, has cast humanity out of the heavenly homeland and into the pilgrimage of this [earthly] exile.

Every day Tobias shared all that he could get with his captive brothers, who were of his race, but he also gave tithes to strangers and proselytes.[3] Likewise in its teachers the people Israel used to distribute the alms of God's word not only to ignorant hearers from its own race, but also to those

1 Tob. 1:5-6; Jeroboam I (922-901 BCE) was the first king of northern Israel after it seceded from the Solomonic empire centered in Judah and its capital Jerusalem. See 1 Kgs. 11:26-16:7, esp. 12:28-31.

2 Shalmaneser V (727-722 B.C.E)

3 Tob. 1:3, 7

Gentiles who wanted to be converted to Israel's way of life. For whatever natural goodness Israel had been able to retain—goodness that the enemy captor[1] had not seized—all this he set before his own people as an example of virtue, but also always gave some portion of saving knowledge to the Gentiles. Thus it is said that Tobias gave strangers a tithe of his own substance.

(1:9) When Tobias became **a man, he took Anna as his wife, a woman of his own tribe.** So also after maturing and increasing in Egypt, the people Israel took the synagogue established by Moses with all its legal ceremonies.[2]

He begot a son by her, assigning his own name to him, because he
[4] knew that the Christ would be born from [Tobias'] own race. As Moses says, *Your God will raise up a prophet for you out of your brethren; him you shall hear as [you would hear] me*;[3] and the Lord said to David, *I shall assign a man from the fruit of your womb upon my throne*.[4] [Tobias] assigned his own name to him by believing and confessing what the Father had said about that man: *And I shall assign him to be my firstborn*,[5] just as he had said of that people, *Israel is my firstborn son*.[6]

---

1 I.e., Satan

2 Because modern scholarly opinion tends to place the origin of the synagogue during the Babylonian exile (587 BCE) at the earliest, Bede's statement that Moses established the synagogue may seem grossly anachronistic. By the term 'synagogue', however, Bede does not mean (as moderns do) a Jewish institution of public worship and instruction. In fact, he attaches two other meanings to the word. Sometimes he uses it to denote that part of God's elect who lived before the time of Christ's incarnation. In this sense the synagogue is, if you will, the 'Jewish church' which existed before Christ's appearance in the flesh and looked to his coming. This seems to be his meaning in the present context and elsewhere in the Tobias commentary. At other times he means by 'synagogue' all Jews who live after Christ's incarnation and yet, not embracing faith in Christ, remain Jews. In this latter sense, the word 'synagogue' represents not a precursor to the Church, but its antithesis. As he refers to it in *On First Samuel*, today's synagogue is the 'synagogue of Satan' (4, 28, 7—*CCSL* 119: 255, 1824-5).

3 Acts 3:22; cf. Deut. 18:15

4 Ps. 132:11 (131:11)

5 Ps. 89:27 (88:28)

6 Ex. 4:22

He taught him **from infancy to fear God and to abstain from every sin,**[1] by believing and confessing that [Christ] would *commit no sin* and that *no deceit* would be *found in his mouth*, but that *a spirit of the fear of the Lord* would fill *him*.[2]

Tobias gave ten talents of silver to his needy tribesman Gabael under his signature.[3] Likewise the people of God through seventy translators entrusted the knowledge of divine law contained in the Ten Commandments to the Gentiles to free them from the poverty of unbelief.[4] Now Tobias gave it under his signature, that is, under the condition that it be repaid when the debtor gets rich or when the creditor asks for it back. Likewise, the Gentiles borrowed God's word from the people Israel through a translation. Now after the Lord's incarnation they understand [God's word] spiritually and practise it so as to acquire the riches of virtues. Surely they will repay the moneylender at the end of the age when they welcome the believing Jews into the unity of the church and entrust Christ's sacraments and open Scripture's mysteries to those who are to be saved.[5]

(1:22-3) The king ordered Tobias to be killed and **all his substance** to be taken away because of the good things he had done, but Tobias **fled naked with his son and wife and lay in hiding, for many loved him.** Likewise, the devil was busy destroying God's people with spiritual death through idolatry. Yet he could not wrest from it its entire treasury of virtues. For it had many holy teachers who cared for its life and welfare. Tobias

1 Tob. 1:10

2 1 Pet. 2:22; Isa. 11:3

3 Tob. 1:17, 4:21

4 By the 'seventy translators', Bede is referring to those seventy men who, according to the traditional story, translated the Hebrew Bible into Greek, thereby producing the Septuagint. The original story is given in the pseudepigraphal *Letter of Aristeas* (ed. Thackeray, 551-606). Since *Aristeas* was written in Greek, Bede would have known this story only through later Latin accounts of it. Such accounts can be found in several ancient works that were either written in Latin or were available to Bede in Latin translation (e.g., Josephus *Ant. Jud.* 12, 2, 11-15—*LCL* 7: 42-59; Eusebius *Hist. Eccl.* 5, 8, 10-15—*LCL* 1: 458-61; and Augustine *De ciu. Dei* 18, 42—*CCSL* 48: 638). Whereas the original *Letter of Aristeas* interprets this act of translation as something done primarily for the edification of Egyptian Greek-speaking *Jews* to express King Ptolemy's appreciation of God's prospering his kingdom (35-8—ed. Thackeray, 557-8), Bede here follows Augustine in interpreting it as something done primarily for the benefit of *Gentiles* who are destined to believe in Christ (*De ciu. Dei* 18, 42—*CCSL* 48: 638, 29-33).

5 Cf. Rom. 11:25-6; Bede *XXX quaest.* 1 (*CCSL* 119: 297, 40-65)

fled with his son and wife because the enemy, no matter how furiously he pursued, could not destroy either the faith in the Lord's incarnation or the synagogue's status[1]—a fact made abundantly clear in the Maccabeans' ordeals.[2]

After the king had been killed by his own sons, all of Tobias' things were restored to him[3] because after the devil had been overcome and condemned by his own evil deeds, which he begot as if they were a wicked child, good fortune very often returned to God's people. Even now, after our Lord's incarnation, we see the condition of the church fluctuate in the same way.

[5] (2:10-11) **Wearied from the burial** Tobias came **to his house** and when **he threw himself down by the wall and slept, some warm dung** fell from **a swallows' nest** into **his eyes** and he became **blind**. Do not be amazed, O reader, that the good deeds of humans sometimes figuratively signify an evil thing, while at other times evil deeds signify a good. If this were forbidden, then one would always have to write *God is light*[4] in bright gold and never in black ink.[5] Yet even if you write the devil's name in white chalk, it still signifies infernal darkness. Tobias' blindness thus represents how, as the Apostle says, *blindness fell partly upon Israel.*[6] He grew tired of burying and went blind because one who tirelessly persists in good works is never deprived of faith's light; while the tired one who neglects to *stay awake, stand in the faith, persist manfully, and be strengthened,*[7] lies down and sleeps in spirit. To such a person is that saying of the apostle aptly applied, *Arise, you who sleep, rise up from the dead, and Christ will enlighten you.*[8] Because of their breezy flight, swallows represent pride and levity of heart, the impurity of which immediately blinds whom it rules. For one who carelessly subjects the mind to the levity of wantonness and pride sleeps as though under a swallows' nest. Now this blindness greatly prevailed over the people Israel when the Lord's coming in the flesh was

---

1 Tobias' wife here functions as an allegory of the synagogue; his son, of Christ's incarnation.

2 2 Macc. 6-7

3 Tob. 1:24-9

4 1 John 1:5

5 Cf. Bede *De octo quaest.* 6 (*PL* 93: 458D-459A), *In Sam.* 2, 10, 25 (*CCSL* 119: 92, 993-1049), *In Gen.* 4, 20, 16 (*CCSL* 118A: 236, 1515-20); Gregory the Great *Moral.* 3, 28, 55 (*CCSL* 143: 148, 7-12)

6 Rom. 11:25

7 1 Cor. 16:13

8 Eph. 5:14

imminent, when the yoke of Roman servitude pressed hard upon them and they were violating the divine law's precepts by profligate living.

Tobias' kinsmen ridiculed him; even his wife reproved him, as if he had served God in vain. Sternly rebuking and teaching them, Tobias turned himself to God in prayer.[1] At that time there were some among that people who with foolish temerity scoffed at the hardships of that same people because it was now far from the ancient blessedness of the holy fathers who once served God nobly. Through all its learned and chosen men that same people used to make every effort to correct such scoffers and applied itself to seeking God's forgiveness so as to gain eternal life. Nor should it seem strange that this same Tobias, who was blind yet also proclaimed God's word, is said to signify those who are reproved yet also chosen. For Jacob the patriarch, by wrestling with the angel, became lame yet also blessed, clearly signifying the unfaithful of his race in [his] lameness, the faithful in [his] blessing.[2]

(3:7-8) **Raguel's daughter Sarah, in a city of the Medes, had been** *[6]*
given to seven husbands, and a demon had killed **them as soon as they would go in to her.** Sarah signifies figuratively the company of nations all of whose teachers knew so much about life in this world, which is formed in seven days, yet knew nothing to say about life eternal. For this reason the devil held them all hostage, inasmuch as they were sold into idolatry until our Lord the true Bridegroom came. The Lord joined this company to himself by his faithfulness after the enemy had been overcome, just as Tobias took Sarah as his bride by the teaching and assistance of the archangel after the demon had been bound. The angel fittingly signifies our Saviour's divinity; Tobias, his humanity. Nor will one marvel at our saying that two persons—an angel and a human—represent the single person of *the mediator between God and humans*[3] when one reads in the expositions of the fathers that this single person of the mediator who suffers to save the world is represented both by Isaac, whose father offered him on

1 Tob. 2:15-3:6
2 Gen. 32:24-9
3 1 Tim. 2:5

the altar, and by the ram that was slain.[1] That person in his humanity was slaughtered like a sheep, yet in his divinity remains immune to suffering along with God [his] Father, even as Isaac returned home alive along with his own father. Now if a ram aptly signifies Christ's humanity and a human being his deity, then why might not a human being much more aptly signify his humanity, and an angel his deity?

(3:25) And so **there was sent the Lord's holy angel Raphael** (whose name is translated as 'medicine of God') to free Tobias from blindness and Sarah from the demon.[2] [In like fashion] was the Lord sent into the world; he said of himself, *A doctor is not needed for the healthy, but for the sick,*[3] and he redeemed the Jewish people from the darkness of unbelief and the Gentiles from the bondage of idolatry. Of him the prophet said, *And his name shall be called Angel of the Great Council.*[4]

The angel appeared to Tobias and offered himself as a companion.[5] Using Tobias the angel would do great things for the people to whom he had been sent. Likewise, God's Son assumed human form to save humankind by living visibly in their midst.

(5:11-13) Tobias introduced the angel to his father and the angel **greeted**
[7] **him** saying, **'May you always be joyful;'** to which the father responded, **'How can I who sit in darkness and see nothing of heaven's light be joyful?' 'Be hearty in spirit,'** he replied, **'your cure from the Lord is at hand.'** Likewise, through miracles he worked in the flesh, our Lord showed the Jews, from whom he had assumed the flesh, that he is the Son of God

1 Gen. 22:1-13; Ambrose *De Abraham* 1, 8, 71 and 77-8 (*PL* 14: 469B, 471BC), *De exc. fratr. Sat.* 2, 98 (*CSEL* 63: 303-4); Augustine *De ciu. Dei* 16, 32 (*CCSL* 48: 536-7), *Enarr. in Ps.* 30, 2 [sermo 2, para. 9] (*CCSL* 38: 208-9). Bede's awareness of the typological connection between the sacrifice of Isaac, on the one hand, and that of Christ, on the other, is probably due not only to these written sources but also to the two pictorial representations, one of Christ carrying his cross and the other of Isaac carrying the wood for his sacrifice, that were placed side by side somewhere in the Jarrow monastery. Benedict Biscop acquired these images on his sixth journey to Rome and brought them to Jarrow in ca. 686 (*Hist. abb.* 9—ed. Plummer, 1: 373; see Meyvaert [1979], 66).

2 Gregory the Great *Hom. in Euang.* 34, 9 (*PL* 76: 1251A-C); Jerome *In Dan.* 2, 8, 16 (*CCSL* 75A: 857, 930-1); Isidore *Etymol.* 7, 5, 13 (ed. Lindsay, vol. 1): 'Raphael interpretatur curatio vel medicina Dei'.

3 Matt. 9:12

4 Isa. 9:6. Bede here uses a non-Vulgate form of this verse derived from the Septuagint (Jerome *In Es.* 3, 9, 6-7—*CCSL* 73: 127, 53-7). He may have encountered it in Gregory the Great *Moral.* 24, 2, 2 (*CCSL* 143B: 1189, 4) or Ambrose *In Luc.* 3, 8 (*CCSL* 14: 80, 130).

5 Tob. 5:5-8

and an angel, that is, a messenger of the Father's will.[1] And he proclaimed the joy of everlasting salvation to them, saying, *Do penance, for the kingdom of heaven is at hand.*[2] And to those despairing of attaining the heavenly light he said, *I am the light of the world. Whoever follows me will not walk in darkness but will have the light of life.*[3]

The angel promises Tobias that he will guide his son to the Median city of Rages and [then] bring him back to him.[4] Although most of the Jews have been blinded, the Lord [similarly] promises the believers among them that he will reveal the mysteries of his incarnation to the Gentile multitudes and then at the end of time, when faith in his divinity everywhere accompanies[5] and animates all things, he will disclose these mysteries more fully to his own people, from whom he assumed flesh. About the journey to the Medes [Christ] said, *I have other sheep that are not of this sheepfold, and I must also lead them*, and so forth.[6] About his return the Apostle said, *Until the fullness of the Gentiles should come in, and so all Israel should be saved.*[7]

(5:18) When Tobias asked the angel where he came from, he replied, **I am Azarias, son of the great Ananias.** 'Azarias' is translated as 'the Lord our Helper'; 'Ananias', as 'the Lord's grace'.[8] The Lord also deeply impresses the fact upon those believing in him that it is he whose coming the prophet desired when he sings, *You, O Lord, are my helper and deliverer; do not delay*;[9] of him the evangelist also says, *We have seen his glory, glory as of the Only-begotten from the Father, full of grace and truth.*[10]

1 The word 'angel' here has the general meaning of 'messenger'. Bede thus does not mean to say that Christ partakes of the same nature with the angels, but simply that Christ is a messenger from God.

2 Matt. 4:17

3 John 8:12

4 Tob. 5:14-15, 20

5 'Accompanies'= *comitante*, the participle of *comitor*, which occurs only eight times in the Vulgate, twice in the fifth chapter of Tobias. The second of these occurrences is in 5:21, where the elder Tobias says to his son, 'Have a good journey, and the Lord be with you on your way, and may his angel accompany (*comitetur*) you.' Since Bede earlier interpreted the accompanying angel as an allegory for Christ's divinity, it seems no accident that he uses this verb in the phrase, 'when faith in [Christ's] divinity accompanies . . . all things.'

6 John 10:16

7 Rom. 11:25-6

8 For 'Azarias', see Jerome *Nom.*, s.v. IV Reg. 'A' (*CCSL* 72: 114, 16); 'Anania', s.v. Ier. 'A' (*CCSL* 72: 125, 12).

9 Ps. 70:5 (69:6)

10 John 1:14

(5:22) **Then,** it says, **when all things were prepared for the journey, Tobias bade his father and mother farewell, and the two set out together**. When the Lord appeared in the flesh, all those things that pertained to the world's redemption were prepared, namely, Christ's virtues, his teaching, temptation, suffering, resurrection, ascension, the sending of the Holy Spirit, the faith of believers, and persecution by unbelievers. By these things the faith and life of the Holy Church are nourished and
[8] strengthened until he brings the life of this age to a close. When these things came to pass in Judea, that *mediator between God and humans*[1] proclaimed the joys of heavenly salvation and peace through the apostles to the people and synagogue, whence he had received his origin in the flesh; and to those who through him were willing to believe and accept these things he gave himself, and in this way also he came to save the Gentiles through these same teachers.[2]

(6:1) **Tobias thus set out and the dog followed him.** When the Lord came to save the nations, holy preachers followed in his footsteps to fulfill what he commanded: *Go and teach all nations*.[3] And so the Lord himself first filled Cornelius' household with the Holy Spirit and Peter duly baptized them with water.[4] Now teachers are [here] called 'dogs' because they defend their Master's spiritual household, wealth, and sheep from thieves and beasts, that is, from unclean spirits and heretical persons.[5]

(6:1-2) Having set out with the angel as guide, Tobias **spent the first night by the river Tigris, and when he went out to wash his feet, behold, an enormous fish sprang up to devour him.** Here again the mystery of the Lord's suffering is plainly signified.[6] For the huge fish that Tobias killed at the angel's prompting, after it tried to devour him, signifies the ancient devourer of humankind, namely the devil, whom the divine power snared while [the devil] was eagerly anticipating the death of the flesh in

---

1 1 Tim. 2:5
2 I.e., the apostles
3 Matt. 28:19
4 Acts 10:44-8
5 Gregory the Great *Hom. in Euang.* 40 (*PL* 76: 1302D); *Moral.* 20, 6, 15 (*CCSL* 143A: 1014-15, 10-34)
6 In the paragraph immediately preceding, Bede also mentions the Lord's suffering as one of several items signified by the things that 'were prepared for the journey' of Tobias and the angel (5:22).

our Redeemer. The river Tigris, which owing to its rapid course takes its name from the tiger, the swiftest beast, indicates the downward course of our death and mortality.[1] In it the enormous fish lay hidden because humanity's invisible seducer *had power over death.*[2] Tobias remained at the flowing Tigris because when the Lord appeared in the world, he led his life among sinners and mortals, yet the water of sin did not touch him nor did the prince of darkness find anything of his own in [the Lord] when he came near. And just as Tobias went out to the river to wash his feet, so the Lord accepted death, to which he owed no debt, so that he might wash all the faithful (that is, his own members) from death's and sin's contagion. The fish fell upon Tobias and wanted to devour him; when the Lord suffered on the cross, the devil—who had instructed that he be crucified—came, hoping by chance to find some wickedness in his soul.

(6:3) **Terrified** of the fish, Tobias **cried out in a loud voice saying, 'Sir, it is coming upon me.'** So also, when the point of death drew near, the Lord *began to fear and grow weary.*[3] He feared not the devil, but did [9]
shudder at death, which *entered the whole world through the devil's envy* through the natural weakness of the flesh.[4] Because of this *he also prayed that if it might be done, the hour might pass from him, and he said, 'Abba, Father, all things are possible for you. Take this cup from me, but [do] not what I want, but what you want.'*[5]

(6:4) **The angel said** to Tobias, **'grab the fish's gill and draw him to you.'** The Lord grabbed the devil and through his own dying took and vanquished the very one that had wanted to take him in death. Now he grabbed his gill so that he might cut off that most vile head from the trapped body with the right hand of his power; that is, so that the loving Redeemer might both sever the ancient enemy's wickedness from the heart of those whom he had wickedly united to himself—and had made as though they were one body with him—and ingraft these into the body of his own Church. For a fish has its gill where its head and body meet. Now just as our Lord

1 Jerome *Loc.* s.v. 'T' [Genesis] (*PL* 23: 923C): '[The Tigris] is called by this name because of its velocity, which equals the exceeding speed of [that] beast when it runs.'

2 Heb. 2:14

3 Mark 14:33

4 Wisd. 2:24

5 Mark 14:35-6

is the head of his Church, and the Church is truly his body, so too is the devil head of all the wicked and they are all his body, his members.[1] So the Lord grabbed that monstrous fish's gill, drew [the fish] to himself, and threw it upon the shore because in shattering the devil's power he openly delivered and confidently uprooted those whom he foreknew to be sons of light from the power of darkness.[2]

Now when he had done this, it says, **the fish began to pant at his feet on the shore.** When the Lord overcame the wicked enemy's iniquity, brought it into the light, and made it apparent to all, the devil still struggled pridefully to stir up persecution among the Lord's elect. These elect are the Lord's feet since by them he who reigns over all things in heaven yet walks upon the earth.

(6:5) **Then the angel of the Lord said to him, 'Disembowel this fish and lay aside for yourself its heart, gall-bladder and liver.'** The Lord disemboweled the fish when he plainly revealed the devil's wickedness to the saints and cut out the secrets, as it were, of his snares. He set aside for himself his heart because he wanted to point out to the saints, from Scripture, the devil's cunning, about which it says, *Now the serpent was more cunning than all the creatures of the earth.*[3] Of that heart Paul also said, *For we are not ignorant of its designs.*[4] He set aside even his gall-bladder because, on account of his zeal for caution, he wanted it to be written and remembered with how much malicious frenzy the devil rages against humankind.[5] He also set aside the liver because he deigned to show us through teachers of truth the seasoned malevolence of Satan's ruminations against us. For they say that the liver's heat and secret strength boil down foods that have been swallowed so that they can be digested.[6] For
[10] when by careful meditation we truly inquire about the order in which those things that we determine to do should be completed, we boil them down, just as we, using the liver's heat, boil down foods taken into the stomach.

1 Eph. 1:22-3, 5:23; cf. Gregory the Great *Moral.* 9, 28, 44 (*CCSL* 143: 487, 23-6) and 13, 34, 38 (*CCSL* 143A: 689, 2-17).

2 Col. 1:13

3 Gen. 3:1

4 2 Cor. 2:11

5 Isidore *Etymol.* 11, 1, 127 (ed. Lindsay, vol. 2): 'For it is by virtue of our spleen that we laugh, our gall bladder that we are made angry, our heart that we are wise, and our liver that we love.'

6 Isidore *Etymol.* 11, 1, 125 (ed. Lindsay, vol. 2): 'The liver (*iecur*) gets its name because fire (*igne*) has its seat there and from there flies up into the head. From there it spreads to the eyes and the other senses and limbs, and by its heat it turns the liquid that it has distilled from food into blood.'

For these necessities are useful medicines, he said. When the ancient enemy's craftiness and deceitful malice are recognized, they become a useful remedy to us. For the more thoroughly we inquire into these things, the more carefully do we avoid them.

(6:6) Tobias **roasted** the fish's flesh, **and they took it with them on their way. The rest they salted, as much as they needed.** The part of the fish that they took with them represents those who were transferred from being the devil's members to Christ's, that is, those who were converted from unbelief to faith. By contrast, the part that they threw out represents those who have heard God's Word yet would rather dwell among their deceiver's dead and rotten members than return to the company of the Saviour. He cooked the fish's flesh in those whom he found to be fleshly-minded, but by the fire of his love he rendered them spiritual and strong. And so the Holy Spirit descended on the apostles in a vision of fire.[1] **The rest,** it says, **they salted.** This pertains especially to the teachers to whom it is said, *You are the salt of the earth.*[2] Now they (that is Tobias and the Angel) salted because the same *mediator between God and humans* both humanly taught the apostles by his speech and divinely granted them the salt of wisdom in their hearts.[3]

They took with them what would suffice until they reached the Median city of Rages, because the Lord gathered to the faith from Judea as many as would suffice for an example of living and a ministry of preaching until he established the Church's foundations among the Gentiles.

The angel suggested that upon entering Raguel's house Tobias ask for Raguel's daughter Sarah to be his wife.[4] Raguel signifies the Gentiles, whom the Lord deigned to visit through his preachers so that he might take a bride from its stock for himself, that is, so that he might make heathendom itself be his Church. Even the name 'Sarah' corresponds to the Church on account of the Sarah who—as wife of Abraham the patriarch—bore Isaac, son of the promise, that is, the free people of the Church. Now the name 'Raguel', which can be translated as 'God is their food' or 'God is their

1 Acts 2:3

2 Matt. 5:13

3 1 Tim. 2:5. According to the Gelasian Sacramentary, salt was placed in the mouths of the newly baptized. This 'salt of wisdom', as it is also called in the Sacramentary, is given as something that is propitious for eternal life (1, 31, 289—ed. Mohlberg et al., 43). See Finn (1992), 93.

4 Tob. 6:10-13

friend,'[1] designates that people who, when the devil's deceit had been conquered, bound themselves and their own to the Lord's fellowship and learned to say, *The Lord feeds me, I shall not want,* and deserves to hear, *Now I shall not call you servants,* but my *friends*.[2]

(6:12) **All his substance is owed to you,** says the angel. So the Father says to the Son, *Ask of me, and I shall give you the nations as your inheritance*, and so forth.[3]

[11] (7:1) **They came to Raguel who gladly received them.** Through the teachers of his Word the Lord went to the people of the nations, who willingly received him, as the Acts of the Apostles testifies in several places.[4]

(7:11) When asked for his daughter, Raguel was at first **terrified, knowing what** had happened to **those seven men.** But when the angel taught that while impure men could not have her, the God-fearing Tobias could, Raguel consented to give her to him.[5] The Gentiles, hearing the word of faith and having been admonished by the apostles so that they might fill Christ's Church throughout the world with their progeny, could not accept the ways and the law of the new faith without a secure examination, knowing that in olden days they had many teachers—being understood here, as it were, by the number seven—who all had known the joys of this life only, but would say nothing certain about eternal things. And because of this, the ruin of eternal death seized those who were without hope of immortal life. But when that Truth which was sounding abroad through the mouths of its teachers taught inwardly, the Gentiles finally understood that fools must say foolish things and that those who had not known the true God must perish, but also that by coming in power to the world the Creator of the world must take charge of the world. And confessing faith in Christ, the Gentiles rejoiced to be sanctified by his sacraments.

(8:2) When Tobias was taken to Sarah in her bedroom, he **brought forth part of the liver from his small bag and placed it on live coals.** When the Lord is gathering the Church from among the Gentiles, at the first moment of her betrothal he commands her in the person of each believer to

---

1 Jerome *Nom.*, s.v. 'R' [Genesis] and s.v. 'R' [Exodus] (*CCSL* 72: 71, 29 and 72: 77, 21-2)
2 Ps. 23:1 (22:1); John 15:15
3 Ps. 2:8
4 E.g., Acts 10:44-8, 13:44-8
5 Tob. 7:10-16

renounce Satan, all his works, and all his pomp and then to confess faith in the Holy Trinity for the forgiveness of sins, which is, as it were, to consume the fish's inmost organs with live coals.[1]

(8:3) After these things had been done, the angel caught and **bound the demon,** because after one renounces the devil and confesses the true faith, forgiveness of sins follows as the water of baptism drives out the devil. Now he bound him because he restrained him from attacking the faithful. For although [the devil] is sometimes permitted to test them so that they may be proven, he is forbidden to overcome them in such a way that they abandon the faith.

He bound him, it says, **in the desert of upper Egypt.** Both the desert and Egypt signify the hearts of the unfaithful, which have been deserted (that is, abandoned) by God and are unworthy of his indwelling. These hearts, explained by the name 'Egypt', have been blinded by the darkness of their own unbelief.[2] For one who is deserted by the divine light's grace is rightly filled by the prince of darkness. And so the angel bound in the desert of Upper Egypt the captured demon who had wanted to kill Tobias *[12]*
because the devil, having been forbidden from plundering the faithful who are their Redeemer's members, is permitted by that same Lord, even our Redeemer, to have dominion only over the unfaithful. Even with respect to the unfaithful he holds the devil bound. For the devil is not even allowed to afflict the impious ones in his power as much as in his insatiable fury he would like.

(8:11) Meanwhile, **as the cocks were crowing**, Raguel and his servants dug a grave because he was afraid the demon had killed Tobias. But after learning that Tobias was safe he ordered it to be refilled with earth at once.[3] The crowing of the cocks is the sound of the preachers who, at morning's [approach], would prophesy to the world that faith's true day was about to come after error's darkness. Some among the Gentiles doubted whether the Lord had truly defeated the ancient enemy and for this reason thought it best to bury and conceal the faith in his name; yet afterwards when the

1 Bede seems here to be alluding to the baptismal liturgy which, before the dipping of the catechumen, calls for the catechumen or his or her sponsor to renounce Satan and his pomp (Gelasian Sacramentary 1, 42—ed. Mohlberg et al., 68). Then, at the baptism itself, the baptizand is dipped three times. The first time, the baptizand or sponsor must confess belief in the Father; the second time, in the Son; and the third time in the Holy Spirit, the holy Church, the forgiveness of sins, and the resurrection of the flesh (Gelasian Sacramentary 1, 44—ed. Mohlberg et al., 74). See also Finn (1992), 103 and 106.

2 Jerome *Nom.*, s.v. 'A'—Acts: 'Egypt is 'darkness' or 'tribulation'' (*CCSL* 72: 143, 28-9).

3 Tob. 8:11-20

light of truth was made known, which is like day dawning and the spreading abroad of the cocks' song—which is the voice of teachers who were accustomed to rise up in their heart's swift flight toward heavenly desires—the Gentiles drove every cloud of doubt from their minds and at the defeat of the enemy recognized Christ truly as the Holy Church's Bridegroom.

(8:22) Rejoicing at Tobias' survival and his daughter's union and marriage, Raguel **had two fat cows and four rams slaughtered and a banquet prepared for all his neighbours and friends.** Rejoicing at their faith in Christ and their call to God, the Gentiles made so much progress in the Lord that from their number there arose teachers and later even martyrs. Such teachers and martyrs are surely the cows, because they bear the gospel's yoke easily[1] in that they beget and suckle by their preaching those also who grow up to bear the same yoke. They are also rams because they are fathers and leaders of those following them. Of these, it is said, *Bring the sons of rams to the Lord.*[2] The cows are fat because the teachers are filled with the grace of heavenly love. Of this [grace] the Psalmist prays, *Let my soul be filled as with the fat of abundance.*[3] Two cows were slaughtered because those who either freely mortify their bodies so as to be made a living sacrifice for Christ or who surrender their bodies to be killed at the hands of unbelievers surely have learned to stand against the enemy *with the weapons of righteousness on the right hand and on the left*, that is, in prosperity and adversity.[4] Four rams were slaughtered because holy teachers and martyrs preserve the four books of the holy gospel by their faith and labour; because they are protected by the four chief virtues—prudence, fortitude, temperance, and righteousness; and because they establish Christ's flock throughout the world, which is divided into four regions. Raguel had the cows and rams slaughtered because the Gentiles showed
[13] that such of their own who had come to the faith were the ones whom the enemy seeks to test because of their exceeding virtue. Unable to conquer those whom he tests, he can only succeed at making martyrs [become] conquerors. Or surely Raguel slaughtered those taught by the Gentiles to *crucify* their *flesh with its vices and desires* for Christ's sake.[5] With their slaughter he prepared a banquet for all his neighbours and friends because

1 Cf. Matt. 11:30

2 Ps. 28:1 (Vulg.). Apart from the Douai-Rheims translation, modern English translations of this Psalm do not contain this reference to 'sons of rams' (cf. Ps. 29:1).

3 Ps. 63:5 (62:6)

4 2 Cor. 6:7

5 Gal. 5:24

the growth, life, suffering, and crowning of the saints bestow joy upon many who are refreshed as though by a feast from their examples.

(8:23) **Raguel entreated Tobias to stay with him for two sabbaths.** We also entreat our Lord to stay with us until we come to the perfection of holy rest by the grace of the Holy Spirit. By that grace we rest both from servile deeds—namely, the sins of the body—and from perverse thoughts of the mind. And resting in our heart and body is he who said, *On whom will my spirit rest if not on one who is humble, quiet, and fears my words?*[1]

(9:3) Tobias bids the angel to take **animals and servants** and to go **to Gabael in Rages of the Medes**, and to give **[Gabael]** back **his signed pledge and** to receive from **him the money** and ask **him to the wedding feast;** and the angel agrees. The faithful members, namely the Lord's [members], ask him to take some believers and commission them to preach the Word.[2] [They ask him] to come among them to gather into his faith nations that have not yet received faith's mysteries, but have heard of it only by report.[3] [They ask him] in his mercy to allow the nations to exchange the talent of the Word, which they have learned by report, for the actual obedience of faith, and so also to be invited by virtue of their belief and upright life, into the Holy Church's wedding feast. At that feast Christ is the Bridegroom; at that feast He has made new wine from water, that is, he gives a spiritual understanding of the Law. And the Lord does not deny their request, but heeding the prayers of those rightly seeking him, he daily gathers new nations into the Church. As we said above, this can be understood specifically of those nations that had received the letter of the

1 Isa. 66:2. Bede's citation of this verse is quite different from the Vulgate. It seems to be an Old Latin reading which Bede probably cited from Gregory the Great (*Moral.* 5, 45, 78 and 18, 43, 68 and 29, 3, 5—*CCSL* 143: 276, 36-9, 143A: 933, 8-9, and 143B: 1438, 29-31; *Hom. in Ezech.* 2, 7, 8—*CCSL* 142: 322, 253-5)

2 Earlier in this commentary, Bede interpreted the younger Tobias as Christ's human nature. Here, in analogous fashion, he interprets Tobias as the body of Christ, which is Christ's church on earth and of which Christ himself is the head.

3 As Bede will explain shortly, Gentile nations which received God's word by way of the Septuagint translation exemplify those nations that had known about faith in Christ 'by report' only.

Law through the seventy translators and so could accept the faith more quickly, insofar as they could lay hold of it through books familiar to them.[1]

(9:6) **Taking four of Raguel's servants and two camels, Raphael went on to the Median city of Rages.** Telling Gabael all about Tobias, Raphael got the money and brought Gabael with him to the wedding feast. Raguel's servants and camels are preachers chosen from the Gentiles through whom the Lord gathers others. They are servants because they
[14] serve the needs of those they evangelize; they are camels because by submitting to brotherly love they carry the burdens of others' weakness. Why there are four servants and two camels was shown earlier where two cows and four rams were slaughtered.[2] [Servants and camels] guide Gabael to Tobias' wedding feast with Raphael's help when holy preachers bring new nations into the unity of Christ's Church with Christ's divine assistance.

(10:1-3) When Tobias **was delayed because of the wedding feast,** his parents were sad **because he did not return to them on the appointed day.** Even now, since Christ delays for the sake of faith in the Gentile Church, the individual Jews that are now converted to faith in him lament deeply in spirit that the Lord has been detained among the Gentiles, and so delays in coming to save them. What Tobias' mother said with great sadness, in poverty and bereft of her husband and son at once, well applies to these Jews:

(10:4-6) **Oh! Oh! my son! Why did we send you to travel! O light of our eyes, stay of our old age, our life's solace, our posterity's hope, we who had everything in you alone should not have let you leave us.** And what Tobias said to console her—**Be silent and do not worry, our son is well; that man with whom we sent him out is very trustworthy**—this applies to those believing Jews who console themselves and their people with [the hope] that at some future time the Lord will surely return

1 Cf. *In Tob.* 1, 9 (*CCSL* 119B: 4, 45-7). Bede here interprets Gabael to be the Gentile nations. Just as Gabael received ten thousand talents from the elder Tobias, so did the Gentile nations first receive report of Christ from the Jews via the Septuagint translation. Gabael's returning of the talents to Tobias represents for Bede the Gentiles giving back their faith to the Jews. Deep in the background of Bede's allegory are echoes of one of Bede's favorite didactic parables, the Parable of the Talents (Matt. 25:14-30). Like the good stewards who return their master's talents with interest, so do the Gentile nations, represented by here Gabael, return to the Jews what the Jews gave them (i.e., the Septuagint translation). Moreover, they return it with interest (i.e., true faith in Christ). Cf. *Ep. Ecg.* 2 (ed. Plummer, 1: 406) and *XXX quaest.* 30 (*CCSL* 119: 321, 60 and 322, 72).

2 *In Tob.* 8, 22 (*CCSL* 119B: 12, 55-9)

to them and all Israel will be saved.[1] They know that the Lord who promises this is very trustworthy. For as we showed above, [the elder] Tobias signifies in Scripture's customary manner both unbelievers because of his blindness and believers because of his faith.[2]

(10:9) Raguel asked Tobias to stay with him longer but Tobias refused, saying, **I know that my father and my mother now count the days, and their spirit is tortured within.** Likewise, when *the full number of Gentiles have entered* none will be able to keep God from meting out salvation to Israel or illuminating its blindness, which has partly happened already.[3] For the divine clemency is mindful of the great sadness and unending sorrow of heart among believing Jews because of the blindness of unbelievers who are Israelites, their kin according to the flesh.

So Raguel sent Tobias back to his parents, giving him Sarah and much
wealth.[4] At the [world's] end, the Church's teachers will send Christ back [15]
along with the Church itself, which has been filled with virtue's riches, to the Jews from whom he assumed the flesh so that faith might enlighten them and the wealth of good works enrich them.

The angel and Tobias went on ahead to Tobias' parents. His wife then followed with his property and slaves after his father's sight was restored.[5] The divine grace goes on ahead to enlighten the blindness of the Jews, and in their own scriptures they will recognize that Christ is true God and man. And after acknowledging the right faith, which is like seeing the angel and their son whom they had not seen for a long time, they will rejoice greatly and by participating in the heavenly mysteries will join themselves to the Holy Church which was gathered among the Gentiles.[6]

(11:9) **The dog, which had also been with them on the road when** the two drew near the house, **ran before them like an approaching messenger and rejoiced with the adoring wag of its tail.** The figure of this dog who is the angel's messenger and companion should not be taken lightly. As we mentioned earlier, it signifies the Church's teachers who by tangling so often with heretics chase away fearsome wolves from the Good Shepherd's

1 Rom. 11:26

2 *In Tob.* 2, 10/11 (*CCSL* 119B: 5, 29-34)

3 Rom. 11:25-6

4 Tob. 10:10

5 Tob. 11:3-8

6 By 'their own scriptures,' Bede intends the Hebrew Bible or, as the Christians call it, the Old Testament. On the Jews seeing Christ as their angel, see *In Tob.* 5, 11/13 (*CCSL* 119: 7, 4-7).

sheepfold.[1] This figure aptly fits them since dogs naturally show gratitude to those who are kind to them and keep a restless watch for the sake of their masters. So the dog ran ahead because the teacher first preaches salvation, and then the Lord as Illuminator cleanses the hearts. The text beautifully says, **like an approaching messenger,** because whoever is a faithful teacher is surely a messenger of truth; and beautifully again, **it rejoiced with the adoring wag of its tail,** a tail inasmuch as what is at the limit or extremity of the body suggests either the extremity of a good work, which is perfection, or perhaps the reward allotted without limit. The dog thus was rejoicing with fawning tail as it visited again the dwellings of the masters from which it had long been absent. So teachers rejoice over accomplishing their work when they realize that by their ministry the Jews will be gathered by the Lord. Even as they promise Christ's coming grace to all the elect, they rejoice over obtaining their eternal reward, shared by all the elect, and they gladden the hearts of those to whom they preach concerning it.

(11:10) And so when the dog announces that Tobias is coming, **his blind father arises and stumbles, then begins to run.** When salvation's word has been heard from the teachers, the Hebrew people will arise from the long sleep of their faithlessness and run with love to the Lord. Yet they will stumble on the steps of works, until having been regenerated in Christ, and instructed, they receive the light of full faith and of good works.

[16] **And Tobias gave his hand to a servant, and hurried to meet his son.** The blind man gives his hand to his servant so that he may hurry to the Lord with the unencumbered foot of charity. For even if he does not yet fully understand the way of faith, he does all that he can to give his consent to one who has known fully the light of truth so that he may come to the Lord.

(11:11) **And receiving him, Tobias and his wife kissed him, weeping for joy.** At last receiving [their] bond with Christ, the Jews will mix their weeping with joy: happy because they believe, sad because they came to the Lord so late.

(11:13) **Then taking some of the fish's gall-bladder Tobias smeared [it on] his father's eyes.** The Lord also reveals more fully to believers how great is the evil of the ancient serpent. For that serpent, who once was eager to devour Christ in his suffering, has himself been struck down for this instead and lost his own members, that is, those he had previously held.

---

1 *In Tob.* 6, 1 (*CCSL* 119B: 8, 5-8)

(11:13-15) **A white film, like an egg's membrane, began to exude from** Tobias' **eyes** after they were smeared **with the fish's gall-bladder,** and he **recovered his sight.** The Jews also will recover the lost light after they recognize the bitter malice of that most depraved enemy. The white film that filled [Tobias'] eyes signifies pride's folly. For *[the Jews] have a zeal for God, but not according to knowledge*, and as it says again, *wishing to establish their own righteousness, they are not subject to the righteousness of God.*[1] For a dark pupil sees, [but] a white one is blind. Likewise, there is no truth in them who seem wise to themselves, saying, *Can we ourselves be blind?*[2], while those inwardly aware of their own fragility and ignorance who know how to say, *My God, enlighten my darkness*,[3] will be blessed in the Lord with the light of life. The white film was rightly likened to an egg's membrane.[4] For surely hope is signified by the egg because it is obviously not yet a living nor animate thing, yet still the bird who laid it hopes it will live, hatch, run, fly. The apostle also said, *Now if we hope for what we do not see, then we wait for it patiently.*[5] And so in the Gospel maxim about the bread, the fish, and the egg, the three greatest virtues are expressed; that is, faith, hope, and love.[6] And so the Jews still have a veil before their heart because they do not perceive Christ's grace.[7] They have a white film because they seem pure and righteous to themselves in comparison to all others, but they have it like an egg's membrane because they prolong their spiritual blindness in the foolish and empty hope that the messiah is yet to be born in the flesh, yet to liberate them, and yet to give
them a great kingdom throughout the world. But those among them from *[17]*
whom the fog of error will be removed will acknowledge that the Christ has come already and redeemed the world by his blood.

(11:16-18) What follows aptly applies to them, for when Tobias got his sight back, **he glorified God with his wife and with all his friends,** saying, **'I bless you, O Lord, God of Israel, for you have rebuked me and saved me and behold I see Tobias my son.' After seven days, his son's wife Sarah arrived.** The seven days signify the light of spiritual grace, which

1 Rom. 10:2-3
2 John 9:40
3 Ps. 18:28 (17:29)
4 Augustine *Quaest. euang.* 2, 22 (*CCSL* 44B: 66, 11)
5 Rom. 8:25; cf. Bede *Hom.* 2, 14 (*CCSL* 122: 277, 180-6)
6 Luke 11:11-12 and 1 Cor. 13:13; Augustine *Quaest. euang.* 2, 22 (*CCSL* 44B: 66, 1-15); Augustine *Serm.* 105, 5, 7 (*PL* 38: 621)
7 2 Cor. 3:15

is received sevenfold.[1] And so after Tobias was enlightened for seven days, his son's wife arrives because after the Jews have been enlightened by faith and have received the grace of the Holy Spirit, the Church will arrive for them in order that there may be *one sheepfold and one shepherd*,[2] and one house of Christ established on one cornerstone.[3]

The wife's many cattle, camels, and goods also arrived. The many faithful and the many virtues of the Church will then be joined to the Hebrews.

And also that money that Tobias received from Gabael. Even the knowledge of the Scriptures, which [the Hebrews] had once loaned to the Gentiles, will be returned to them at that time.

(11:20-1) **Tobias' relations came, congratulating him for all the good things that the Lord had done for him, and for seven days** they feasted with him. This is what Moses said in the song, *Rejoice, O Gentiles, together with his people*.[4] They feast together seven days because they rejoice in spiritual gifts and powers.[5]

When the angel is ready to return to heaven, he explains more fully to them who he is, why he came, and that he is about to return to God.[6] At that time also the Lord will disclose more fully to that same people,[7] as it progresses [spiritually], the rewards of knowing him, revealing and showing everyone that he is in the Father and the Father in him.[8] And so the angel returns to God, while Tobias stays with his father. Likewise, the elect

1 Isa. 11:2-3. The Gelasian Sacramentary prescribes that immediately following the baptism, the officiating presbyter sign the infant on the head with chrism. Then, the bishop gives the infant the sevenfold gift by imposing his hands on the child with these words: 'Almighty God, Father of our Lord Jesus Christ, who has regenerated your servants from water and the Holy Spirit (cf. John 3:5) and has given them the remission of all sins: Lord, send upon them your Holy Spirit, the Paraclete, and give them the spirit of wisdom and understanding, the spirit of counsel and might, the spirit of knowledge and faithful devotion, and fill them with the spirit of fear of God (cf. Isa. 11:2), in the name of our Lord Jesus Christ, with whom you live and reign always God with the Holy Spirit throughout every age of ages. Amen.' (1, 44—ed. Mohlberg et al., 74; transl. Finn [1992], 106). See Augustine *Serm. dom. in monte* 1, 4, 11 (*CCSL* 35: 9, 188-96) and *Serm.* 248, 5 [in diebus Paschalibus, 19] (*PL* 38: 1160); Isidore *Etymol.* 7, 3, 13 (ed. Lindsay, vol. 1); Hilary of Poitiers *In Matt.* 12, 23 (*SC* 254: 292).

2 John 10:16

3 Eph. 2:20; 1 Pet. 2:5-6

4 Deut. 32:43; Rom. 15:10

5 *In Tob.* 11, 16/18 (*CCSL* 119B: 17, 70-1)

6 Tob. 12:6-20

7 I.e., the Jews

8 Cf. John 14:10

also understand the Lord to be equal with the Father in his divinity, and consubstantial with us in his humanity.

(13:1) Then **opening his mouth, the elder Tobias blessed God.** Acknowledging God's severity and mercy, he reminded the faithful always to proclaim the benefits and fear the scourges of God. And filled with the spirit of prophecy he sang in praise of many things[1] concerning our mother *[18]*
the heavenly Jerusalem.[2] Likewise, when the Jewish people have converted to the faith at the end of the age, they will have many teachers and prophetic men who will rouse the minds of their kindred toward heavenly desires until the heavenly homeland's eternal joys resound in abundance for them.

(14:5) **In his dying hour** the elder Tobias **summoned his son Tobias and Tobias' seven sons, his grandchildren, and told them** that Nineveh's destruction was nigh, as was the renewal of Jerusalem and the land of Israel.[3] At that time also all of the faithful and upright teachers among the Jews, who live in this world yet are about to leave it, will warn their kindred that the end of the world is near and that the future life's bounties are coming soon. Moreover, they shall warn especially those whom they consider as reborn by the Lord's favour and see filled with the gift of the sevenfold Spirit, which is like the fact that the sons of the younger Tobias are seven in number and young men too, that is, strong in faith and overcoming the devil.

(14:12-13) **Guide your steps,** he said, **that you may leave** Nineveh; **for I see that its iniquity shall bring its end.** This is to say to his hearers among the faithful, 'Guide your heart's intention so that you may forsake the desires of this world and of earthly ways and seek heavenly things with your whole mind.' For it is well known that the multitude of the wicked and the transgression of God's precepts throughout the world are so great that they can be stopped only by destroying that world, as it once was in the flood, and by annihilating all humankind.

(14:14-15) Tobias thus **left Nineveh with his wife, and children, and children's children and returned to his in-laws and found them in good old age.** This the Lord does daily and will do until the end of the age when he abandons those whom he has not recognized as his own, so that he might visit and enlighten the hearts of those he has predestined to eternal life.[4]

1 Tob. 13:2-22
2 Gal. 4:26
3 Tob. 14:6-8
4 Rom. 8:29; Eph. 1:5

For he finds such as these in good old age when he rejoices that by his grace they have devoted themselves to good works for so long. By contrast, he sees in a bad old age, and so will pass by, those who though living longer are still childish in their judgement, not to be venerated for the lustre of their good deeds like one is for gray hair, but are doubled up under the weight of their vices. Of such as these Isaiah says, *A boy shall die after a hundred years, a sinner of a hundred years shall be cursed.*[1] Those who have lived childishly for many years and have never sought to put off a spirit of levity will justly be subject to condemnation for their sins.

He found them healthy, it says, **in good old age and he took care of**
[19] **them and closed their eyes and took possession of all the inheritance of Raguel's house.** Our Lord and Saviour also takes care of the ones he knows have persisted in the health of good works. For by closing the heart's eye to the allure of this present life he lifts them to contemplation of the perpetual light and leads them to heavenly things after this life is over. His is the inheritance about which the prophet sings to him, *Arise, O God, judge the earth, for you will inherit among all the nations.*[2]

(14:16-17) **And after he had lived** many **years in fear of the Lord, all his kindred joyfully buried him.** Tobias' burial signifies the end of the whole world, when our Lord with his whole body—which is the Church he has redeemed—shall enter into eternal rest,[3] with the angels rejoicing over the fellowship of redeemed human beings and assigning each one, their Maker's members as it were, to the heavenly homeland's various mansions in accordance with the variety of their merits.[4]

And all his generation persisted in good life and holy behaviour. All over the world and throughout this entire age, this is that one generation of those seeking the Lord and looking for the face of Jacob's God.[5] About this generation it also says, *The generation of the righteous will be blessed.*[6] Yet what life is better, what behaviour holier than one which forever remains in the glory of its Maker?

So that they were welcomed as much by God as by all the land's inhabitants. Having been led to the heavenly homeland, humanity's [elect] will be welcomed by God, whose grace has redeemed them, and also by the

1 Isa. 65:20
2 Ps. 82:8 (81:8)
3 Col. 1:24
4 Cf. John 14:2
5 Ps. 24:6 (23:6)
6 Ps. 112:2 (111:2)

angels whose number they will complete and to whom they will be linked in brotherly fellowship forever.[1] In fact, these are the inhabitants of that land, about which the Lord says, *Blessed are the meek, for they shall possess the land.*[2] Longing to see this land the Psalmist said, *I believe that I shall see the good things of the Lord in the land of the living.*[3]

1 In saying that the number of redeemed human beings will complete the number of the angels, Bede is alluding to Augustine's teaching that the number of redeemed human beings will match the number of fallen angels, thus filling up the quota of redeemed rational creatures. In a curious interpretation, Augustine understands the gospel assertion that resurrected human beings will be 'equal to angels' (Luke 20:36) as meaning *not* that resurrected human beings will be equal to the angels in stature or goodness, but that they will be equal in number to the number of fallen angels (Augustine *Enchir.* 9, 29—*CCSL* 46: 65, 17-32).

2 Matt. 5:4

3 Ps. 27:13 (26:13)

THIRTY QUESTIONS ON THE BOOK OF KINGS: INTRODUCTION

The 'Book of Kings'

Bede's title, *Thirty Questions on the Book of Kings*, may confuse some modern readers of Scripture who think that the Hebrew Bible contains not one book of Kings, but two, and that these two books of 1 and 2 Kings are sandwiched between 2 Samuel and 1 Chronicles. For Bede, however, 'the Book of Kings' designated neither what we know as 1 or 2 Kings nor both together. Rather, it designated what now to us are the four biblical books of 1 and 2 Samuel, and 1 and 2 Kings.[1] Yet Bede's Book of Kings was divided into four parts, which he designates as 1-4 Kings. His 1 Kings corresponds exactly to our 1 Samuel; his 2 Kings to our 2 Samuel; his 3 Kings to our 1 Kings; and his 4 Kings to our 2 Kings. For the purposes of this work, we shall use the modern designations for these books when giving a Scriptural citation and shall use Bede's term, 'the Book of Kings', to refer to all four books together. Bede's *Thirty Questions* thus addresses questions of interpretation in all four books. Questions 1-6 deal with passages from 1 Samuel; 7-10, from 2 Samuel; 11-17, from 1 Kings; and 18-30, from 2 Kings.

1 The Septuagint, which saw all four books as a unity, called these books 1-4 *Basileiai*, which may be translated as 1-4 Kingdoms or 1-4 Reigns. When translated into Latin, these titles became 1-4 Regnorum. But in his Prologue to Samuel, Jerome rejected the term 'Regnorum' [=*Kingdoms*] in favor of 'Regum' [=*Kings*], arguing that since these books dealt not with the kingdoms of separate nations, but only with the one kingdom of Israel, the plural designation of 'kingdoms' was misleading. Thus, in the Vulgate these books become known as 1-4 Regum [=1-4 Kings], which is what Bede calls them (*Biblia Sacra Vulgata* 364-5).

One is hard pressed to explain why Bede almost always referred to all four of these biblical books as the single Book of Kings,[1] especially in light of the fact that he refers to the first two (i.e., 1 and 2 Samuel) also as a single book: the Book of Samuel.[2]

The Exegetical Style of the Thirty Questions

Bede's *Thirty Questions* is a series of thirty responses to questions that were put to him by Nothhelm, whom Bede describes in his *Ecclesiastical History* as 'a godly priest of the Church in London'.[3] When Bede was compiling the Kentish materials for his *Ecclesiastical History*, the Abbot Albinus of St. Augustine's monastery, which was at that time just outside Canterbury, sent Nothhelm to Bede at Jarrow with materials relating to the Roman mission in Kent.[4] Either on this visit or in some later correspondence, Nothhelm also provided Bede with some of Gregory the Great's correspondence which he had copied while in Rome. In 735, the year of Bede's death, Nothhelm was consecrated Archbishop of Canterbury. He died in 739.

Whereas many of Bede's biblical commentaries elucidate almost exclusively the figurative or allegorical sense of a work of Scripture, the *Thirty Questions* is devoted largely to explicating the plain or historical sense of certain difficult passages in the Book of Kings. In only about five of the thirty questions does Bede attempt any allegorical exegesis at all, and even in those questions, a more literal exposition typically precedes his allegorical interpretation.[5] The whole tenor of the *Thirty Questions* thus tends to bear out Paul Meyvaert's assertion that the literal sense of Scripture was of much greater interest to Bede than it was to an exegete like Gregory the Great. Moreover, anyone who reads Question 4—which is concerned with how long the ark remained in Kiriath-jearim—or Questions 11-13—which deal with the dimensions of Solomon's Temple—will clearly see what

1 Cf. Bede *De tab.* 1 (*CCSL* 119A: 29, 937), *XXX Quaest.* Prol. (*CCSL* 119: 293, 1-2); *XXX Quaest.* 11 (*CCSL* 119: 303, 1); *XXX Quaest.* 18 (*CCSL* 119: 311, 17); *XXX Quaest.* 27 (*CCSL* 119: 317, 4); *In Ezr.* 3 (*CCSL* 119A: 351, 476); *In Marc.* 3, 12 (*CCSL* 120: 593, 2013). One of the few places where Bede refers to these four books in the plural is in the list of his works that he published at the end of his *Ecclesiastical History*, where after referring to *Thirty Questions* on the *book* of Kings (*in Regum librum*) he goes on several lines later to refer to his summaries of lessons on the *books* of Kings (*in libros Regum*) (*Hist. Eccl.* 5, 24—ed. and transl. Colgrave and Mynors, 568). I am grateful to Paul Meyvaert for these references.

2 E.g., *In Ezr.* 2 (*CCSL* 119A: 307, 800-1).

3 *Hist. eccl.* Praefatio (ed. and transl. Colgrave and Mynors, 4)

4 Bede *Ep. Alb.* (Plummer, 1: 5)

5 See QQ. 1, 12, 14, 16, and 30 below.

Meyvaert means when he says of Bede: 'Problems of chronology and measurement clearly delight him.'[1]

In *Thirty Questions*, however, one wonders whether Bede's attention to such problems reflects equally Nothhelm's interests. Although little is known about Nothhelm's schooling, Lapidge and others have demonstrated that the Canterbury school, under the leadership of Archbishop Theodore and his friend Hadrian, had a keen interest in Scripture's literal sense—an interest which included those 'problems of chronology and measurement' that a careful reading of Scripture posed.[2] A possible link between Nothhelm and the Canterbury school may well be found in the person of Albinus, who was educated in the Canterbury school, as Bede notes in the Preface of the *Ecclesiastical History*, and who, as Hadrian's successor as abbot at St. Augustine's, dispatched Nothhelm to Jarrow with the Kentish materials for Bede's *History*. Moreover, Bede implies that Nothhelm was more than Albinus' passive emissary when he relates that Nothhelm delivered some of Albinus' information to Bede by 'his own mouth' (*ipsius Nothelmi uiva uoce*). As Albinus' trusted disciple, who was later dispatched to comb the Roman church's archives for materials on Gregory the Great, Nothhelm the priest seems to have been a considerable scholar in his own right and one whose interests typically tended towards the historical. As such, one is not surprised to find that most of Nothhelm's thirty questions to Bede concern themselves with Scripture's literal, historical sense.

Although Bede's Preface to Nothhelm gives the impression that the *Thirty Questions* is nothing more than a long personal letter from a scholar to an eager student, the treatise really belongs to the old and established literary genre of the *quaestio*. Dating back to classical times, works of this genre attempt to elucidate the meaning of difficult passages from sacred or highly venerated literature. Aristotle's *Homeric Problems*, for example, consists of a list of difficulties in Homer and answers to them. After Aristotle, the Peripatetics, Stoics, and Neoplatonists continued to employ this genre to explain Homer until the beginning of the fourth century CE[3] By that time, certain Christian authors had adopted this genre for biblical exegesis. Like the works devoted to Homer, the Christian *Quaestiones* focused attention upon difficult isolated passages of Scripture and usually preferred historical, philological, and etymological explanations to allegorical ones. Prominent Christian examples of this genre include Eusebius

1 Meyvaert (1976), 47
2 Bischoff and Lapidge (1994); Lapidge (1995)
3 Pfeiffer (1968), 69-70

of Caesarea's *Gospel Questions and Solutions*, Jerome's *Hebrew Questions on Genesis*, Ambrosiaster's *Questions on the Old and New Testaments*, Augustine's *Questions on the Heptateuch*, and Isidore of Seville's *Questions on the Old Testament*. What distinguishes a biblical *quaestio* from a biblical *commentarium* is the disputatious quality of the *quaestio*. Whereas the *commentarium* is the general interpretation or discussion of a particular biblical work, the *quaestio* specifically seeks to resolve Scripture's ambiguities or contradictions, or to make sense of that which seems nonsensical in it. As Isidore of Seville puts it, 'Now *problemata*, which are called *propositiones* in Latin, are *quaestiones* that have something needing to be resolved by disputation. And a *quaestio* is a questioning because [in it] is sought (*quaeritur*) whether something exists, what it is, and what its distinguishing characteristics might be.'[1]

Sources and Date

In composing *Thirty Questions*, Bede drew upon a number of earlier authorities. The several earlier Latin treatises on parts or all of the Book of Kings include Isidore of Seville's *Questions on the Old Testament*, the *Commentary on 1 Samuel* attributed to Gregory the Great, such remarks of Gregory on the Book of Kings as were recorded by his notary Paterius, and a Latin translation—probably by Rufinus—of Origen's *Homily* 1 on Hannah.

Bede seems to have known little or nothing of these works. Perhaps he knew of Gregory the Great's commentary, although it did not circulate widely under Gregory's name and there is now some question as to whether Gregory actually wrote it.[2] Frequent similarities of interpretation between Gregory's and Bede's separate commentaries on 1 Samuel have led Dom David Hurst to conclude that Bede used this commentary.[3] Against Hurst, Meyvaert argues that because Bede customarily makes generous use of verbatim borrowings from Gregory, the total absence of such borrowings from this commentary shows that Bede did not have it.[4]

1 *Etymol.* 6, 8, 14-15; cf. 6, 8, 5 (ed. Lindsay, vol. 1)

2 *In Libr. 1 Reg.* (*CCSL* 144: 49-614). On the question of authorship, see De Vogüé (1996).

3 CCSL 119, Praefatio (p. v): 'Expositionem Gregorii Magni eiusdem libri primi Regum Bedae notam constare uidetur.'

4Meyvaert (1976), 64, n. 23

Perhaps Bede knew of the commentary, but not as a work by Gregory.[1] There are only two places in the *Thirty Questions* which show any possible dependence upon it.[2] Moreover, both of these exhibit a general similarity of ideas which were commonly known and shared by other Christian Latin writers of late antiquity. There is thus no need to assume Bede's direct dependence on the earlier source. There is no evidence that Bede knew about or used either Paterius' extracts from Gregory's works or Origen's *Homilies* on 1 Samuel.

Even if Bede had had all of these earlier commentaries at his disposal, he would have had little use for them since they seldom address those particular passages from Kings about which Nothhelm inquires. In short, Bede is largely commenting upon passages for which there has been no previous commentary. Yet for many of the questions, Bede is able to find other kinds of sources which assist him in answering Nothhelm's queries. The authority upon which Bede relies most often is Scripture itself. That is, Bede commonly uses one passage from Scripture to shed light upon the problem in Kings which he is considering. So, for example, he uses the clearer sense of the idiom 'to let one's face fall to the ground', which is found in Job 29:24, in order to shed light on its obscurer sense in 1 Sam.

1 The fact that the work was not known to be Gregory's may be due either to the fact that Gregory did not actually write it, as De Vogüé alleges, or to Gregory himself. According to Richards (1980), Gregory worried that publishing his work would open him up to charges of vainglory and he feared his views might become distorted through the transmission of faulty texts (48-9). In fact, he had been so concerned about the scribal accuracy of abbot Claudius of Classis—the very one who had transcribed Gregory's comments on 1 Samuel into the Commentary as we presently have it—that he recalled that commentary, as well as others, to be corrected (Gregory the Great *Ep.* 12, 6—*CCSL* 140A: 975, 31-42; cf. Verbraken [1956], 213-17).

2 The first place is Question 1 where, in commenting upon the prophecy concerning the downfall of Eli's house and the appointment of a new faithful priest (1 Sam. 2:35-6), Bede follows Gregory in interpreting the fallen remnant of Eli's house as an allegory for the Jews, who though rejected now, will confess Christ and be brought into the Church at the end of the age (cf. *CCSL* 119: 297, 47-51 and *CCSL* 144: 158, 1473-80). One suspects, however, that the similarity of Bede's interpretation to Gregory's can be attributed either to their similar outlook or to their common use of Augustine's *City of God* which makes the same point in its discussion of these two verses (17, 5—*CCSL* 48: 565, 127-30 and 565, 149 - 566, 153). It is not surprising that both Gregory and Bede would see Eli, an Old Testament priest who has been rejected by God, as a type of the latter day Jews whom God has rejected temporarily so as to save the Gentiles.

The second place where one might suspect Bede of relying on Gregory's commentary is Question 3, where with Gregory Bede explains an obscure Scriptural passage by appealing to the distinction between the words *populus* and *plebs* (cf. *CCSL* 119: 298, 9-11 and *CCSL* 144: 271, 2661-6). Still, this distinction was such a common one that there is no need to assume that Bede learned it from Gregory.

3:19;[1] or again, he uses a fuller and clearer parallel account in 1 and 2 Chronicles to illuminate the more difficult one in Kings.[2] Finally, he also uses Scripture to solve both chronological and geographical problems that are pertinent to the question at hand.[3]

After Scripture itself, Bede relies most heavily upon those writings of Jerome which illuminate Scripture's literal sense. Indeed, Q. 15 is little more than an extended excerpt from Jerome's *Commentary on Ezekiel*. Besides relying on Jerome's Old Testament commentaries, Bede also draws heavily from Jerome's *Book of Places* and his *Book on the Translation of Hebrew Names* for geographical and etymological information.

Two other of Bede's sources bear special mention. The first is the Jewish historian Josephus whose *Antiquities* expands and embellishes certain of the accounts in the Book of Kings. Bede is most heavily dependent on Josephus in Questions 11-14, which have to do with the plan of Solomon's temple. Moreover, his use of Josephus' *Antiquities* in Q. 10 indicates that Bede was drawing upon a Latin translation of Josephus that sometimes differs significantly from the Greek original. Finally, Bede draws heavily upon the work of Isidore of Seville, yet never mentions him by name. Indeed, the whole of Bede's explanation in Q. 9 seems to hinge on the derivation of the word *teredo* (wood worm) which Bede gets from Isidore's *Etymologies*.

The text of *Thirty Questions* offers no direct clue as to when Bede might have written it. It must have been completed before 731, since Bede mentions it in his oft-quoted autobiographical note in the *Ecclesiastical History*.[4]

From its style and content, Laistner placed the *Thirty Questions* among Bede's latest biblical commentaries. Presuming that the order in which Bede commented upon the works of Scripture at this time corresponds to their canonical ordering, Laistner dated the *Thirty Questions* to about 725, between Bede's *Commentary on Ezra and Nehemiah* and his *On the Temple*.[5] Recently, however, Paul Meyvaert has called into question Laistner's presumption, noting that the time at which Bede wrote *Thirty Questions* seems to have been determined more by the timing of Nothhelm's

1 *XXX Quaest.* 2 (*CCSL* 119: 297-8)

2 *XXX Quaest.* 14 (*CCSL* 119:306, 1-7)

3 E.g., *XXX Quaest.* 4 (*CCSL* 119: 298, 3-11) and 26 (*CCSL* 119: 317, 1-10).

4 5, 24 (ed. and transl. Colgrave and Mynors, 568-9)

5 Laistner and King (1943), 62. Deanesly (1961) conjectures, without supporting argument, that *Thirty Questions* was composed just after 716 (161).

request than by any more general timetable that Bede might have been following.[1]

Meyvaert himself dates *Thirty Questions* to about 715 and offers a much more detailed and compelling argument than Laistner did. Comparing and contrasting those sections of *On 1 Samuel* and *Thirty Questions* in which Bede comments upon the same passage of 1 Samuel, Meyvaert concludes that Bede wrote *Thirty Questions* at some point between the time that he began *On 1 Samuel*, probably 713 or 714, and the time that he completed it, in about 717.[2] Of the two arguments, Meyvaert's is much the more sophisticated, although it should be noted that Laistner also dated *Thirty Questions* on the basis of the Latin style which Bede exhibited there—a style which Laistner asserted, but did not argue, belonged to the more mature Bede.

The present translation is based on the critical edition prepared by David Hurst for *CCSL* 119. That edition, in turn, is based on three ninth-century manuscripts and one manuscript which may date back to the eighth century (Koninklijke Bibliotheek 16 at The Hague). Bede's *Thirty Questions* was first published in 1563 by John Heerwagen in the Basel edition of Bede's collected works.

1 Meyvaert (1997)
2 Ibid.

THIRTY QUESTIONS ON THE BOOK OF KINGS

PREFACE [293]

I, Bede, send greetings to my most beloved brother Nothhelm.[1] With the Lord's help and to the best of my ability I have taken care to explain, dearest brother, the matters that you sent for personal clarification about the Book of Kings, with the following distinction. Thirty of the propositions that seem the more difficult, I am including for you in this volume and have assigned each a short chapter heading so that it might be located more easily. But at the same time I am sending to Your Fraternity, on other sheets collected separately, the other things that you noted down with them—names and phrases that can be explained more easily and briefly.[2] Although I knew of several passages in that book much more puzzling than those you thought I should examine, I also know how it often happens that one who has already understood perhaps many more obscure things, because he found them sufficiently explained in the discussions of great authorities, still continues to be uncertain and doubtful about the meaning of certain easier passages which may not have been thought worthy of investigation by those who have pondered the profounder ones. It is also the case that not everyone can possess all that the Fathers have written and that Scripture's difficult passages thus remain unknown to readers, not because teachers have not explained them, but because their explanations are either unavailable to inquirers, or, if available, are not understood by them, as is repeatedly the case with several passages whose answers you sought and received from me. Because I have, with these answers, devoted

1 Nothhelm was Archbishop of Canterbury from 735 to 739. Since, however, the *Thirty Questions* was written before the *Ecclesiastical History*, and thus before 731, we know that Bede addressed the *Thirty Questions* to Nothhelm when he was a priest of London.

2 David Hurst suggests that these 'names and phrases' refer to Bede's *Names of Places*, which is his glossary of place names mentioned in 1 Samuel (*CCSL* 119: v = PRAEFATIO). In two ancient manuscripts, as well as in Hurst's *CCSL* edition, this *Names of Places* is appended to the end of Bede's *On First Samuel* (*CCSL* 119: 273-87). By contrast, Laistner and King suggest that these 'names and phrases' refer to Bede's *Eight Questions* which Bede never intended for publication (*PL* 93: 455-62; *Hand-List* [1944], 156, n. 70).

myself to fulfilling your requests, following in the footsteps of the Fathers,[1] I pray that you and the brethren who serve the Lord with you in those parts, paying the debt owed our devotion, will remember to intercede for our health both in soul and body; and also, that you will not refuse to send us quickly a better explanation of anything about which I have written here, if you should find it—which could very easily happen. Fare well dearest brother in Christ.

[294] CHAPTERS

1. And I shall raise up for myself a faithful priest, etc.
2. Not one of all his words fell to the ground.
3. And [God] struck down seventy men of the people, and fifty thousand of the common people.
4. From the day that the ark remained in Kiriath-jearim, days were multiplied, etc.
5. What Jonathan said to David, 'If I live, you shall show me the Lord's kindness,' etc.
6. What Abigail said to David, 'For if someone at any time shall rise, and persecute you,' etc.
7. And he commanded them to teach the children of Judah the bow.
8. And he defeated Moab and measured them with a line.
9. He is like a very tender little wood worm.
10. And he went down, and slew a lion in the midst of a pit.
11. What is said about the temple, that it was thirty cubits in height, while in the Book of Chronicles it is held to be one hundred and twenty.
12. The door for the middle side was in the right portion of the house.
13. And he covered the house with a panelled ceiling of cedar.
14. And since the carrying-poles stuck out, their ends could be seen from outside in the sanctuary, etc.
15. Solomon made a solemn feast, and all Israel with him.
16. In his days Hiel of Bethel built Jericho.

1 This expression, 'following in the footsteps of the Fathers' (*uestigia patrum sequens*) is one of Bede's favorites. With characteristic modesty, he typically uses it to show how much he depends upon the Fathers for his own exegesis and to stress his lack of originality. Bede also uses this expression or its equivalent twice in *On the Song of Songs* and once in *On First Samuel* (Prologue and 6—*CCSL* 119B: 180, 503 and 359, 4; Prologue—*CCSL* 119: 10, 53-4). For more references to Bede's use of this phrase, see Meyvaert (1976), 62-3, n. 7.

17. May the gods do these things to me, and even more, if the dust of Samaria shall supply enough handfuls for all the people that follow me.
18. Let one third of you enter on the sabbath and keep watch on the king's house.
19. And he brought forth the king's son, and put the diadem and the testimony upon him.
20. And no audit was done on these men who received money, etc.
21. In the valley of the saltpits he slew [men] from Edom.
22. He restored the borders of Israel from the entrance of Hamath, etc.
23. And each nation made its own god.
24. Where is the god of Hamath and Arpad?
25. Do you want the shadow to advance ten lines? etc. [295]
26. She dwelt in Jerusalem in the Second.
27. And he defiled Tapheth, which is in the valley of the son of Hinnom.
28. And he removed the horses that the kings of Judah had given to the sun.
29. Also, the high places at Jerusalem on the right side of the Mount of Scandal, etc.
30. And he took all Jerusalem and all its rulers, etc.

1 [296]
(1 Sam. 2:35-6)
AND I SHALL RAISE UP FOR MYSELF A FAITHFUL PRIEST, ETC.

This is what the prophet said to Eli on God's behalf, **And I shall raise up for myself a faithful priest who will do the will of my heart and soul, and I shall build him a faithful house, and it will walk all the days before my anointed.**[1] Samuel must be understood as a figure of the Lord, Savior, and true High Priest for this clear reason: just as Samuel succeeded the dead

1 'anointed' = *christus*. Modern readers sometimes forget that the term Christ as applied to Jesus is not his last name, but a title meaning 'the anointed one'. When Bede reads *christus* in this passage, he clearly has Jesus Christ in mind, yet in its general sense 'my anointed' here refers to any Israelite king.

The Vulgate text of this verse fails to identify precisely the subject of the clause 'will walk all the days before my anointed.' In this respect, it correctly translates the same ambiguity of the original Hebrew. Some modern English translations give 'he' (i.e., the faithful priest) as the subject (e.g., KJV, D-R, JB, NRSV), while others give 'a faithful house' (e.g., NEB, REB). Later in this Question, Bede indicates unambiguously that he understands its subject to be 'a faithful house', which is why the ambiguity has here been resolved in this way.

Eli to the priesthood, having been chosen not from Aaron's lineage, but from another household, namely Levi's (for Samuel was son of Elkanah, son of Jeroham, son of Eliel, son of Toah, son of Zuph, son of Elkanah, son of Joel, son of Azariah, son of Zephaniah, son of Tahath, son of Assir, son of Ebiasaph, son of Korah, son of Izhar, son of Kohath, son of Levi, son of Israel, as the Book of Chronicles narrates) so also did the *mediator of God and humans*[1] take his fleshly origin not from Levi, but from another tribe, namely Judah, so that he might be our priest.[2] He offered the Father a sacrifice other than what the Law required, namely his own flesh; he left for us heirs of his priesthood other than those of Aaron's line, namely the sons of grace of the New Covenant, gathered from every Gentile nation. Surely what God said, as if speaking in a human manner, **who shall do according to my heart and soul**, can be rightly understood both of Samuel, since as a human he obeyed God's will in all things, and of the Lord and Savior, since as the only-begotten Son he was privy to the Father's mysteries in all things, according to what he plainly testifies of himself saying, *For I do nothing by myself, but I speak those things as the Father has taught me and he who sent me is with me and has not left me alone because I always do what pleases him.*[3] For him the Father builds a faithful house and we are that house if we hold firmly to the faith and to the hope of glory until the end. And this house **will walk all the days before** its **Anointed**, namely that same High Priest. For surely the Holy Church will never cease to make progress in the growth of its members until the world's end. But how can we understand it being said of Samuel that **a faithful house which will walk all the days before the Lord's anointed** (that is, Samuel) **will be built for him**, when we read in the following pages that Samuel's sons
[297] turned from his ways,[4] turned aside after gain, and perverted justice, unless perhaps we understand Samuel's 'house' here to be the Israelite people, who would go on serving the Lord all the days of Samuel's priesthood? About this house it is written, *And all the house of Israel rested following the Lord,*[5] and a little later, *Then the children of Israel put away the Baalim and Ashtaroth, and only served the Lord.*[6]

1 I.e., Christ; 1 Tim. 2:5

2 1 Chr. 6:34-8

3 John 8:28-9

4 1 Sam. 8:3

5 1 Sam. 7:2; cf. Bede *In Sam.* 1, 2, 34-5 (*CCSL* 33, 909-13)

6 1 Sam. 7:4. These verses describe the blessed state of Israel during Samuel's judgeship. As such, they highlight the contrast between this blessed time and that later time of calamity when Israel instituted the monarchy. The Baalim and the Ashtaroth are Canaanite gods whom the Israelites worshipped when they abandoned faith in God.

What follows, **And it will come to pass that whoever remains in your house will come to have prayers said for him, and will offer a silver coin and a roll of bread**, is being partially fulfilled in the present age and will be completely fulfilled at the world's end. For some Jews, if only a few—of the common stock as well as the priestly—now flee daily to the Church for refuge, but when the *whole number of the Gentiles* has entered, then *all Israel will be saved.*[1] Moreover, that one who is said to remain in [Eli's] house signifies those Jews yet to be saved. When Eli's priesthood passes away, that one will have to come to the Church and offer to a Christian priest, for his own sake, the coin of a confession which is consecrated to God, contained in the creed, concise in [its] formulation, but unexcelled in power.[2] For it often happens that silver symbolizes the heavenly word's clarity, just as gold symbolizes spiritual wisdom's radiance. And after the Law's animal sacrifices have been abandoned, that one will also offer the bread of the redemptive sacrifice[3] **and will say, Send me forth, I pray, to the priestly part,**[4] namely, to that people which shines with Christ as its priest and to whom Peter said, *You are a chosen people, a royal priesthood.*[5] The next phrase, **that I might consume a morsel of bread** *also expresses aptly that kind of sacrifice about which that same Priest says, 'The bread that I shall give is my flesh, for the life of the world.'*[6] *Because he had said earlier that he gave nourishment to Aaron's house from animal victims,* which *were what Jews sacrificed under the Old Covenant, he thus said here*

1 Rom. 11:25-6. Following Augustine and Isidore of Seville, Bede believed that we are living in the world's sixth and final age, which he called the *aetas decrepita*, the 'world's old age' (*De tempor.* 16, *CCSL* 123C: 601, 21; cf. Augustine *De ciu. Dei* 22, 30—*CCSL* 48: 865, 124-40; Isidore *Etymol.* 5, 38, 5—ed. Lindsay, vol. 1). The sixth age lasts from Christ's incarnation until the end of history. The sixth age itself, however, he divides into three stages of salvation history. In the first, redemption is offered to a portion of Israel; in the second, to the Gentiles; in the third, to all Israel. One can see that Bede here understands his own time as belonging to the end of the second stage. Although the Gentiles are still being converted to Christ, as the Anglo-Saxon conversion proves, Bede yet expects the final conversion of the Jews, or 'all Israel', as he refers to them here. For a more complete account of Bede's understanding of the six ages, see Davidse (1982) and Brown (1987), 37-8.

2 Cf. Augustine *De ciu. Dei* 17, 5 (*CCSL* 48: 565, 127-30 and 565, 149 - 566, 153)

3 The text from this point until the end of Q. 1 is identical to Bede's *On First Samuel* 1, 2, 36 (*CCSL* 119: 33, 931 - 34, 940).

4 1 Sam. 2:36

5 1 Pet. 2:9; cf. Augustine *De ciu. Dei* 17, 5 (*CCSL* 48: 565, 140-1); Bede *In Sam.* 1, 2, 36 (*CCSL* 119: 33, 931-3)

6 Augustine *De ciu. Dei* 17, 5 (*CCSL* 48: 565, 145-7); Bede *In Sam.* 1, 2, 36 (*CCSL* 119: 33, 933-6)

that one should ask for a morsel of bread to eat, *since bread is the sacrifice of Christians under the New Covenant.*[1]

2
(1 Sam. 3:19)
NOT ONE OF ALL HIS WORDS FELL TO THE GROUND.

What is said about Samuel after he relayed the message that he had received from God that night to Eli the next morning, **Not one of all his words fell to the ground**, signifies that none of these words he spoke was invalid, but that all he said was accomplished in fact.[2] For useless words, words that should be regarded as of no account and spurned in everyone's
[298] eyes, fall to the ground. Accordingly, blessed Job said, *The light of my countenance did not fall to the ground,*[3] doubtless because he was accustomed to maintain so solemn a countenance that he never succumbed to base jocularity; and yet as often as he showed his exceeding happiness to those around him, he surely did so always for their benefit.[4]

3
(1 Sam. 6:19)
AND [GOD] STRUCK DOWN SEVENTY MEN OF THE PEOPLE, AND FIFTY THOUSAND OF THE COMMON PEOPLE.

And [God] struck down seventy men of the people, and fifty thousand of the common people. This is said about those who were not of levitical stock yet dared to look at the Ark of the Lord as it returned from

1 Augustine *De ciu. Dei* 17, 5 (*CCSL* 47: 566, 153-8); cf. Bede *In Sam.* 1, 2, 36 (*CCSL* 119: 33, 936 - 34, 940).

The phrase 'he had said earlier' refers to what the Lord said several verses before to Eli through the mouth of the prophet, 'And I chose [Aaron] out of all the tribes of Israel to be my priest . . . and I gave to your father's [i.e., Aaron's] house all of the sacrifices of the sons of Israel' (1 Sam. 2:28).

Following Augustine, Bede allegorizes the silver coin, the priestly part, and the mouthful of bread, respectively, as the Christian confession of faith, the true Church, and the bread of the Christian eucharist.

2 What Samuel said, at God's command, is found in 1 Sam. 3:11-14. Using Samuel as a mouthpiece, God prophesies to the priest Eli concerning the downfall of Eli and his sons because Eli had failed to keep his sons from greedily appropriating for themselves sacrificial meat dedicated to God (1 Sam. 2:12-17).

3 Job 29:24

4 Cf. Gregory the Great *Moral.* 20, 3, 6 (*CCSL* 143A: 1005, 1 - 1006, 35); see especially, 1006, 11-16.

the land of the Philistines. 'People' and 'common people'[1] usually are taken to mean one and the same thing, as both are customarily translated from the same Greek word, which is λαός.[2] But they seem to mean different things here inasmuch as 'men' is also used in the first part of this verse.[3] (By the way, what your codex has, 'seventy two,' is definitely wrong.)[4] For the word 'men' signifies those of a nobler birth, so that the meaning may be that seventy nobles of the people were struck down and fifty thousand of the

1 'people' = *populus;* 'common people' = *plebs*

2 Λαός is a Greek word for 'people' or 'nation'. Bede's statement raises the question of how he knew that the single Greek word λαός was translated sometimes by the Latin *plebs*, sometimes by *populus*. It is known that Bede had access to a manuscript of Acts which gave the Greek and Latin versions in parallel columns (Laistner [1935], 257). Although it is not known how fluent Bede was in Greek, he must have known enough to look at a Latin word in one column and find its Greek counterpart in the other. To cite just one of many examples that could be adduced solely from Acts, he could have seen λαός rendered as *populus* in Acts 3:11, but as *plebs* in Acts 3:23.

Bede seems to assume that the Vulgate's *plebs* and *populus* here translate the LXX's λαός. But they translate ἄνδρες, which means 'men'.

3 Here Nothhelm's question seems to be, 'What does Scripture mean in this passage by saying that seventy of the *populus* (people) were struck down and fifty thousand of the *plebs* (common people)?' Bede argues that while *populus* and *plebs* are usually taken to be synonyms, in this case their juxtaposition designates a social distinction between the aristocracy (*populus*) and the common folk (*plebs*). How does Bede come to this conclusion? He notes that the meaning of the word 'men' (*uiros)* in this verse's first clause—which Bede has not quoted in the heading for this chapter ('And God struck down some of the *men* of Bethshemesh because they looked at the Ark of the Lord'—1 Sam. 6:19a)—is meant to parallel its meaning in the next clause, 'And he struck down seventy *men* of the people.' He notes that the word 'men' (*uiri*), which is used in both phrases, can and does here mean not simply 'male', but 'a man of excellence', or a nobleman. The use of *uiri* with *populi* in the phrase *de populo septuaginta uiros* (='seventy men of the people'), but not with *plebs* in the phrase *quinquaginta milia plebis* (='fifty thousand of the common people'), reinforces for Bede the notion that *populi* here has aristocratic connotations. Thus, these seventy are not just any seventy, but seventy noblemen. With much less scholarly argument, the Kings commentary traditionally attributed to Gregory the Great also notes that the *populus/plebs* distinction in this verse denotes a class difference: 'nobles in the cities are included in the name *populus*, while the rest are *plebs*, who are without nobility' (*In I Reg.* 3, 130—*CCSL* 144: 271, 2661-3).

Bede saw rightly the problem of the text before him. His solution, however, differs from that of all modern critics. A literal translation of the Hebrew and the LXX versions would read, 'of the people seventy men, fifty thousand men,' which does not make much sense. Jerome's somewhat literal Latin translation of the Hebrew seems to make sense of this phrase by introducing the *populus/plebs* distinction, which is neither in the Hebrew nor the LXX. Modern English translations (e.g., NRSV, NEB) typically solve the problem by concluding that the received Hebrew text was corrupted somewhere in the process of transmission. Josephus' version of this verse, for example, seems to say nothing of the fifty thousand figure, which modern critics conclude is probably a later gloss. See *Ant. Jud.* 6, 1, 4 (*LCL* 5: 172) and note *b.*

4 Nothhelm's copy of this verse apparently had *binos* for *uiros*.

common folk. For in Exodus the people stood afar off and prayed and *only Moses ascended to the Lord*[1] so that the people should not suffer thus.[2]

4
(1 Sam. 7:2)
FROM THE DAY THAT THE ARK REMAINED IN KIRIATH-JEARIM, DAYS WERE MULTIPLIED, ETC.

From the day that the ark remained in Kiriath-jearim, days were multiplied; in fact, it was now the twentieth year; and all the house of Israel came to rest following the Lord.[3] This should not be taken to mean that the ark remained in Kiriath-jearim for twenty years—that is, until the

---

1 Ex. 24:2

2 Cf. Bede *In Sam.* 6, 19 (*CCSL* 119: 56, 1878-9). Bede is drawing upon an analogical passage to explain why so many were struck down. In Exod. 24:1-2, God permits only Moses to ascend the mountain and expressly forbids the seventy elders of Israel from doing so. Like Mount Sinai in Exodus, the Ark of the Lord in 1 Samuel is depicted as being God's special dwelling place, and thus a place of awesome power and holiness. As such, the seventy people and the fifty thousand common people should have kept themselves at a safe distance from it.

3 In this Question, Bede does not give a single definitive explanation for this verse, but offers two alternatives. In question is whether the phrase 'twentieth year' refers to the last year in which the ark remained in Kiriath-jearim or to the last year in which Israel rested following the Lord.

Supposing first that it refers to the length of time during which the ark remained at Kiriath-jearim, Bede is chiefly concerned to show what happened to the ark at the end of this twenty-year period. He quickly dismisses the theory that this period ended when David removed the ark from Abinadab's house to Jerusalem, his new capital, after his kingship was extended beyond Judah to include all of Israel (2 Sam. 6:1-19). By pointing out that Saul had already removed the ark from Kiriath-jearim to do battle with the Philistines (1 Sam. 14:18) long before David brought the ark to Jerusalem, Bede argues that Saul's removal of it—not David's—must mark the end of that twenty-year period. To understand Bede's logic here, one must note the significance that he attaches to Scripture's statement, 'the ark remained in Kiriath-jearim.' Bede clearly understands this statement to mean that the ark remained there *continuously*. By citing Saul's removal of the ark from Kiriath-jearim (1 Sam. 14:18), Bede can easily disprove the theory that the ark remained continuously at Kiriath-jearim between its first arrival there (1 Sam. 7:1-2) and David's removal of it to Jerusalem after Saul's death (2 Sam. 6:1-19). Thus Bede's view of the history of the ark during this period is this: the ark arrived in Kiriath-jearim and remained there continuously in Abinadab's house for twenty years until Saul removed it to do battle with the Philistines (1 Sam. 7:1-2; 14:18); after the battle, Saul returned it to Kiriath-jearim where it remained for an unspecified period of time until David carried it to Jerusalem (2 Sam. 6:1-19).

Next, supposing that the phrase 'twentieth year' refers not to how long the ark was in a particular location, but to how long it had been since Israel had come to rest following the Lord (7:2), Bede uses the testimony of Josephus to show that this twenty-year period included all of Samuel's twelve-year rule and the first eight years of Saul's twenty-year reign, after which time Saul and his followers forsook the Lord (*CCSL* 119: 299, 18-28).

eighth year of David's reign, when a gathered throng of the people brought the ark to Jerusalem.[1] For one finds in what follows that in Saul's time it was carried out of that city and brought to the camp when Saul fought against the Philistines. As in fact it is written, *And Saul said to Ahijah, 'Bring the ark of God,'; for the ark of God was there with the sons of Israel on that day.*[2] Because it is known that David brought it to Jerusalem, having [299] taken it from Abinadab's house where it is said to have been put, one must conclude that in Saul's day it was brought back from the camp and carried into the city just mentioned.[3] From there it was later brought to Jerusalem during David's reign. Thus, the meaning of the sentence in question is that in the twentieth year of its being stationed at Kiriath-jearim the ark was moved from there because of the war in Saul's reign; or perhaps, that it was the twentieth year since what was still the whole house of Israel came to rest following the Lord; that is, by casting out its idols and serving him alone. For no one who attends to sacred history is ignorant of the fact that Israel did this during all of Samuel's rule[4]—which, as Josephus attests, lasted twelve years—and during the first part of Saul's reign which, as the same historian affirms, he held for twenty years.[5] But later, when the spirit of the Lord left Saul and an evil spirit stirred him especially to persecute

1 Since Scripture does not say that the ark was brought to Jerusalem during the eighth year of David's reign, one wonders how Bede obtained this bit of information. He seems to have done so by logical inference. 2 Sam. 2:11 states that David first reigned over Judah alone for seven and a half years at Hebron before becoming king of all Israel. David thus became king of all Israel during the eighth year of his reign over Judah. Bede assumes logically enough that David would have both moved the capital and sent for the ark at Kiriath-jearim at this time, that is, immediately upon this extension of his kingdom. (2 Sam. 5:13, 6:1-2).

2 1 Sam. 14:18

3 1 Sam. 7:1; 'the city just mentioned,' i.e., Kiriath-jearim.

4 'Samuel's rule' = *praesulatus Samuhel*. Bede typically uses *praesulatus* to describe a specifically priestly or religious form of leadership (e.g., *Hist. Eccl.* 5, 2—ed. Colgrave and Mynors, 456). His use of the word here in conjunction with Samuel underscores Samuel's priestly and prophetic authority. It contrasts with *regnum*, the word that Bede uses to designate Saul's specifically royal authority.

5 Josephus *Ant. Jud.* 6, 13, 5 and 6, 14, 9 (*LCL* 5: 312 and 356). Although Josephus seems to rely almost exclusively upon the Hebrew Bible as his source for the events related in the Books of Samuel and Kings, and thus is privy to no source that Bede does not have, Bede nevertheless often treats Josephus' sometimes creative construal of these early biblical facts and events as authoritative, as he does here.

Bede's claim that Saul's reign lasted twenty years in all is derived from the Latin edition of *Ant. Jud.* 6, 14, 9. The Greek edition of this passage indicates that his reign lasted forty years in all (*LCL* 5: 357, n. *f*).

the blameless and righteous David, there must have been a part of Israel's army or people which to some extent colluded with Saul in his malice.[1]

5
(1 Sam. 20:14-17)
WHAT JONATHAN SAID TO DAVID, 'IF I LIVE, YOU SHALL SHOW ME THE LORD'S KINDNESS,' ETC.

When Jonathan was pained to see David worn down by his own father's unjust persecution,[2] he said to David, **If I live, you shall show me the Lord's kindness, but if I die, you shall never withdraw your kindness from my house, when the Lord shall have rooted out the enemies of David, every one of them from the earth.** Scripture goes on to say, **Jonathan therefore made a covenant with the house of David**, and immediately adds, **And the Lord required [it] from the hand of David's enemies.**[3] It surely said this by way of anticipation, here interposing into the story what happened much later, when the kingship passed to the house of David after Saul had been killed and when God punished with a just vengeance those who had unjustly persecuted the innocent David. For here the Lord required [it] from the hand of David's enemies because they harried a holy man; then later they were forced to pay the penalty for the hatred with which they had raved against him for so long. This can be understood equally of Absalom, Sheba son of Bichri, and the rest of David's

1 Assuming that the twentieth year designates the time during which Israel rested following the Lord, Bede concludes that some Israelites must have served as Saul's accomplices in malice, for had they not, then all the house of Israel would have rested following the Lord for longer than the twenty-year period, thus contradicting the testimony of the biblical verse here in question.

2 Jonathan's father was Saul, the first Israelite king (ca. 1020-1000 B.C.E.).

3 This is the phrase that is chiefly under scrutiny in this chapter. As will be seen, Bede interprets the phrase 'And the Lord required it of David's enemies' to mean that the Lord 'required'—in the sense of 'demanded'—David's enemies to live under the same covenant of peace with David under which Jonathan had agreed to live. The 'it' that is required should thus be interpreted to mean the covenant: the Lord required the covenant of David's enemies. That is, the Lord required David's enemies to abide by that covenant. Because they did not abide by it, but rather persecuted David, they were punished with death.

These verses are difficult. Modern biblical translators have resolved the problem by not taking what the Hebrew text says as literally as Jerome and Bede do. They typically argue that the word 'enemies' in the phrase 'required it from the hands of David's enemies' is a corrupt addition and that the passage should be emended to read 'required it from the hands of David,' so that David is the one who is bound by this covenant, not his enemies. Such an emendation renders this passage perfectly comprehensible. Bede, however, will here try to extract a meaning from the more difficult unemended literal reading. Cf. McCarter (1980), 337, note for 20:16.

enemies.[1] On the other hand, if you want to know what the Lord required of David's enemies, from the sentence cited above (where it is said that Jonathan made a covenant with the house of David) it can (if I am not mistaken) be deduced *mutatis mutandis*[2] that he required this [covenant] of [300]
David's enemies; that is, [he required it] because they had not been willing of themselves to enter into a covenant of peace with one whom they saw the Lord was with. For that reason Scripture seems by a foreshadowing to interpose that sentence here so that Jonathan's testimony, in which he said, **When [the Lord] shall have rooted out David's enemies, every one of them from the earth,** would prove true, since David's enemies indeed were removed from the earth—not by David himself taking vengeance on his adversaries, but by God judging in David's favor.

The following is rightly added, **And Jonathan swore again to David, because he loved him, for he loved him as his own soul**, in order that he who indeed loved David with so perfect a love, according to God's law, might be shown to be immune from the downfall of David's enemies. Although death snatched him away so that he could not rule an earthly kingdom in common with David as he had hoped, he doubtless received a partnership in the heavenly kingdom with [David], whom he always loved for his glorious virtues.[3] For he too was a man of virtues.

1 Absalom was David's rebellious son who attempted but failed to usurp his father's throne (2 Sam. 15-18). Despite David's orders to spare Absalom, Joab, the commander of David's army, murdered him while Absalom's head was held fast in an oak (2 Sam. 18:9-18). Sheba, son of Bichri, also revolted against David. Pursued by Joab, Sheba met a violent end at the hands of the people of Abel, who so feared the destruction that Joab would bring upon their city in pursuit of Sheba that they cut off Sheba's head and threw it over the city wall to Joab (2 Sam. 20).

2 *Mutatis mutandis* ('when the things to be changed have been changed') here translates the phrase ἀπὸ κοινοῦ, a grammatical technical term meaning that a word expressed in one phrase is also understood in another. Bede thus argues that the sentence in question can be understood by considering it in tandem with the previous sentence. Both have to do with the making of a covenant with David's house.

3 Jonathan was killed along with his father Saul in a battle against the Philistines on Mount Gilboa (1 Sam. 31:1-2).

6
(1 Sam. 25:29)
WHAT ABIGAIL SAID TO DAVID, 'FOR IF SOMEONE AT ANY TIME SHALL RISE, AND PERSECUTE YOU,' ETC.

When Abigail's husband had insulted David, for he had been rendered senseless by his foolishness and drunkenness,[1] she pleaded for herself and her household saying, **For if someone at any time shall rise, and persecute you, and seek your soul, my lord's soul[2] will be kept, as it were, in the bundle of the living, with the Lord your God; but the souls of your enemies shall be whirled, as with the violence and whirling of a sling.** With a glorious comparison she distinguishes the condition of the righteous from the lot of the reprobate. For she calls the souls of the righteous 'living' to imply a contrast between them and the souls of the condemned which have been seized with spiritual death, in accordance with that saying of the prophet, *The soul that sins shall die.*[3] She likens the former souls to a bundle, the latter to a sling's stone; for a bundle is tied so that the whole will abide and be preserved, while a stone is prepared and put in a sling so that it may be cast away. For the more the elect are persecuted in this world and chastised by the blows of afflictions, the more closely do they unite themselves to each other in mutual love, so that being united to one another they may be saved in eternity by their Redeemer's hand. Conversely, the more the reprobate abandon themselves like children to their own pleasures in this life, the further are they flung away in the time to come from the glory of the divine vision, so that it is aptly said of them, *And they are cast*
[301] *off from your hand.*[4] Abigail marvelously describes the heavenly Protector's almighty providence when she says that the holy man's soul is kept with him, as though in the bundle of the living. For as it is easy for anyone to hold a bundle of grass or hay in one's hand, so does the strength of our Lord and Saviour effortlessly preserve all the elect throughout the earth from the beginning to the end of the world. And so, none of them perish for any reason at all, in accordance with what he himself said of the elect in the Gospel, using sheep as an allegory, *And they follow me; And I shall give them everlasting life, and they never will perish, and no one will pluck them*

1 Nabal, the name of Abigail's husband, means 'fool' in Hebrew (1 Sam. 25:25); Jerome *Nom.* I Reg. N (*CCSL* 72: 104, 12-13) [=Nabal]. There is a reference to Nabal's drunkenness in 25:36.

2 'Soul' here means simply 'life'. When Abigail says 'my lord's soul', she means David's life.

3 Ezek. 18:4

4 Ps. 88:5 (87:6)

from my hand.[1] As a bundle is held together as one by some sort of tie, so is the whole assembly of saints bound to each other by one and the same faith, hope, and love, and enclosed by one rampart of divine protection. The literal sense is clear enough: although David's enemies pursued him, his soul was always kept safe in the portion of the living, but when adversities pressed upon his enemies, they would be disturbed by upheaval, driven from their own territory, and even carried away from mortal existence, like a stone whirled round by a sling.

7
(2 Sam. 1:18)
AND HE COMMANDED THEM TO TEACH THE CHILDREN OF JUDAH THE BOW.

It is written of David, when he was grieving over the murder of Saul and Jonathan, **And he commanded them to teach the children of Judah the bow**. Since David now knew that the Philistines had many archers (in fact, Saul had perished mostly as a result of their blows),[2] he gave this order so that his own soldiers would also learn this same skill of war so as to defeat the Philistines next time. It then says, **as it is written in the Book of the Upright.**[3] They say that this book is nowhere to be found today, not even among the Hebrews. This is the case also with the Book of the Wars of

1 John 10:28

2 The 'mostly' here is explained by elements in the story of Saul's death that Bede assumes Nothhelm knows well. 1 Sam. 31:3 relates that Saul was mortally wounded by the Philistine archers. To avoid being mocked and finished off by the approaching Philistines, Saul killed himself by falling on his sword (31:4). Bede thus says that Saul died mostly because of the Philistine archers since, although their arrows did not finally kill him, they did precipitate his suicide.

3 Although Bede may not have known it, the Book of the Upright, or the Book of Jashar, was an ancient Hebrew poetry anthology. It contained David's lament over the death of Saul and Jonathan (2 Sam. 1:19-27) as well as the poetic verses mentioned in Josh. 10:12-13 and 1 Kgs. 8:12-13. It does not make much sense that David's command for his soldiers to learn archery should be included in a poetry anthology. For that reason, most modern translations prefer to follow the LXX, which has David commanding the people to learn not archery, but the song of lament over the death of Saul and Jonathan. It would certainly make sense that such a song should be preserved in a poetry anthology. Unlike the LXX, the Hebrew Bible specifies the bow as that which is learned, not the lament. Trying to keep as closely as possible to literal Hebrew meaning, Jerome's Vulgate retains the Hebrew reference to the bow. Since Bede here has the Vulgate reading before him, he needs to account for its reference to the bow. In the prologue of *Thirty Questions* Bede commends Nothhelm for noticing difficulties in Scripture that others pass over. Here is an instance where Nothhelm raises a question that has puzzled biblical scholars and translators for generations.

the Lord (which the Book of Numbers mentions[1]); the poems of Solomon; Solomon's very learned treatises on the nature of all trees and herbs as well as beasts of burden, birds, reptiles, and fish; what is mentioned in the Book of Chronicles, *Now the rest of Solomon's acts from first to last are written in the words of Nathan the prophet, and in the books of Ahijah the Shilonite, and in the vision of Iddo the seer against Jeroboam the son of Nebat*;[2] and the many such volumes that Scripture surely proves existed, but that clearly do not exist today. For when the Chaldeans destroyed Judea, a raging fire consumed its library, which had been assembled long before, as well as that province's other treasures. By his diligence, Ezra, High Priest[3] and prophet, later restored from that [library] a few books now contained in Holy
[302] Scripture.[4] Consequently, this is written of him, *Ezra went up from Babylon and he was a nimble scribe in the law of Moses*[5] (nimble, that is, because he devised shapes of letters that were more easily written than those that the Hebrews had used up until that time),[6] and this, in the Persian king's

1 Num. 21:14

2 2 Chr. 9:29

3 Neither the Vulgate version of Ezra nor any other patristic writer refers to Ezra as a 'high priest' (*pontifex*). Meyvaert (1996), 875 concludes that Bede's source here is a version of the apocryphal Esdras books that Bede found in the Codex Grandior (1 Esd. 9:39-40 and 50 = 3 Esd. 9:39-40 and 50). It is noteworthy that Bede does not refer to Ezra as *pontifex* in his later Ezra commentary, a fact which suggests, as Meyvaert notes, that between writing *Thirty Questions* and *On Ezra*, Bede came to realize that the apocryphal Esdras books were not reliable historical sources (876).

4 Bede means to say here that Ezra restored some of the books, not all of them. He clearly believes that Ezra did not restore the writings that Bede just mentioned, all of which were permanently lost in the fire at the Jerusalem library. Bede's source for Ezra's restoration of the sacred books is most likely 2 Esd. 14:19-48 (4 Esd. 14:19-48); cf. 2 Kgs. 25:9. On the availability of 2 Esdras in Bede's time, see Meyvaert (1996), 874. Before Bede, Isidore also makes mention of the burning of the Jerusalem library in *Etymol.* 6, 3, 2 (ed. Lindsay, vol. 1). Wearmouth-Jarrow's famous Latin pandect, the Codex Amiatinus, also preserves this tradition concerning Ezra. There, in the upper margin of the famous Ezra miniature folio (f. V^{r}), the caption reads: *Codicibus sacris hostile clade perustis / Ezra dō feruens hoc reparauit opus* [When the sacred codices were burned by the enemy devastation / Ezra, in his ardour for God, restored this work] (Bruce-Mitford [1969], 11). Meyvaert (1996), 877 argues that Bede himself composed this caption.

5 Ezra 7:6

6 In 2 Esd. 14, the Holy Spirit causes Ezra to dictate the lost Books of the Law to five men who were said to have written what they heard in characters they did not understand (14:42). These characters are generally taken to refer to the Aramaic script which, according to tradition, Ezra is supposed to have designed; see Myers (1974), 326. Bede likely learned that Ezra was the designer of this new script from Jerome, who in the so-called 'Helmeted Prologue' to his Vulgate translation of the Books of Samuel and Kings said, 'And it is certain that Ezra the scribe and teacher of the law, after Jerusalem had been taken and the temple had been rebuilt under Zerubbabel, invented the other letters which we now use, although up until that time the characters of the Hebrews and the Samaritans were the same' (Jerome *Prol. in Reg.—Biblia Sacra* [1975], 364). Cf. 2 Esd. 14:24.

letter, *Artaxerxes, king of kings, to Ezra the priest, the most learned scribe of the law of God of heaven, greeting.*[1]

8
(2 Sam. 8:2)
AND HE DEFEATED MOAB AND MEASURED THEM WITH A LINE.

What is written about David, **And he defeated Moab and measured them with a line, levelling them to the ground**, should be understood as hyperbole. For it could not have happened that the people living on the land were so abased that they seemed on a level with the contours of the land itself when a measuring line was stretched overhead.[2] Instead, in this verse Scripture wanted to emphasize the immense abasement of a captured and oppressed nation; hence it says that they were levelled to the ground. It is as though the people were so weakened and despised by God that they were of no more use living on that land than is that land which has no people. You have several examples of this kind of discourse in the Scriptures, as in the Gospel, *But there are also many other things that Jesus did; if they were written one by one, the world itself, I think, could not contain the books that would be written.*[3] For how could the world not contain books that are able to be written in the world? But to indicate the magnitude and multitude of the Lord's deeds, Scripture wanted to use such a phrase. Another example is David's lamentation, *They were swifter than eagles, stronger than lions.*[4] Very similar to this is that line of secular literature, *They could surpass*

---

1 Ezra 7:12

2 Unlike Bede, McCarter interprets this verse not as hyperbole, but as literally true. Believing that this verse describes a method of choosing prisoners to be executed, McCarter translates the Hebrew of this verse as, 'He also defeated the Moabites and, making them lie down on the ground, measured them off by line—two lines were to be put to death and one full line was to be spared' (*II Samuel* 242 and 247, n. 2). Another reference to 'measuring with a line' occurs in Herodotus' *Histories* 1, 66, in which the Delphic oracle tells the Spartans that they will 'measure out with the line' (διαμετρήσασθαι) the fair plain of Tegea. Thinking this meant that they would triumph over the Arcadians in battle, they engaged the Arcadians, lost, and were themselves captured and 'measured with a line' as they worked the plain of Tegea (*LCL* 1: 76-8). See Scott (1913), 481.

3 John 21:25

4 2 Sam. 1:23. This lamentation was for the death of Saul and Jonathan. Bede cites this verse as an example of hyperbole in his textbook on rhetorical figures (*De sch. et trop.* 2, 2, 11—*CCSL* 123A: 161, 173-6).

the snow in brilliance, the winds in speed.[1] Where it said that they were measured with a line, it used 'line' as an allegory for 'lot' inasmuch as the dimensions of fields are typically measured by a line, whence it is written, *And by lot did he divide the land for them by a line of distribution.*[2] Moreover, the meaning is that David divided the Moabites' regions for heirs of his choosing as freely as some landholder divides his own fields as he pleases with a line drawn from there to here. **And he measured with two lines, one for killing and one for making alive.** This saying signifies by allegory that since no one offered resistance, David held in his power those whom he could either kill as rebels, or spare as subdued subjects.

[303]

9
(2 Sam. 23:8)
HE IS LIKE A VERY TENDER LITTLE WOOD WORM.

This is what is said about the wisest chief of David's valiant men, whose name is not even mentioned in the Book of Kings but is given in the Book of Chronicles as Jashobeam and is there remembered as Hachamoni's son:[3] **He is like a very tender little wood worm.**[4] Here is designated at one and the same time the man's valour in war and his unassuming gentility. For a tender little wood worm's entire body seems fragile and also very small, yet it eats up the strongest kind of wood by destroying and rotting it. (For it gets the name 'worm' by wearing down the wood).[5] In a similar way, that man seemed friendly to all at home, even quiet and humble, yet showed himself as firm and unstoppable to an enemy when battling for the common good.

1 Vergil *Aen.* 12, 84 (*LCL* 2: 304)

2 Ps. 78:55 (77:54, iuxta LXX)

3 1 Chr. 11:11

4 The meaning of the Hebrew text for this verse is extremely obscure. The Hebrew passage that Jerome's Vulgate renders as 'he was like a very tender little wood worm,' recent translations render as 'he wielded his spear' (cf. NRSV, NEB). One modern commentator says that the Hebrew of this text 'will not yield to interpretation,' yet nevertheless dismisses the Vulgate translation that Bede used as 'quaint but not enlightening' (McCarter [1984], 489-90). Nevertheless, Bede's inspired imagination and etymological learning led him to an interpretation which by the standards of Bede's time was both sensible and edifying.

5 Bede here explains how the worm got its Latin name, *teredo*. Noticing the likeness of this name to *tero*, the Latin verb 'to wear down', Bede assumes that the name of the former derives from the latter. This assumption is not original to him. He probably received it from Isidore: 'The Greeks call wood worms *teredonas* because they eat [wood] by wearing [it] down [= *terendo*]' (*Etymol.* 12, 5, 10—ed. Lindsay, vol. 2).

10
(2 Sam. 23:20)
AND HE WENT DOWN, AND SLEW A LION IN THE MIDST OF A PIT.

It is said of Benaiah, **And he went down, and slew a lion in the midst of a pit, in the time of snow**. Josephus narrates more clearly how this may have happened.[1] For surely the pit was quite deep, and in the wintertime when all things are covered with snow, it also would have been made level with the ground by the snow's great accumulation.[2] When the lion, unaware of the danger, stumbled onto the pit, it fell in and was trapped there; loudly it roared; up ran the people to see what the commotion was. Since Benaiah also approached with others to see that spectacle, he immediately leapt down into the pit and smote and killed the attacking lion in the midst of the snow.[3]

---

1 *Ant. Jud.* 7, 12, 4 (*LCL* 5: 528-30)

2 Although Bede cites Josephus' fuller and clearer account of this story in the previous sentence, what he says here seems to be based on his own inference and not on anything that Josephus specifically says (cf. the Latin edition of Josephus *Ant. Jud.* 7, 12, 4—ed. Froben, 210). For example, Bede's statement that the pit was quite deep is not found in Josephus. By contrast, his statement that the snow would have obscured the true depth of the pit, and even made it appear level with the area around the mouth of the pit, must in some way derive from Josephus' reporting that the mouth of the pit was blocked by snow (*Ant. Jud.* 7, 12, 4—*LCL* 5: 528-30).

3 Neither Josephus nor the Vulgate explicitly states, as Bede does here, either that the lion was unaware of the danger or that others came with Benaiah to see the lion in the pit. While the latter item remains a mystery, the former might plausibly be explained by considering the *editio princeps* of the Latin Josephus (ed. Froben, 210). There one reads a detail not given in the Greek Josephus, namely, that the lion lay in the pit 'concealed and invisible' [*latebat absconsus nec apparebat*]. Perhaps Bede's manuscript had *absconsum* instead of *absconsus*, which would indicate that the pit, not the lion, lay hidden and invisible to the lion, as Bede here explains it. Alternately, Bede may have simply inferred that just as no one was able to see the lion concealed in the pit, so too was the pit itself concealed to the lion before the lion stumbled into it. In any case, Bede seems to assume that the snow acted like a natural version of the standard way of trapping wild animals, that is, by covering a pit with some fragile material that is level with the ground.

11
(1 Kgs. 6:2)
WHAT IS SAID ABOUT THE TEMPLE, THAT IT WAS THIRTY CUBITS IN HEIGHT, WHILE IN THE BOOK OF CHRONICLES IT IS HELD TO BE ONE HUNDRED AND TWENTY.

Of the building of the Temple in the Book of Kings it is said that **[the Temple] was thirty cubits in height**, while in the Book of Chronicles it is written, *Moreover the height was one hundred and twenty cubits.*[1] It must be known that these passages by no means disagree, but both are true. For as Josephus' history suggests, there were thirty cubits from the ground floor
[304] to the middle storey,[2] and again thirty cubits from the middle to the third.[3] The height of the side chambers[4]—which were connected to the Temple on

1 2 Chr. 3:4; cf. Bede *De templo* 1 (*CCSL* 119A: 161, 558-62)

2 Bede's reference here to the Temple's middle storey [*medium caenaculum*] must derive from 1 Kings 6:8, 'The door for the middle side was on the right side of the house, and by a spiral stairway they went up to the middle storey [*medium caenaculum*] and from the middle to the third.' Bede here takes the 'middle storey', or *medium caenaculum*, to refer to the second level of the main Temple building. All modern authorities, however, believe that in the verse just cited, the middle and third storeys refer to different levels of the side chambers, not of the main building. If Bede believed, on the basis of his reading of 1 Kings 6:8, that the main building was divided into three storeys, then on what authority does he base his conviction that the side-chambers are also divided into three storeys? It must be Josephus' *Ant. Jud.* 8, 3, 2: 'And all around the Temple he built thirty small chambers .... And above these were built other chambers and again still others above them, equal in proportion and number, so that they reached a combined height equivalent to that of the lower building' (*LCL* 5: 606).

3 Bede here does his best to harmonize the conflicting accounts of Josephus and Chronicles, on the one hand, and 1 Kings on the other. While both Josephus *Jewish Antiquties* 8, 3, 2 and 2 Chr. 3:4 state that the Temple was one hundred twenty cubits high, 1 Kgs. 6:2 states that it was only thirty cubits high. Josephus also states that the Temple was divided into two major levels, each sixty cubits high. Because Bede erroneously believed that the three storeys mentioned in 1 Kgs. 6:8 referred not to the side chambers, but to the main Temple building, he assumed that what Josephus referred to as the lower house was itself comprised of two levels, each thirty cubits high. Here Bede makes what seems to be a totally novel assumption, but one which enables him to affirm the truth of not only both Chronicles and Kings, but also of Josephus. He thus ends up with a Temple that has, on the one hand, two houses or levels, an upper and a lower (*Ant. Jud.* 8, 3, 2—*LCL* 5: 604-6) and, on the other, three storeys (1 Kgs. 6:8). The first two are thirty in height, the third is sixty. He thus concludes that the altitude of thirty cubits given in 1 Kgs. 6:2 refers to the distance between the ground floor and the panelled ceiling at the top of the first storey. See Appendix I below.

4 Bede here uses *porticus*—a fourth declension noun—to refer to all the side chambers. These encircled the Temple on three of its sides and had three storeys [*caenaculi*]. The Vulgate refers to these as *latera*; the Latin Josephus as *paruulae domus* (ed. Froben, 223). This plural form of *porticus* is not to be confused with the singular form, which Bede uses to refer to the Temple's porch at the east entrance (*XXX Quaest.* 12—*CCSL* 119: 304, 7). For more on this term and Bede's use of it in his description of the Temple precinct's outer courts and buildings, see Meyvaert (1996), 853-4.

the southern, western, and northern sides—rose to the the third storey, which taken altogether is sixty cubits. From that point there were another sixty up to the house's highest roof. Consequently, its total height was one hundred and twenty cubits.[1]

12
(1 Kgs. 6:8)
THE DOOR FOR THE MIDDLE SIDE WAS IN THE RIGHT PORTION OF THE HOUSE.

The door for the middle side was in the right portion of the house. This does not indicate, as some think, that the door by which one would have entered the Temple was built on the southern portion, that is in the midsection of the south wall. Were that the case, Scripture would simply have said, 'The door of the house was placed facing south.'[2] In fact, the door by which one entered for the Temple's daily services was to the east, as Josephus relates,[3] and the porch on the Temple's front also faced the east so that the rising equinoctial sun would cast its rays unobstructed—first through the doors of the Temple and then through the doors of the oracle—upon the ark, which was in the holy of holies.[4] But the stairway that led to the upper house, and from the upper to the third,[5] was on the Temple's south side (for this is the house's right portion).[6] This stairway was

1 Cf. Bede *Hom.* 2, 25 (*CCSL* 122: 375, 267-70) and *De templo* 1 (*CCSL* 119A: 161, 560-4 and 166, 785-93)

2 Cf. Bede *De templo* 1 (*CCSL* 119A: 165, 745-50)

3 Josephus *Ant. Jud.* 8, 3, 2 (*LCL* 5: 609): 'And the king contrived a stairway to the upper storey through the thickness of the wall, for it had no great door on the east as the lower building had, but it had entrances through very small doors on the sides.'

4 Josephus *Ant.* 3, 6, 3 (*LCL* 4: 370, 115; ed. Blatt 233, 5-6); cf. Bede *De templo* 1 (*CCSL* 119A: 161, 573-6). Bede's statement about the sun's first rays striking the east side of the Temple derives from Josephus' testimony about the Tabernacle. By inference, Bede concludes that such would have also been the case for the Temple. Bede shows his immense astronomical knowledge by revising Josephus' account slightly to limit this phenomenon to the equinoctial sun. I am grateful to Paul Meyaert for this insight.

5 Bede seems here to think that the stairway led to two upper floors or houses directly over the lower house. Because modern scholars reject as fantastic the testimony of Chronicles and Josephus that the Temple was 120 cubits high—testimony that Bede regarded as true—they see this stairway as connecting the three storeys of the Temple's side chambers.

6 Isidore explains that a temple's so-called 'right side' (*dextra pars*) denotes that side facing south (*Etymol.* 15, 4, 7—ed. Lindsay, vol. 2). Bede need not be drawing upon Isidore here. It may have been a well-known fact to both that whenever one refers to the right side of a temple, the south side is meant. Both Isidore and Bede used the word 'temple' (= *templum*) to refer to a church and not just to the Jerusalem Temple, although Bede does so quite rarely (e.g., *Hist. eccl.* 5, 7—ed. Colgrave and Mynors, 470; *Hom.* 2, 24—*CCSL* 122: 359, 23-4).

concealed and had a little door low down on the east side at the very corner of the right wall.[1] Thus it is suitably added, **And by a spiral stairway they went up to the middle storey and from the middle to the third.** The design of this ascent commends to us a most noteworthy mystery. For it is clear that this Temple, which Solomon made, figuratively denotes the body of Christ, the peaceable king, not only that body which is his entire Church,[2] but also that most holy body that he assumed from the Virgin so that he might be the Church's head.[3] Now **the door for the middle side was in the right portion of the house.** From that door one would ascend secretly from the lower parts to the middle storey and from the middle to the third.[4] For when the Lord suffered on the cross, *one of the soldiers opened his* right *side with a spear, and immediately blood and water flowed forth.*[5] Now these are the blood of redemption and the water of our washing.[6] Once

1 In other words, this stairway and the door by which one entered it was situated at the southeast corner of the Temple. Bede also cites this verse (1 Kgs. 6:8) in *Homilies* 2, 1 (*CCSL* 122: 190-1, 244-6). In the translation of this homily by Martin and Hurst, the phrase *latus medium* has been rendered as 'the middle of the side.' Translating *latus medium* in this way puts the stairway and its door in the center of the Temple's south wall. This, however, contradicts what Bede says here, namely, that the door was located in a corner. Although Bede does not say so here, his *Homilies* 2, 1 shows that he sees the door to this stairway as being on the Temple building's inside wall (*CCSL* 122: 190, 240, transl. in Martin and Hurst, 2: 10). Cf. Bede *De templo* 1 (*CCSL* 119A: 165, 752).

2 Cf. Col. 1:24

3 Cf. Col. 1:18

4 In this Question, Bede is so concerned to explain the phrase 'right portion of the house' that he does not sufficiently explain an equally problematic phrase, namely, *latus medium* ['the middle side']. Whereas the Vulgate probably intends *latus medium* (1 Kgs. 6:8) to refer to the middle storey of the Temple's side chambers, Bede reads *latus medium* in another way. In this Question, he always employs the word 'side' [*latus*] in connection with the Temple building itself, and never to indicate its side chambers. (As can be seen in Question 11, Bede refers to the side chambers collectively as *porticus*.) Bede here indicates, though somewhat obscurely, that he understands the Vulgate's *latus medium* in 1 Kgs. 6:8 to refer to the middle or second storey not of the side chambers, but of the Temple building itself. Against the Vulgate, Bede himself prefers the phrase *medium caenaculum* ['middle storey'], which he uses here, to *latus medium*.

5 John 19:34; cf. Bede *De templo* 1 (*CCSL* 119A: 166, 760-2)

6 I.e., the blood of the eucharist and the water of baptism; cf. Augustine *Tract. in Joh.* 120, 2 (*CCSL* 36: 661, 8-12). Bede's allegory here hinges on the double meaning of 'right side' as pointing literally to the right (or south) side of the Temple and allegorically to the right side of Christ's body which, according to Bede, was the side pierced by the soldier at the Crucifixion (John 19:34). Although the biblical text does not specify which of Christ's sides was pierced, Bede states in Book 1 of *De templo* that the Holy Church believes it to have been Christ's right side (*CCSL* 119A: 166, 762-4). On Bede's symbolic use of the 'right' side, see Ward (1990), 104-5.

cleansed from this life we lead on earth and consecrated by these mysteries, we shall advance in the life to come to the spirit's rest[1], as though to an upper house. And freed from the flesh, once we have ascended to the spirit's rest, we shall further look for our flesh to be raised on the day of resurrection, as though it were ascending to an uppermost storey.[2]

13 [305]

(1 Kgs. 6:9-10)

AND HE COVERED THE HOUSE WITH A PANELLED CEILING OF CEDAR.

What is said, **And he covered the house with a panelled ceiling of cedar**. A panelled ceiling consists of boards fastened beneath the beams with nails and they often display the marvelous ornamentation of its painting to onlookers.[3] Now there were three panelled ceilings in the Temple: the first was thirty cubits above the floor; the second, sixty cubits—level with the top of the side chambers; and the third, which was atop the entire building, one hundred twenty cubits. For roofs of buildings in Palestine, as in Egypt, do not have ridge beams. Instead, they are made flat, suitable for sitting or even walking on, whence the Lord says in the Gospel: *What you have whispered in the ear shall be proclaimed on the houseuops.*[4] For such is a quite suitable place from which a preacher may proclaim the Word either to listeners sitting beside him or situated below. About such a roof Solomon also says in Proverbs, *It is better to dwell on the corner of a* ***doma*** *than in the same house with a contentious woman.*[5] For the Greek word *doma* is 'roof' in Latin.[6] Furthermore, those side chambers around the Temple also had three decorated ceiling panels. The first was twenty cubits from ground level; the second, forty; the third, sixty.

1 Bede believed that between the time of bodily death and the time of the Last Judgement, the souls of the saints enjoy a heavenly rest as they await the resurrection of their bodies at the Last Judgement. Cf. *In Hab.* (Hab. 3:16) (*CCSL* 119B: 404, 652-5), *Hom.* 2, 1 (*CCSL* 122: 191, 259-62), *Hist. eccl.* 5, 12 (ed. Colgrave and Mynors, 492-5), and Carroll (1946), 184-5.

2 Cf. Bede *De templo* 1 (*CCSL* 119A: 166, 767-77)

3 Cf. Josephus *Ant. Jud.* 8, 3, 2 (*LCL* 5: 607-8) and Bede *De templo* 1 (*CCSL* 119A: 167, 832-5). On Bede's usage of the term *laquearia*, which here is translated as 'panelled ceiling', see Meyvaert (1979), 71, esp. n. 5. On the connection between Bede's description of the Temple and his description of possible parallel features, like ceiling paintings, in the churches of Wearmouth and Jarrow see Holder (1989), 123-5.

4 Matt. 10:27; Luke 12:3. Cf. Bede *De templo* 1 (*CCSL* 119A: 169, 886-9) and *In Ezr.* 3 (*CCSL* 119A: 370, 1250-2). See Meyvaert (1979), 70.

5 Prov. 21:9

6 'roof' = *tectum*

Now the roofs of these also had been made flat. For the thirty side chambers below, the thirty in the middle, and the thirty on top were partitioned not with walls but with boarded panels in such a way that each of the ninety side chambers was five cubits in breadth and length, but twenty in height. The Book of Chronicles mentions these side chambers frequently, but Josephus explains more fully in what order they were arranged.[1]

What follows, **And he built a boarded barrier five cubits high on top of the entire house**, is what Moses commanded in Deuteronomy: *When you build a new house, you shall make a wall around the roof so that if anyone should slip and fall, no blood will be shed in your house and you will not be guilty.*[2] For instead of railings, a boarded barrier had been erected on the very top of the Temple's walls so that if any climbed to the upper storey and carelessly approached the roof's edge, they would not die in a fall to the lower storeys. This is what King Ahaziah is found to have suffered later when he became fatally ill after falling through an upper storey's railings.[3] Most people called such barriers, walls, or railings 'parapets'
[306] when they were positioned for the safeguarding of life.[4] And what is added, **And he covered the house with cedar timber**, designates the topmost covering of the whole structure. That covering is a boarded floor laid on top of those beams, to which the above-mentioned topmost panelled ceiling was nailed from below.[5]

1 Actually, Chronicles contains no references to *porticus* ('side chambers'), at least not in the Vulgate. Instead Chronicles denotes these chambers as *cellaria* ('treasuries') and *cubicula* ('inner chambers'), as Bede later notes in *De templo* 1 (*CCSL* 119A: 167, 795-9). Cf. Josephus *Ant. Jud.* 8, 3, 2 (*LCL* 5: 606). See Appendix I below.

2 Deut. 22:8; cf. *De templo* 1 (*CCSL* 119A: 168, 849-55)

3 2 Kgs. 1:2; cf. *De templo* 1 (*CCSL* 119A: 163, 669-72). Ahaziah fell off his own house in Samaria, not off the Temple.

4 Cf. Meyvaert (1979), 71; cf. Bede *De templo* 1 (*CCSL* 119A: 163, 669-72 and 168: 851-9). The phrase 'the safeguarding of life' translates *tutelam uitae*. Hurst's edition, however, has *tutelam uiae*. In a private communication, Paul Meyvaert suggested that the reading of *uitae*, as opposed to *uiae*, seems the more likely in light of Bede's comment elsewhere that the specific purpose of these railings was to prevent death, or, put positively, to safeguard life (*In Ezr.* 3 —*CCSL* 119A: 370, 1254-5).

5 Cf. Bede *De templo* 1 (*CCSL* 119A: 169, 884-6)

14
(1 Kgs. 8:8)
AND SINCE THE CARRYING-POLES STUCK OUT, THEIR ENDS COULD BE SEEN FROM OUTSIDE IN THE SANCTUARY, ETC.

Where the ark is brought into the holy of holies, it says, **And since the carrying-poles stuck out, their ends could be seen from outside in the sanctuary, just in front of the oracle, but not from farther out.**[1] This is written more clearly in the Book of Chronicles, where it says, *Because the ends of the poles that carried the ark were very long, they were visible from just in front of the oracle, but if someone were a bit farther out, they could not be seen.*[2] Here it must be noted that although the ends of the carrying-poles were visible to those who, being just in front of the oracle, had drawn nearer to contemplate more attentively, it was impossible for their ends to have protruded outside the oracle. For surely when the oracle was closed and the curtain hung before the doors, these poles must have been concealed completely inside, along with the ark and the cherubim. Now this could not have happened had the poles, by sticking out too far, not left room to extend the doors to their closing position. For good cause and in consideration of a great mystery, Scripture took care to explain fully the poles' position. For it is agreed that the Temple's outer house designates the Church in pilgrimage on earth, while the holy of holies designates the inner happiness of the heavenly homeland. Likewise, the ark, which has been brought into the holy of holies, is a type of the humanity assumed by Christ and led within the veil of the heavenly court, while the ark's carrying-poles prefigure the preachers of the Word through whom [Christ] became known to the world.[3] A golden urn containing manna was in the ark because *all the fullness of divinity dwells bodily* in the human Christ.[4] In the ark also was Aaron's branch which had flowered again after having been cut down because the power to sentence everyone belongs to him whose sentence was seen to have been removed in suffering's humiliation.[5] The tablets of the covenant were also there, for in it *are hidden all the treasures of wisdom and*

---

1 Bede uses the word 'sanctuary' to denote the main part of Solomon's Temple, which only the priests could enter. Bede uses the term 'oracle' to designate the holy of holies, that part of the Temple which contained the ark of the covenant and which was accessible only to the High Priest once a year.

2 2 Chr. 5:9

3 Cf. Gregory the Great *Reg. Past.* 2, 11 (*SC* 381: 254, 28-32) and Bede *De tab.* 1 (*CCSL* 119A: 16, 455-7)

4 Col. 2:9; cf. Heb. 9:4 and Bede *De tab.* 1, 4 (*CCSL* 119A: 17, 472-4)

5 Num. 17:1-13; cf. John 5:27

knowledge.[1] Poles were fixed to the ark for carrying it, because teachers who once laboured for Christ's Word now rejoice in the present vision of his glory.[2] For what one of these [teachers] said about himself—*I desire to*
[307] *die and be with Christ*—he surely meant to be understood of all who share in his work.[3] The poles' ends were not always visible from outside the oracle, but only when the oracle's doors were opened. (Nor were they visible to everyone, but only to those desiring to draw nearer and gaze more intently at the things within). Only those entering the oracle were permitted to see what the ark was and how it was stationed, because none of the saints still stationed in this life—though they lift their minds to a very great height—will fully behold their Redeemer's glory, but only the citizens of that [heavenly] homeland. The poles were also hidden away with the ark in the oracle because all the elect who are now perfect, having preceded us out of the world away from human turmoil, are also hidden under the cover of God's face.[4] Yet just as the pole tips were seen sometimes by those approaching the oracle when it was opened, so does the divine grace offer up for contemplation a glimpse of the heavenly citizens' joy both to the more perfect and to those making every effort to purify their spiritual sight.[5] Surely such contemplation is granted in no way to them that retreat even a little, because the further they stay outside on account of their wandering minds,[6] the less will they behold inner joys.

1 Col. 2:3. The contents of the ark listed in Heb. 9:4. Cf. Bede *De tab.* 1, 4 (*CCSL* 119A: 17, 480-5).

2 For Bede, teachers include the apostles, church fathers, and evangelists of every sort.

3 Phil. 1:23

4 Ps. 31:20 (30:21)

5 The intended parallel in this sentence is between the tips or ends [*summitates*] of the ark's carrying poles and the glimpse [*aliquid extremum*] of heavenly joy.

6 The *Rule of St. Benedict* has some harsh words for wanderers. It condemns the gyrovagues, or wandering monks, as 'slaves to their own wills and gross appetites'; it also expressly forbids monks to wander outside the walls of the monastery, 'because this is not at all good for their souls' (*Reg. Ben.* 1, 11 and 66, 7—ed. Fry, 170 and 288). Although Bede may not have this passage of Benedict's *Rule* specifically in mind, it serves to exemplify cenobitic monasticism's general contempt for the wandering monk, who here functions as a parallel for the monk's wandering mind (*mens uaga*). Cf. Mayr-Harting (1976), 7.

15
(1 Kgs. 8:65)
SOLOMON MADE A SOLEMN FEAST, AND ALL ISRAEL WITH HIM.

Solomon made a solemn feast, and all Israel with him, a great multitude from the entrance of Hamath to the brook of Egypt, before the Lord. [This passage] designates the promised land's northern border by 'the entrance of Hamath' and its southern border by 'the brook of Egypt' (or 'torrent,' as Chronicles calls it).[1] On this subject, I think the reader would welcome a fuller quotation from the words of St. Jerome.[2] *This is written in the Book of Numbers, where in a few words, all the promised land is bounded by four borders: 'The southern region shall begin at the wilderness of Zin, which is by Edom, and shall have the saltiest sea*[3] *as its border on the east; the border shall wind south by the ascent of the Scorpion*[4] *and so cross into Senna,*[5] *and then run southward to Kadesh-barnea. From there it shall go out to the town called Addar,*[6] *then extend to Azmon, then turn up from Azmon to the torrent of Egypt and then end at the shore of the Great Sea.'*[7] Instead of this, the prophet Ezekiel's last vision says this: *'And the south side southward is from Tamar even to the waters of Mariboth,'* (that [308]
is, *of strife*), *'at Kadesh, and from the torrent to the Great Sea.'*[8] This means that the immense wilderness of *Zin, which is next to Edom, and on the Red Sea,*[9] *extends its border through the ascent of the scorpion, Senna, and Kadeshbarnea and the town,* or estate, *of Addar, and from Azmon to the*

1 2 Chr. 7:8

2 What follows in the rest of this question is a long quotation, edited and reworked by Bede, from Jerome's *On Ezekiel* (14, 47, 15-20—*CCSL* 75: 720-7, 1296-1488). In it Jerome uses the description of the borders of Israelite territory given in Num. 34:3-12 to illuminate a like description in Ezek. 47:15-20. Bede need not have quoted Jerome at such length since Nothhelm's question only concerns the promised land's western border. In this Question, italic type indicates a citation from the passage in Jerome's Ezekiel commentary; quotation marks enclose scriptural citations.

3 I.e., the Dead Sea

4 In modern Bibles this place is designated as the ascent of Akkrabbim.

5 In modern Bibles Senna is Zin and is explained as a now unknown place that gave its name to the Wilderness of Zin (cf. *NOAB*, Map 2, T2).

6 In modern versions, Hazar-addar.

7 Num. 34:3-5. The Great Sea denotes the Mediterranean Sea.

8 Ezek. 47:19

9 In Jerome's time, 'Red Sea' was a term that designated not only what we term the Red Sea today, but the entire Arabian and Persian Gulfs. Here he must specifically be referring to what we call today the Gulf of Aqaba.

torrent of Egypt, which flows into the sea at the city of Rhinocorura.[1] *This boundary line on the south begins at Tamar*[2]*—which is a city in the wilderness that Solomon erected with marvelous buildings and today is called Palmyra, named for the Hebrew word 'amar' which means 'palm-tree' in our language.*[3] *From there the border goes to the waters of strife at Kadesh, which is doubtless in the desert, and then coincides with the torrent flowing into the Great Sea, which stretches to the shores of Egypt and Palestine.* The Book of Numbers continues, *'And the west side shall begin at the Great Sea and be bounded by its coast,' that is, from sea to sea, namely from the torrent which flows into the sea at Rhinocorura, to that place* where *the city Hamath*[4] *of Syria is.*[5] Ezekiel also associates this name with the [western] side, saying, *'And the side toward the sea is the Great Sea from the border straight on until you come to Hamath,'*[6] *which is now called Epiphania because its name was changed by Antiochus, cruelest of tyrants, Epiphanes being his surname.*[7] *'But as for the north border,'* it says, *'its boundary-line shall begin at the Great Sea, and reach to the most high mountain; from there you shall come to Hamath, to the borders of Zedad; from there the boundary shall go to Ziphron, and end at the town of Enan;* these shall be the boundary-lines on the north side.'[8] *The Hebrews say that the northern side begins from the Great Sea, which extends along the shores of Palestine, Phoenicia, and Syria (which is called Coele*[9]*), and Cilicia, and extends beyond Egypt to Libya. Because it says*

1 MAP 2, T2 (*NOAB*)

2 MAP 4, X7 (*NOAB*)

3 Jerome is confusing the Tamar that is to the south of the Dead Sea (MAP 4, X7, *NOAB*) with the Syrian city of Tadmar, known later as Palmyra (MAP 6, G4, *NOAB*.)

4 Hamath; see note for Num. 34:1-29 on entrance of Hamath (*NOAB*, 210), and MAP 5, Y2 (*NOAB*).

5 Num. 34:6

6 Ezek. 47:20

7 Antiochus Epiphanes was a Seleucid ruler of Syria during the first quarter of the second century B.C.E. In his zeal to Hellenize wherever he could, Antiochus tried to exterminate Judaism, attacking Jerusalem and spoiling its Temple in 168 B.C.E. He also made the observance of Jewish customs a capital crime and instituted pagan cults. Because of these repressive policies, Jerome calls him 'the cruelest of tyrants.' His policy toward Judaism sparked the Maccabean revolt described in 1 and 2 Maccabees. The city which was named for Antiochus Epiphanes, Epiphania (formerly Hamath), lies on the Orontes River on the present-day site of Hamah in Syria. Cf. *XXX quaest.* 22 (*CCSL* 119: 315, 2-7).

8 Num. 34:7-9

9 Coele Syria, also known as Syria major, was the name given to the northern province of Syria in order to distinguish it from the southern province, Syria Phoenice. Both were created by the Roman emperor Septimius Severus (193-211 CE). Coele Syria corresponds roughly to the northern half of the modern nation of Syria. Syria Phoenice, or simply Phoenicia (as Bede here calls it), corresponds roughly to what is today Lebanon and southern Syria.

that the border extends to the most high mountain, the Hebrews assert that the mountain signifies either Amanus or Taurus, which seems quite likely to us.[1] *'From there,'* it says, *'the boundary shall go to Ziphron,' a city called Zephyrium today, a town of Cilicia. What follows, 'and the town of Enan', which the Hebrews write as Hazar-enan,* meaning *'court of the spring', is the border with Damascus.* Thus Ezekiel says, *'And the boundary-line from the sea to the court of Enan,'* or Hazar-enan, *'shall be the border of Damascus,* and from the north to the north, this is the north side.'[2] *'From there,'* it says, *'they shall draw the boundary on the east side from the town of Enan to Shepham, and from Shepham it shall go down to Riblah facing the spring; from there it shall go eastward to the Sea of Chinnereth, and* [309] *extend to the Jordan, and finally end at the* saltiest *sea.'*[3] *Thus from the northern boundary, namely at the court of Enan, the border extends to Shepham, which the Hebrews call Apamea,*[4] *and from Apamea it goes down to Riblah which is now called Antioch of Syria. In order that you might know that Riblah signifies this city, which is now the noblest in Coele Syria, there follows 'facing the spring', which clearly signifies Daphne.*[5] *The above-mentioned city enjoys very abundant waters from that spring. 'From there,' it says, 'the border goes eastward to the sea of Chinnereth,'*[6] that is, *to the Sea of Tiberias.*[7] *It is said to be a sea even though it has fresh water, because Scripture employs the idiom 'sea' for any large body of water. 'And it shall extend,' it says, 'to the Jordan and finally end at the sea,'*[8] *either at the Dead Sea or, as others reckon, at the tongue of the Red Sea on the coast where Ahila lies.*[9]

1 These two mountains are actually mountain ranges: Amanus on the border of Cilicia and Syria, and Taurus in southern Cilicia, near the Mediterranean coast.

2 Ezek. 47:17

3 Num. 34:10-12

4 Map 12, G3 (*NOAB*)

5 Daphne was a grove and sanctuary of Apollo near Antioch in Syria.

6 Num. 34:11

7 Sea of Chinnereth and Sea of Tiberias were different names for what we now call the Sea of Galilee. 'Sea of Chinnereth' was its designation in ancient Israel, 'lake of Gennereth' in New Testament times. 'Sea of Tiberias' is a name that derives from the name of the city that Herod Antipas built on this body of water's western shore in 20 C.E. (*WHA* 20).

8 Num. 34:12

9 MAP 12, F5, 'Aila' (*NOAB*). By 'tongue of the Red Sea', Jerome intends the Gulf of Aqaba. Ahila (or Aelana) was the ancient site on or very near which the modern city of Aqaba is founded.

16
(1 Kgs. 16:34)
IN HIS DAYS HIEL OF BETHEL BUILT JERICHO.

It is said of the time when Ahab reigned, **In his days Hiel of Bethel built Jericho; he laid its foundations in Abiram, his firstborn; and he set up its gates in Segub, his youngest son**. The apparent sense is that when the above-mentioned city's builder began to lay its foundations, his firstborn, named Abiram, died; and that after the city had been built, when he tried to fortify its gates, he lost his youngest son, named Segub. Joshua predicted that this would happen when, after Jericho's destruction, he made it anathema by cursing it, saying, *Cursed be the man before the Lord that shall raise up and build the city of Jericho, and in his firstborn may he lay its foundation, and in the last of his children set up its gates.*[1] Because Hiel is translated as 'living for God' and Bethel as 'house of God',[2] Hiel of Bethel restores Jericho's walls (which Joshua had destroyed and cursed) whenever any who have taken up the religious life in the Church resume doing the evil deeds for which the Lord Jesus forgave them on the day of [their] baptism and whenever they who have renounced the devil's pomp return to it by wanton living, or prefer false doctrines or Gentile fables to the Church's truth in which they were instructed.[3] They are like one who left Bethel to rebuild Jericho's ruins. Such a one, who has been cursed before the Lord's face, rightly loses both his firstborn in the foundation of a wicked city and his youngest in setting up its gates, because he forsakes not only the foundations of faith, from which he should have begun erecting good
[310] buildings, but also the gates of good works, by which he should have been perfected. I have explained these things allegorically so that you might recall the truth of the Apostle's statement: *all things happened to them in a figure; and they are written for us.*[4]

1 Josh. 6:26

2 Jerome *Nom.* Gen. B (*CCSL* 72: 62, 18) [=Bethel] and IV Reg. A (*CCSL* 72: 113, 8) [=Hiel, s.v. Ahihel]. Jerome gives two meanings for 'Hiel'. One is 'living for God', which Bede mentions here; the other is 'seeing God' (=*uidens deum*).

3 In Bede's allegory, Hiel (=living-for-God) represents those who, in Bede's words, have 'taken up the religious life.' Likewise, Bethel (=house-of-God) represents the Church. For Bede, those who have committed themselves to the Church and then leave it by abandoning faith and its attendant good works are like Hiel leaving Bethel. Bede's phrase 'renouncing the devil's pomp' derives from the Church's baptismal liturgy (Gelasian Sacramentary 42—ed. Mohlberg et al., 68, 6-10).

4 1 Cor. 10:11

17
(1 Kgs. 20:10-11)
MAY THE GODS DO THESE THINGS TO ME, AND EVEN MORE, IF THE DUST OF SAMARIA SHALL SUPPLY ENOUGH HANDFULS FOR ALL THE PEOPLE THAT FOLLOW ME.

When King Benhadad of Syria besieged and began to attack Samaria, he said, **May the gods do these things to me, and even more, if the dust of Samaria shall supply enough handfuls for all the people that follow me.** This saying has the following meaning. In accordance with the custom of cities, Samaria must have had earth [piled] next to its interior walls and nearly level with them so that the walls would not, for want of a supporting embankment, be destroyed by the repeated blow of a ram, swung by hostile hands. On the outside, the walls' height loomed high above the level ground, especially since, as Scripture states, that same city was situated on a hilltop.[1] So the proud king, terrorizing the besieged city, said that he had so great an army with him that even if each of his soldiers contributed only a single stone, or a clod of earth, or a log to build a rampart against the city, it would still rise to a height level with the top of that city inside the walls; thus fighting in this way, they could send javelins and torches from it against the city from level ground.[2] Israel's king countered such rash arrogance with a modest reply, saying: **'Tell him: "Let not the girded boast as though he were ungirded."'** For it is one thing to be girded, another thing to be ungirded, and yet another not to be girded. For, indeed, he is girded who, with belt around him, advances; he is ungirded who has just taken off his belt and is ready, for instance, either to enter the bath or climb into bed, or perhaps put on another tunic; he is not girded who, having recently put on his tunic has not yet secured himself by putting on his belt. So also on a military expedition he who has been rightly stationed is called 'girded', that is, armed; he who, when the battle is over, returns home a conqueror is rightly called 'ungirded' because when arms have been put down he doubtless enjoys the leisure of a longed-for peace; and he who has not yet begun either to fight or prepare himself for a struggle is rightly said to be

1 1 Kgs. 16:24

2 Most modern commentators interpret the phrase 'handfuls of dust' very differently from the way that Bede does here. They see the handfuls of dust as being taken away from Samaria to the extent that Samaria will no longer exist (Gray [1970], 423). Bede's explanation, by contrast, hinges on his knowledge that Samaria is located atop a hill or mountain and on his consideration of the problem of attacking such a high place from without.

'not girded'. Thus Israel's king said to Syria's king, who was boasting as if he had already taken Samaria, even though he had only begun to surround it, **'Let not the girded boast as though he were ungirded.'** It is as if he had plainly said, 'Do not boast as though you have already won the contest. For since you are stationed on the frontline, you cannot know whom victory will favor.' Truly indeed had he spoken. For no sooner had the struggle
[311] begun than Benhadad returned home, not triumphing over conquered enemies, but fleeing with his army slaughtered.

18
(2 Kgs. 11:6-8)
LET ONE THIRD OF YOU ENTER ON THE SABBATH AND KEEP WATCH ON THE KING'S HOUSE.

This is what the priest Jehoiada said to the priests and Levites in the Temple as he brought forth Joash, Ahaziah's son whom Jehoiada had been rearing secretly in the Temple during Athalia's six-year reign: **'Let one third of you enter on the sabbath and keep watch on the king's house, let another third be at the gate of Sur, and let the final third be at the gate behind the dwelling of the shieldbearers—and you shall keep a watch on the house of Messa; but let that two-thirds of you that [usually] leave on the sabbath keep watch around the king at the Lord's house. And you shall surround him with your weapons ready.'** These and the rest of the sayings and deeds mentioned in this passage are better understood if one has a fuller understanding of those places in the Temple where [the incident] occurred.[1]

Apart from surrounding porticos adjoining it on all sides, that Temple had inside walls sixty cubits long and twenty cubits wide.[2] (This is the first measurement mentioned in the Book of Chronicles.)[3] This entire perimeter was enclosed in a court that was three cubits high and that had an entrance

1 Meyvaert (1996), 853-8 argues convincingly that Bede based the following description of the Temple and its precincts upon descriptions of the Temple in Scripture and in Josephus as well as upon the image of the Temple that Cassiodorus placed in the Codex Grandior. That codex was available to Bede at Wearmouth-Jarrow. Meyvaert offers a reconstruction of the Temple complex as he thinks it would have appeared in the Codex Grandior (857). For a drawing based solely on the description of the Temple complex that Bede gives in this Question, see Appendix II below.

2 The Temple had a porch on its east front and side chambers on its other three sides. In describing the Temple, Bede uses the word *porticus* to denote both the east porch and the side chambers on the north, west, and south sides.

3 2 Chr. 3:3

on the [Temple's] east side.[1] Scripture mentions this court in the Book of Kings as follows, *And he built the inner court with three rows of polished stones, and one row of cedar beams.*[2] It calls this the inner court because other outer courts were built around it.[3] Later in Chronicles Scripture says this: *He also made the court of the priests, a great hall, and doors that he covered with bronze in the hall.*[4] Surely Scripture calls this [inner court] 'the court of the priests' because it had been made to keep others away from the Temple's entrance and to mark [the Temple] off as a place where only priests were permitted. Now this court was very near the Temple wall on the southern, western, and northern sides; but on the eastern side, where it also had a staired entrance, this court extended a long way out from the Temple since it had to accommodate on that side the altar of the holocaust, two sets of five lavers for washing the sacrifices, the bronze vessel in which the priests washed themselves when they were about to enter for the office, and troops of priests sacrificing and Levites singing.[5] Moreover, this court was surrounded on all sides by a very long rectangular building.[6] The lower part of its inner wall, the one that faced the Temple from the world's four *[312]*
quarters, was built on arches all the way around, while the outer wall had been founded with firm solidity and also had bronze doors, as the passage we recalled earlier said, *and doors that he covered with bronze in the hall.*[7]

---

1 Josephus *Ant. Jud.* 8, 3, 9 (*LCL* 5: 623). Bede's terminology can be somewhat confusing. He here uses the word 'court' (*atrium*) specifically to designate the wall or structure which encloses the space surrounding the court of the priests. Usually, he calls the enclosed space itself a court.

2 1 Kgs. 6:36

3 Scripture gives no description of the outer courts. Apparently taking the Codex Grandior's drawing of Temple complex as authoritative, Bede describes the outer courts of Solomon's Temple in much the same way that Josephus described the rebuilt Temple of Herod. This latter Temple is described by Josephus in *Ant. Jud.* 15, 11, 3-5 (*LCL* 8: 188-205) and *Bel. Jud.* 5, 5, 1-2 (*LCL* 3: 254-61).

4 2 Chr. 4:9

5 A holocaust is a whole burnt-offering; see 2 Chr. 4:1. A laver is a basin for washing, of which there were 'twice five' or ten; cf. 2 Chr. 4:6b and 1 Kgs. 7:38-9. On the bronze vessel, see 2 Chr. 4:2, 6.

6 'Building' here translates *aedes*. Usually translated as 'temple', *aedes* corresponds to the Greek ἱερὸν. In New Testament Greek, ἱερὸν designates the Temple's sacred precincts, including various auxiliary courts, side chambers, and porticos, while ναὸς designates the Temple proper. Bede here uses the Latin *templum* to denote what is intended by the the Greek ναὸς (i.e., the Temple proper); and he uses *aedes* to denote the various auxiliary structures which—when taken together—comprised the courts around the Temple. Since *templum* and *aedes* can both be translated as 'temple', *aedes* is here translated as 'building' to distinguish it from the Temple proper. This building is meant to be a synonym for 'the great hall' which was mentioned above in Bede's citation of 2 Chr. 4:9.

7 2 Chr. 4:9

This building had also been fortified with great porticos and separated into suitable upper storeys. Outside this building was yet another that surrounded the first one in like fashion, and around it was even a third.[1] Built in the same way, [this third building] surrounded everything inside in length and breadth.[2] In only one respect did it differ from the above mentioned buildings: its eastern and northern walls had no doors because they both were part of the city walls. Now these are the [three] courts about which the Psalms sing, *You who stand in the house of the Lord, in the courts of the house of our Lord.*[3] And since that house of the Lord[4] had been constructed at a higher elevation, the further out the [outer] courts were built, the higher were their walls, naturally having their foundations proportionally deeper so that the farthest out were four hundred cubits high. Yet they did not even come close to rivalling the Temple's height. Chronicles mentions all these things in a general way: *And David gave to Solomon his son a description of the porch, the Temple, the treasuries, the upper floor, the inner chambers, and the house for the mercy seat; and also of all the courts, as he conceived them, and the surrounding chambers which were for the treasuries of the house of the Lord and for the treasuries of the consecrated things.*[5] The passages from Josephus and the picture sketched by the ancients delineate more fully the plan of how these things were made.[6]

1 The second building forms the outer wall of the court of the women; the third likewise forms the outer wall of what Bede designates as the court of the Gentiles. See Appendix II below.

2 Bede also refers to these buildings (*aedes*) and courts (*atria*), which surround the Temple proper, in his Ezra commentary (*In Esr.* 2—*CCSL* 119A: 333, 1804-11).

3 Pss. 134:1 (133:1), 135:2 (134:2)

4 I.e., the Temple proper, as opposed to the surrounding walls or buildings.

5 1 Chr. 28:11-12

6 Josephus *Ant. Jud.* 8, 3, 2-9 (*LCL* 5: 604-24); *Ant. Jud.* 15, 11, 3-5 (*LCL* 8: 188-205); *Bel. Jud.* 5, 5, 1-2 (*LCL* 3: 254-61).

Bede had seen a picture of Solomon's Temple in what Bruce-Mitford (1969), 8-9 believes to have been the Codex Grandior, Cassiodorus' Latin pandect which Ceolfrith brought from Rome to Wearmouth-Jarrow (*De templo* 2—*CCSL* 119A: 192, 28 - 193, 52; *Hist. abb.* 2, 15—ed. Plummer, 1: 379; *Vit. Ceol.* 20—ed. Plummer, 1: 395).Unfortunately, any illustration of the Temple that Bede might have had is now lost. Although it has been alleged by Bruce-Mitford and others that fol. IIv-IIIr of the Codex Amiatinus, another Latin pandect at Wearmouth-Jarrow in Bede's time, shows a picture of Solomon's Temple, Meyvaert points out that Amiatinus here actually depicts the tabernacle (Bruce-Mitford [1969], 3; Meyvaert [1979], 71-2, n. 7; O'Reilly [1995], lii-lv).

Meyvaert (1996), 833-4 has noted that when Bede's reference to this 'picture sketched by the ancients' is contrasted with his later parallel reference in *De templo*—in which Bede specifically identifies Cassiodorus as responsible for this picture—one discovers that between the time of his writing of the *Thirty Questions* and *De templo*, Bede discovered precisely who was responsible for the picture in the Codex Grandior, perhaps from a remark in Cassiodorus' commentary on Psalm 86. See *De templo* 2 (*CCSL* 119A: 192, 28-30 and 193, 48-52).

Now with the buildings so arranged, the High Priest alone entered the holy of holies with the blood of the sacrifice once a year;[1] only purified priests went inside the sanctuary in front of the holy of holies; all priests and Levites went into the inner court;[2] Israelite men customarily convened under the open sky, or if a storm threatened, in the buildings placed around this court[3] to pray or hear the word; in the third row of courts the Israelite women stood under the sky to pray or, if weather did not permit, they went under the roofs of the surrounding buildings; next, in the outermost row of courts entered such Gentiles as had happened to convene for prayer. There also, after the Dispersion, the Israelites just returning from Gentile regions were purified for seven days before seeking to enter the holy places within.[4] Such floors as were between or within the courts were all covered with variegated stone.[5] Now the doors in the buildings were aligned with each other so that even those who stood in the outermost places could see the Temple. Now there were twenty-four troops of priests, Levites, and door- [313] keepers who in as many weeks succeeded each other by turns on the sabbath.[6] At that time, a new troop would enter for service. After the sabbath, the troop that had served the previous week returned home.[7]

But because it was necessary to increase the army around the young king, this High Priest took those ready to enter the Temple for weekly duty and also retained those who had just served their week so that they might not depart; he also assembled others at Jerusalem, including Levites from all the cities of Judah together with the chiefs of Israel's families, having despatched captains of hundreds for this purpose, as Chronicles narrates.[8] When he was ready to lead out the king's son, he divided them as follows. First, all who had just fulfilled their sabbath duties and were ready to leave

1 Heb. 9:6-7; Lev. 16:15, 34

2 I.e., the court of the priests. Its inner boundary was the Temple's outer walls; its outer boundary was the wall three cubits high, mentioned by Bede earlier in this Question.

3 I.e., the inner court or court of the priests.

4 The Dispersion refers to the scattering of the Jewish people throughout the ancient Mediterranean world. It began when some of the the Jewish exiles in Babylon did not return to Judah after their captivity had ended in 538 B. C. E. Jews who thus chose to live outside Palestine nevertheless often made a pilgrimage to Jerusalem and its Temple. It is these to whom Bede refers here.

5 2 Chr. 3:6

6 2 Chr. 23:8; Josephus *Ant. Jud.* 7, 14, 7 (*LCL* 5: 554-7) and *Vit.* 1 (*LCL* 1: 2-3). This weekly alternation is not explicitly mentioned in Scripture. It represents the custom in Josephus' own time (*LCL* 5: 557, note d).

7 Thus, on the Sabbath itself, the Temple had a total of two troops of priests.

8 2 Chr. 23:1-2

were divided into two parts and each was to stand armed around the king in the inner places of the court; a remaining multitude, namely those who were not of levitical stock, were to guard the outer doors of the courts against the queen's fury in case she tried to do some mischief. Secondly, those priests, Levites, and door-keepers who had just come for the sabbath were divided into three parts and were to keep watch on the king's house, the palace, so that when the army[1] assembled, the queen might not hold the palace against the king; they were also to guard the gate of the dwelling-place of the shieldbearers through which one descended from the Temple to the palace, as is said later, *and they brought the king from the house of the Lord: and they came by the way of the gate of the shieldbearers into the palace, and he sat on the throne of the kings.*[2] One may also see there both the gate of Sur and the house of Messa, which are mentioned along with the gate of the shieldbearers.[3] It calls the king's guardians 'shieldbearers', a fact to which the Book of Chronicles attests when it tells how Rehoboam had bronze shields made to replace the golden ones and adds, *And he delivered them to the captains of the shieldbearers, who guarded the entrance of the palace.*[4] In that book all these events are recounted more clearly, *A third of you priests, Levites, and porters that come to the sabbath shall be at the gates, and a third at the king's house, and a third at the gate that is called the Foundation; but let all the rest of the people be in the courts of the house of the Lord. And let none except the priests and those Levites who minister enter the house of the Lord; let only them enter, because they are sanctified, and let all the rest of the people keep the watches of the Lord. And let the Levites be round about the king, each with his arms,*[5] and so forth.

1 I.e., the army that Jehoiada was assembling to guard the young king.
2 2 Kgs. 11:19
3 2 Kgs. 11:6
4 2 Chr. 12:9-10
5 2 Chr. 23:5-7

19
(2 Kgs. 11:12)
AND HE BROUGHT FORTH THE KING'S SON, AND PUT THE DIADEM AND THE TESTIMONY UPON HIM.

What follows is said of that same one:[1] **And he[2] brought forth the king's son, and put the diadem and the testimony upon him.** By 'diadem' is meant the royal crown; by 'testimony', the divine law's decrees. By these [314] latter the king is taught what to do and how to live. Accordingly it says more clearly in Chronicles, *And they put the diadem on him and gave him the law to hold in his hand.*[3] Surely a great and wholesome prudence dictated that after the tyrannical and impious queen's execution, the discipline to be observed in God's law should be committed to the rightful king's son, the heir to the throne, at the same time as the insignia of kingship, so that he who sees himself as exalted to rule over the people might remember that he himself is to be ruled and subject to divine laws.

20
(2 Kgs. 12:15)
AND NO AUDIT WAS DONE ON THESE MEN WHO RECEIVED MONEY, ETC.

In the passage where Joash (the king just mentioned) repaired the Lord's Temple, it is said: **And no audit was done on these men who received money to pay the workmen; and yet they handled it honestly**. This shows the devotion of those about whom this passage speaks. Such was their zeal for religion that everyone confidently expected them to handle the Lord's money without any suspicion of fraud and to pay each workman, as required, the money that had been legitimately withdrawn from the treasury for building the house.

1 I.e., the young king Joash, son of king Ahaziah, who was mentioned at the very end of Q. 18, immediately preceding.

2 I.e., Jehoiada the priest.

3 2 Chr. 23:11

21
(2 Kgs. 14:7)
IN THE VALLEY OF THE SALTPITS HE SLEW [MEN] FROM EDOM.

It is said of Amaziah, king of Judah: **In the valley of the saltpits he slew ten thousand men from Edom, and took Petra in battle, and called its name Joktheel.** The valley of the saltpits was where they made salt either by cutting down, drying, and burning brine-soaked hay—as happens in many places—or by boiling salt water from wells and hardening them to salt by cooking, or by any other way in which salt is usually made.[1] We read that Joab also slew twelve thousand Edomites in that same place.[2] Nor should it be neglected that the old edition[3] has given Gemela as the name of the region instead of the valley of saltpits.[4] Now Petra is a noble city of Arabia also in that same land of Edom. It is called Recem in the Book of Numbers and the Syrians call it by that name today.[5] Joktheel, the name that the conquering Amaziah gave it, is translated as *assembly of God* or

---

1 The latter method of making salt, by boiling down salt water, was fairly common in antiquity; cf. Pliny *Nat. Hist.* 31, 39, 81 (*LCL* 8: 426-7). The former method, by burning hay that was grown in saltwater marshes, does not appear to be found in any classical source. It seems to be a method that was used only in more northerly climates. The sunless climate of northern Europe and the low concentration of salt in sea water made impractical the extraction of salt by Mediterranean methods that depended upon evaporation by the sun. Because salt, however, is found in more concentrated form in sea plants and other burnable shore refuse, these materials were burned and their ashes leached to obtain salt (Multhauf [1978], 25). Since Bede's monastic brethren at Wearmouth-Jarrow had easy access to the North Sea coast, he is describing here a method of making salt that was more likely to have been practiced in his native Northumbria than in ancient Judah.

2 Ps. 60, opening ascription (59:2); cf. 1 Sam. 8:13.

3 By 'old edition', Bede means one of the Bible's several Old Latin versions which were used by the Latin-speaking Christians of the West in the early Christian centuries. Because the manuscripts of the Old Latin Bible differed so greatly from each other, Jerome was induced to produce his Vulgate translation of Scripture in the late fourth and early fifth centuries. According to Laistner, Bede had access to 'one or more versions' of the Old Latin Bible ([1935], 257). In his *Hist. abb.* 15, Bede identifies one of these Old Latin Bibles as the Latin pandect that was brought from Rome to Wearmouth-Jarrow by Ceolfrith (ed. Plummer, 1: 379). Although Bruce-Mitford identifies this Old Latin pandect as Cassiodorus' Codex Grandior, not everyone agrees with his claim (Bruce-Mitford [1969], 8; cf. Hunter Blair [1971], 222).

4 Jerome *Loc.* (*PL* 23: 903A): 'Gemela is a district of the Edomites which Aquila and Symmachus translate as "the valley of salt."'

5 Num. 31:8; Jerome *Loc.*: 'Petra, a city of Arabia in the land of Edom, which is also called Joktheel, is called Recem by the Syrians' (*PL* 23: 915C); cf. Josephus *Ant. Jud.* 4, 7, 1 (*LCL* 4: 552-3); see MAP 12, G-4 (*NOAB*).

God.[1] In faith he determined that it be forever remembered as a place that was taken by the assembly of God's people, or else, with God's help.

22 [315]
(2 Kgs. 14:25)
HE RESTORED THE BORDERS OF ISRAEL FROM THE ENTRANCE OF HAMATH, ETC.

It is said of Jeroboam, king of Israel, **He restored the borders of Israel from the entrance of Hamath, unto the sea of the wilderness.**[2] *Hamath, which is now named Epiphania was Israel's northern border, while the sea of the wilderness*—which is called *Araba* in Hebrew—designates the Dead Sea *which* extends *five-hundred eighty stadia in length, as far as Zoar of Arabia, and one-hundred fifty in width, as far as the neighborhood of Sodom.*[3]

1 Jerome *Nom.*, IV Reg., 'I' (*CCSL* 72: 116, 3-4)

2 Jeroboam II (786-746 B.C.E.)

3 On Hamath/Epiphania, see Bede *XXX quaest.* 15 (*CCSL* 119: 308, 32-7).

The dimensions that Bede here gives for the Dead Sea come ultimately from Josephus *Bel. Jud.* 4, 8, 4 (*LCL* 3: 140-3). He may have obtained them directly from Josephus or via Adamnan's *De locis sanctis* 17, 18 (*CCSL* 175: 215, 24-6). Isidore of Seville gives a similar description of the Dead Sea, but puts its length at seven hundred eighty stadia (*Etymol.* 13, 19, 3-5—ed. Lindsay, vol. 2). On Bede's dim view of Isidore's reliability, which in this instance seems justified, see Meyvaert (1976), 58-60; for an opposing view, see McCready (1995). A stadion is roughly 12/100 of a mile. Thus, according to Bede and his ancient sources, the Dead Sea is approximately 67 miles long and 17 miles wide. In reality, it is about 53 miles long and 10 miles wide.

It is curious to note that in his *Names of Places*, Bede not only gives completely different dimensions for the Dead Sea, but also gives those dimensions in Roman miles instead of stadia (*CCSL* 119: 283, 377-80). He states that the Dead Sea's length is 100 Roman miles (= 92 English miles) at its maximum and 70 Roman miles (= 64 English miles) at its minimum; and that its width is 25 Roman miles (= 23 English miles) at its maximum and 6 Roman miles (=5 1/2 English miles) at its minimum. Bede's sources for these dimensions are not apparent. The figures that he gives for the maximum length and minimum width match exactly Pliny's figures (*Nat. Hist.* 5, 15, 72—*LCL* 2: 274-5); the figure that he gives for the minimum length comes close to the figure for the length that he gives in this Question. His figure for the maximum width does not seem to derive from any known source.

23
(2 Kgs. 17:29-31)[1]
AND EACH NATION MADE ITS OWN GOD.

It is said of those nations that were brought to Samaria by the king of the Assyrians: **And each nation made its own god and they put them in the temples at the high places that the Samaritans had made, each nation in the city where it dwelt; for the men of Babylon made Succoth-benoth, the men of Cuth made Nergal, and the men of Hamath made Ashima. And the Avvites made Nibhaz and Tartak.** Now in the *Book of Places* we read that Benoth and Nergal were cities built in the region of Judea by Samaritans who had migrated from Babylon; the town of Ashima likewise was built by those who had come there from Hamath, while Nibhaz and Tartak were cities established by the Avvites in the same region of Judea.[2] By what follows in this passage, it seems that one can discern the names of the idols also that these nations previously had served in their own land. For when it is said, **And each nation made its own gods**, there is added, as though to complete the thought, **For the men of Babylon made Succoth-benoth**, which means the booths of Benoth. (If I am not mistaken, the translator would have done better to render 'Succoth' into the Latin as

---

1 The Scriptural passage with which this Question deals falls in a larger narrative that explains the origin of the Samaritans (2 Kgs. 17:1-41), those people who subsequently dwelt in what was once the northern kingdom of Israel. The account of Samaritan origins given in 2 Kgs. 17 is told from the standpoint of the southern kingdom of Judah. It is thus the Judah-istic, or Jewish standpoint. According to this account, the Samaritans do not really belong to God's chosen people, despite the fact that they live on what was once Israelite territory. Instead, they descend from Babylonians and Syrians who were settled there by Shalmaneser, king of Assyria, in the late eighth century B.C.E. The Samaritans themselves opposed this Jewish view, claiming to be descendants of native Israelites. Bede here obviously takes up the Jewish viewpoint put forth in Hebrew Scripture. Moreover, he infers from Jerome's *Book of Places*, that the names of the various sites settled by the original Samaritans derive from the names of the gods whom they had previously worshipped in Babylon and elsewhere (2 Kgs. 17:30-1).

2 The *Book of Places* is Jerome's *Liber Locorum* (= *Loc.*), in which all of the place names here mentioned are cited: Ashima (*PL* 23: 876A), Benoth (*PL* 23: 884B), Nergal and Nibhaz (*PL* 23: 914A), and Tartak (*PL* 23: 926B).

'booths' and to give 'Benoth' by itself as the idol's name).[1] And in the same way that it is shown that Adramelech and Anamelech were idols of the city Sepharvaim (since this is clearly said in the words that follow, **And they that were of Sepharvaim burnt their children in fire, to Adramelech and Anamelech the gods of Sepharvaim**), so too would it seem to follow that Nergal was the idol of the men of Cuth, Ashima of the men of Hamath, and Nibhaz and Tartak of the Avvites.

24 *[316]*
(2 Kgs. 18:34)
WHERE IS THE GOD OF HAMATH AND ARPAD?

What Rabshakeh said, among other utterances by which he blasphemed God, as he was crying out against Jerusalem, **Where is the god of Hamath and Arpad? Where is the god of Sepharvaim, Hena, and Ivvah? Have they delivered Samaria out of my hand?**[2] This shows that the Samaritans worshipped the gods of all these cities or nations, and that because these were idols instead of gods, the worshippers of vanity were deservedly

1 Bede suggests that Jerome should have translated the Hebrew differently here than he did. In the Vulgate text of 2 Kgs. 17:30, Jerome translates Succothbenoth as the one-word name of a Babylonian deity. In Jerome's *Book of Places*, however, *Benith* (=Bede's *Benoth*) is listed as a place-name occurring in the Book of Kings. Of it Jerome says, 'The Samaritans who came from the region of Babylon built Benith' (*PL* 23: 884B). Since no place with the simple name of *Benith/Benoth* occurs in Jerome's Vulgate translation of Kings (or the entire Vulgate for that matter), Bede logically assumed that Jerome meant to equate *Benith* with the last two syllables of the name Succothbenoth. Thus, Bede concludes, Jerome thought that the *Benoth* of *Succoth-benoth* indicated a place name. If that were the case, however, then why did Jerome not indicate that in the Vulgate by treating Benoth there as a separate word? This is Bede's quandary, and instead of trusting Jerome's Vulgate text, Bede prefers to correct that text in light of what Jerome says about *Benoth* in the *Book of Places*. Moreover, Bede inferred that since all the other place-names listed in 2 Kgs. 17:30-1 derive from the name of foreign deities, then the placename *Benoth* must also. *Benoth*, therefore, must indicate the name not only of a place, as Jerome says, but also of a deity. If that is the case, however, then what does *Succoth* mean? He learned, probably from Jerome's *On Hebrew Names*, that it means 'booths' (*PL* 23: 790). Bede thus uses Jerome against Jerome, appealing to the authority of Jerome's reference works to argue against his translation of 2 Kgs. 17:30.

2 Following the Septuagint, Jerome translated the Hebrew רבשקה (*rabsaqe*) as the proper name *Rabshakeh* (2 Kgs. 18:19). Modern English translations, however, translate this not as a name, but as a title, meaning 'chief officer'. At any rate, the one whom Bede, following Jerome, here calls Rabshakeh is clearly a high-ranking Assyrian official who in this passage is trying to convince the people of Jerusalem to submit to the will of the Assyrian king Sennacherib (704-681 B.C.E.), and not to trust in the protection of Yahweh, as King Hezekiah wants them to do. Rabshakeh here reminds Jerusalem that the gods of other territories proved wholly incapable of resisting Assyrian conquests.

overthrown. Now Hamath, a city of Coelesyria, which is now called Epiphania, is near Emesa, as we said above.[1] Arpad is the city of Damascus; Jerome also writes that it was conquered by the king of the Assyrians.[2] *Sepharvaim*, which as a plural word-form meaning 'books' or 'letters', *is the name of the places from which Assyrians migrated before they settled in Samaria*, as we find in the *Book of Places*.[3] Indeed in Isaiah where it is plainly said, *Where is the god of the city of Sepharvaim?*[4], this word also seems to be the name of a city, although it is spoken of in the plural as are Thebes and Athens. For Hena and Ivvah the old edition gives the name Henaugivvah, as though it were a single city, and it certainly is thus written in Hebrew; indeed, because the letter 'u', which is placed in the middle of the name, signifies the conjunction 'and' among the Hebrews, it can be so separated as to be read 'Hena and Givvah', as Aquila translated it, or as 'Hena and Ivvah' as our translator renders it.[5]

25
(2 Kgs. 20:9-10)
DO YOU WANT THE SHADOW TO ADVANCE TEN LINES? ETC.

The prophet Isaiah said to king Hezekiah, **'Do you want the shadow to advance ten lines, or to go back by as many degrees?'** The terms 'degrees' and 'lines' here signify the same thing, namely, the different hours of the day that we usually mark twelve to the day on a sundial. Or, as Jerome

1 See *XXX quaest.* 22 (*CCSL* 119: 315). Coelesyria, meaning 'Hollow Syria', designates the land between Mt. Lebanon and Mt. Hermon. The entrance of Hamath is the lowland between these two mountains that leads northward to Hamath. Cf. s.v. 'Emath', in Jerome *Loc.* (*PL* 23: 859-928).

2 The *PL* reading, which has 'Jerome' (*Hieronymus*), is here preferable to the *CCSL* reading, which has 'Jeremiah' (*Hieremias*); cf. *PL* 91: 731C and *CCSL* 119: 316, 9. Although Jeremiah makes mention of Arpad (49:23), it is Jerome—not Jeremiah—who says that Arpad was conquered by the Assyrian king (*Loc.*, *PL* 23: 876D).

3 Jerome *Loc.* (*PL* 23: 922D). Bede derives the meaning of 'Sepharvaim' as 'books' or 'letters' from Jerome's *On Hebrew Names* (*CCSL* 72: 118, 17).

4 Is. 36:19, 37:13

5 The letter 'u' is the transliteration of the Hebrew character ו (*waw*), which is a conjunction meaning 'and'. Bede's knowledge of this point of Hebrew vocabulary derives from Jerome's *In Es.* 11, 37, 8-13 (*CCSL* 73: 437, 28-32).

Aquila was a Hellenistic proselyte to Judaism who lived during the second century. Having learned Hebrew and rabbinic exegesis, he translated the Hebrew Bible into Greek. A quite literal translation of the Hebrew, Aquila's version was intended to replace the Septuagint as the official version of Scripture among Hellenistic Jews.

'Our translator' is Jerome, translator of the Hebrew Bible and Greek New Testament into the Latin Vulgate.

says, *The degrees were mechanically constructed in such a way that the shadow, as it passed through each, marked off an hour's length.*[1] Now it was the tenth hour of the day when the prophet said these things to the king. He thus says, **Do you want the shadow to advance ten lines?** (He meant by this that the sun would move eastward above the earth through the sky's northern quadrant, although by its daily custom it would take its course below the earth.) **Or [do you want]** the shadow **to go back by as many degrees?** (He meant by this that the sun would retreat in retrograde movement back through the southern quadrant toward the east.) But the king said, **It is easy for the shadow to advance ten lines, but I do not want it to do that; instead let it go back ten degrees.** For surely he saw *[317]*
that it would be a greater miracle for the sun to take a course contrary to its usual one than for it to fly high toward the east, as though about to make the morning of the next day without an intervening night. For by doing the latter, it would simply advance as it usually does, though in a much higher orbit (namely, above the earth).[2] For those who live on the isle of Thule, which is far beyond Britain, or in the remotest frontiers of the Scythians, see this happen on certain days every summer.[3] For the sun, which to the rest of the world has set and is below the horizon, nonetheless appears to them above the horizon all night; and it is quite plain how it returns low in the sky from west to east until at the proper season, it is returned to the whole world in a sunrise that all can see.[4] Ancient histories and people of our own age who have come forth from those parts abundantly attest to this

1 Jerome *In Es.* 11 (*CCSL* 73: 445, 44-6). Bede's reference to the synonymous meaning of 'degrees' and 'lines' as well as his claim in the next sentence that this conversation between Isaiah and King Hezekiah occurred at the tenth hour of the day, which is about 4 p.m., also derive from Jerome's commentary on Is. 38:4-11, which contains a parallel version of this story (*In Es.* 11—*CCSL* 73: 444, 41 - 445, 44 and 445, 47).

2 I.e., above the earth's horizon. Bede is referring to a situation in which the sun would not sink below the horizon during the night hours.

3 In *De Natura Rerum* 47, Bede copies Pliny almost verbatim, putting Thule and Scythia in the northernmost regions of the earth (*CCSL* 123A: 231, 39-40; cf. Pliny *Nat. Hist.* 6, 39, 219—*LCL* 2: 500-1). Whereas Scythia is located at the northeastern extreme, Thule is at the northwestern. It is unclear where Bede thought these places to have been. He may have identified Thule either with Iceland, a Shetland Island, or part of Scandinavia. What is important to Bede, however, is not the exact locations of these places, but the fact that each is so far north that it experiences perpetual daylight during parts of the summer months.

4 By the 'the proper season', Bede means that time sufficiently past the summer solstice when the sun begins to set and rise again in an alternation of day and night.

fact.[1] By the same token, those who inhabit remoter southerly climes have never seen the sun move backward from west to east through the southern sky.

26
(2 Kgs. 22:14)
SHE DWELT IN JERUSALEM IN THE SECOND.

It is said of Huldah the prophetess that she **dwelt in Jerusalem in the Second**. The Book of Chronicles explains what this [i.e., *Second*] means when it relates the following about the aforementioned king Hezekiah: *With great diligence he built up the entire wall, which had been broken down, and he erected towers, and another wall on the outside.*[2] Zephaniah also remembers this place, saying, *a voice crying from the fish gate, and a howling from the Second.*[3] The old edition gave *Masena* as if it were the proper name of a place; but surely [the Hebrew word] *masena* is translated as 'second'.[4] Therefore, understand the saying that the prophetess lived *in the Second* to mean 'within the quarter of the second wall'.

1 The key to understanding Bede's logic in this Question hinges upon understanding his comparison of what happens on a sundial located in the hotter and milder regions with what happens on a sundial located in the earth's northernmost places in midsummer. Anyone who goes sufficiently far north on June 21 will see the sun twenty-four hours a day. In the morning, the sun is in the eastern sky and ascends through the southern sky, reaching its peak at noon. In the afternoon it descends through the southern sky, moving westward. It continues to descend as it moves west, but does not sink below the horizon. At evening, therefore, the sun does not set. Instead, it moves eastward across the northern sky, reaching its lowest point on the horizon at midnight. Moving eastward from that point it continues to ascend until at 'dawn' it begins to move westward again. For Bede, the miracle of moving the shadow on the sundial ahead ten lines would simply have duplicated what naturally happens every summer in the far north. The greater miracle, he concludes, would have been to have the shadow go backwards ten lines, a wholly unnatural phenomenon that occurs nowhere on earth, ever. He presumes that it was logic of this kind that led King Hezekiah to call the first miracle easy and, therefore, to ask for the latter one.

2 2 Chr. 32:5. This passage from 2 Chronicles is crucial to Bede's explanation of the name of the district or quarter called the Second. Bede understands the 'other wall' that Hezekiah is said to have built as a *second* wall in addition to the first wall that Hezekiah is said to have repaired. Hence the name, the Second. Bede seems to be getting this idea from Jerome who, in his commentary on Zephaniah 1:10, states that the Second signifies a gate associated with a second wall (*CCSL* 76A: 666, 391-6).

3 Zeph. 1:10

4 *Masena* is Bede's transliteration of a Hebrew word which modern scholars now transliterate as *mishneh* (משנה). Bede's translation of the word as 'second' is taken from Jerome's *On Hebrew Names* (*CCSL* 72: 116, 16).

27
(2 Kgs. 23:10)
AND HE DEFILED TAPHETH, WHICH IS IN THE VALLEY OF THE SON OF HINNOM.

It is said of King Josiah, **And he defiled Tapheth, which is in the valley of the son of Hinnom, so that no one might consecrate a son or daughter to Molech there by fire.**[1] Frequent mention of these places is made in Scripture, especially in the Book of Kings and in the prophet Jeremiah.[2] For the valley of Hinnom, or of the son of Hinnom, is by Jerusalem's east wall;[3] a most lovely grove is watered there by the fountains of Siloam. And Tapheth, or Topheth (for it is written both ways), was a place in that same

1 As part of a general program of religious reform, King Josiah (640-609 B.C.E.) sought to purge Judah of pagan cults, including the cult of Molech which was reputed to have practiced human sacrifice.

2 The Book of Jeremiah mentions Tapheth and the valley of the son of Hinnom together in 7:31, 7:32, and 19:6. In addition, it mentions Tapheth by itself in 19:11-14 and the valley of the son of Hinnom in 19:2 and 32:35.

3 Bede's statement here does not quite fit the usual terminology for Jerusalem geography. The Valley of Hinnom typically refers to the valley that lies to the west and south of Jerusalem, not to the east, as Bede here claims. That valley does, however, merge into the Valley of Kidron, which runs from north to south just east of Jerusalem's eastern wall. Bede seems to be using the name 'Valley of Hinnom' to include what is usually called the Valley of Kidron. Because these two valleys converge, Bede seems to have thought of them together as a single semicircular valley that begins next to Jerusalem's western wall, curves around southwestern and southeastern corners of Jerusalem, and then ends along its eastern wall next to the Temple mount.

In *On the Holy Places*, Bede writes, 'Gehenna runs alongside the eastern wall of the Temple, and of Jerusalem itself. Also called the Valley of Jehoshaphat, it extends from north to south. The brook of Kidron runs through it when it rains' (5, 2—*CCSL* 175: 261, 13-16). As Bede will explain shortly, 'Gehenna' is the New Testament's Greek name for the Valley of Hinnom. This description of the Valley of Hinnom from *On the Holy Places* conforms perfectly to what Bede says of it in this Question. In both places he describes Hinnom as running along Jerusalem's eastern wall.

Yet note how in the passage just cited from *On the Holy Places*, Bede does not use the term 'Valley of Kidron', but speaks only of a brook of Kidron which runs through the Valley of Hinnom. This nomenclature is inconsistent with terminology that Bede uses in his other works. For example, in Bede's index of *Place Names*, which he appends to his *On First Samuel*, he writes, 'The brook of Kidron, or Valley of Kidron, is between the Mount of Olives and Jerusalem' and a little later, 'The Valley of Jehoshaphat, also called the Valley of Kidron, is adjacent to Jerusalem's eastern wall and belongs to the tribe of Benjamin' (*CCSL* 119: 286, 501-2 and 287, 517-18). One can thus see that whereas Bede identifies the Valley of Jehoshaphat with the Valley of Hinnom in *On the Holy Places*, he identifies it with the Valley of Kidron in *On First Samuel*. Similarly, he has the Brook of Kidron flowing through the Valley of Hinnom in *On the Holy Places* and through the Valley of Kidron in *On First Samuel*. One way to explain this inconsistency is to assume that Bede somehow saw the Valley of Kidron as an integral part of the longer Valley of Hinnom.

[318] valley near the Fuller's Pool, which Scripture remembers, and near the Akeldama field which even today is shown to be to the south of Mount Zion.[1] And because Tapheth was a delightful place, where *even today the charm of its gardens can be enjoyed,* they used to make sacrifices to demons on an altar set up there.[2] In an unholy fire they would *consecrate their own children and give them as a whole-offering,*[3] as is written of King Ahaz in the Book of Chronicles, *It was he who burned incense in the valley of Benhinnom, and consecrated his sons in the fire.*[4] Now Benhinnom means 'son of Hinnom'. Moreover, the valley of Hinnom is called 'Gehinnom' in Hebrew. From that word, hell's torment is given the nickname 'Gehenna' in the New Testament, no doubt because just as those in the valley of Hinnom perished in the very place that they served idols, as the prophets attest, so too are sinners punished in eternal damnation with the very sins that they have committed. In fact, when Jeremiah reports that the Lord had commanded him, saying, *Go to the valley of the son of Hinnom, which is by the entrance of the earthen gate*, he says not long after, *This place shall no more be called Topheth or the valley of the son of Hinnom, but the valley of slaughter, and I will shatter the deliberation of Judah and of Jerusalem in this place and destroy them by the sword.*[5] In like manner, Isaiah quite plainly calls hell 'Topheth'. For after he described the devil's everlasting ruin, referring to him as the 'Assyrian', and saying, *For struck with the rod, the Assyrian shall tremble at the Lord's voice, and the rod's path, which the Lord shall bring down upon him, shall be established,* he immediately added how and where he would perish, saying, *For Topheth was prepared recently, prepared deep and wide by the king.*[6] Well did he say, *and wide,*

1 2 Kgs. 18:17; Is: 7:3; 36:2. Scripture never actually mentions a Fuller's Pool. Instead, it talks about a Fuller's Field. Jerome, however, in his *Book of Places* does mention a Fuller's Pool in his description of Taphet: 'Even today in the suburban parts of Aelia there is a place that is thus named [i.e., Taphet]. It is by the Fuller's Pool and the Akeldama Field' (*PL* 23: 926B). Since Bede mentions a Fuller's Pool, he must be following Jerome here. Aelia Capitolina is the Gentile city that the Romans founded on the ruins of Jerusalem after the Bar Kochba rebellion in 135 C.E.

Akeldama means 'field of blood' and is mentioned in Matt. 27:8 and Acts 1:19. Bede *De loc. sanc.* 3, 2 (*CCSL* 175: 259, 7-9) and Jerome *Loc.* (*PL* 23: 877B).

2 Jerome *In Hier.* 2, 45, 2 (*CCSL* 74: 83, 18)

3 Ibid. 2, 45, 3 (*CCSL* 74: 84, 6-7)

4 2 Chr. 28:3

5 Jer. 19:2, 6-7

6 Is. 30:31-3

because Topheth is translated as 'width'.[1] *Its food,* he said, *is fire and much wood; the Lord's breath is kindling it like a torrent of brimstone.*[2] So Josiah defiled Tapheth, scattering either the bones of the dead there—as the following verses show him doing at other places of idols—or every other kind of unclean thing.[3] As a result, the place would seem more suitable for abomination than for delight to all who looked on it.[4]

28
(2 Kgs. 23:11)
AND HE REMOVED THE HORSES THAT THE KINGS OF JUDAH HAD GIVEN TO THE SUN.

The following passage about that same King Josiah says: **And at the entrance of the Lord's Temple he removed the horses that the kings of Judah had given to the sun**; and a little later it says: **and he burned the sun's chariots with fire**. This passage shows that the Jews at that time were given over to every superstition of Gentile idolaters, so much so that in order *[319]*
to venerate the sun, which they believed was a god (just as the Gentiles did), they added horses and chariots to [the sun's] image that they had made, and this [they did] in the courts of the Lord's Temple! For Gentiles typically either paint or fashion a likeness of the sun by putting a beardless boy on a chariot and harnessing to it horses that seem headed heavenward in [their] course. They use a boy's image for the sun because the sun experiences no old age through the ages, as though it were being born daily with each new rising. Bishop John of Constantinople thinks that their ascribing of horses and chariots to the sun is taken from the miracle of Elijah the prophet since

1 Bede probably derives this from Jerome's claim that Topheth is a Hebrew word for 'width' (*In Hier.* 2, 45, 3—*CCSL* 74: 84, 21-2). This claim sees dubious. Although it is difficult to know what Jerome had in mind, he may think that the consonantal radical for 'Topheth' (תפת), is related to the word 'phatah' (פתה), which means 'open' or 'wide' (F. Brown et al., [1972], 834a).

2 Is. 30:33

3 2 Kgs. 23:14

4 Bede is referring to the effect that Josiah's defiling of Tapheth had upon the natural beauty of the place, a beauty to which Bede alluded earlier in this Question.

he was taken up to heaven by a fiery chariot and fiery horses.[1] Now the sun is called *helios* in Greek, as Sedulius shows when he sings of Elijah's ascent, saying,

> How well the brilliant sky serves as Elijah's shining highway,
> and how deservedly radiant is he in his name!
> And worthy of his reward was he, (for if one letter and accent
> of his Greek name are changed, it is the sun).[2]

Because of this, and because it was rumored among the Greeks that the Israelites had divine writings, when the Greeks heard the Israelites proclaim that Elijah was carried to the heavens by a fiery chariot and fiery horses, or when they saw this depicted on a wall with other things, they were deceived by a similarity of name into believing that the sun's passage through the heavens was hereby meant.[3] They thus changed a miracle divinely done into proof— contrived by human folly—of an error. By imitating them, the Jews themselves managed to seem no less foolish in any respect than the most foolish of Gentiles.

1 2 Kgs. 2:11. Bede is appealing to the authority of John Chrysostom, a Greek Father who was bishop of Constantinople from 398 to 404. The passage to which Bede refers, however, belongs to a homily that is falsely attributed to Chrysostom. This homily, *De ascensione Heliae*, belongs to a larger collection of thirty-eight homilies, of which only sixteen are definitely attributable to Chrysostom. This homily, however, seems to have been written first in Latin, not Greek, and thus cannot be authentic. The entire collection may have been compiled and partly authored by Pelagius' disciple Anianus, deacon of Celeda (fl. 5th century). Anianus may have also translated Chrysostom's authentic sermons from Greek to Latin. Before Bede, this collection was known to Augustine, Pope Leo the Great, and Cassiodorus. The passage to which Bede here alludes reads as follows: *Hinc* [i.e., the ascension of Elijah] *poetae atque pictores in figuranda solis imagine exempla credo sumpsisse . . . sol enim graeco nomine Helios appellabatur. Unde Helias uere Helios . . . .* ['I believe that poets and painters have used Elijah's ascension as a model for their figurative depictions of the sun. For the sun is called Helios in Greek. Whence Elijah is really Helios . . . .'] (ed. Gelen, 1: 649-52 as cited in Wilmart [1917-18], 311, n. 1). Pseudo-Chrysostom and Bede, following him, make their argument hinge upon the similarity between *Helias*, the Latin name for Elijah, and *Helios*, the Greek word for sun. See also Quasten and di Berardino (1983-6), 3: 431 and 4: 493.

2 Sedulius *Pasch. Car.* 1, 183-6 (*CSEL* 10: 29). Sedulius was a Christian Latin poet who probably wrote in Italy during the first half of the fifth century. See Quasten and di Berardino (1983-6), 4: 321-6.

3 The similarity of name to which Bede refers is the similarity between *Helias* (=Elijah) and *Helios* (=the sun).

29
(2 Kgs. 23:13)
ALSO, THE HIGH PLACES AT JERUSALEM ON THE RIGHT SIDE OF THE MOUNT OF SCANDAL, ETC.

The passage that follows a little later, **Also, the high places at Jerusalem on the right side of the Mount of Scandal,** and that continues until, **the king defiled and broke the statues in pieces**, is about that same king,[1] and its meaning is clearer than day. For Scripture customarily gives the name 'high places' to designated sites on wooded hills where [the people] either used to sacrifice to demons or offer victims also to the Lord, enticed by the beauty of such sites and unlawfully abandoning the altar in the Temple. Thus in this book it is often said of kings who were less than completely righteous, *But he did not remove the high places*.[2] It calls the mountain of the idol the 'Mount of Scandal'[3] since Scripture, of course, customarily gives idols the name 'scandal' either because God is scandalized by them or because they bring scandal and ruin to their worshippers.[4] This is *[320]*
indicated later in that same verse where it says, **Solomon king of Israel had built these [high places] for Astarte the idol of the Sidonians, and for Chemosh the scandal of Moab, and for Milcom the abomination of the children of Ammon**. If I am not mistaken, it is also plainly shown there (how I wish it were not!) that Solomon never fully repented of the acts of idolatry which he had committed. For had he borne fruits worthy of repentance,[5] he would have been concerned above all to remove from the holy city the idols he had built and not to leave behind, as things wisely and rightly done, those deeds that he, for all his wisdom, had wrongly done and

1 I.e., Josiah

2 E.g., 2 Kgs. 15:35

3 The KJV and RSV translate the Hebrew text here as 'Mount of Corruption'; the NRSV as 'Mount of Destruction'; the NEB and JB prefer the Septuagint version, which reads 'Mount of Olives'. The Vulgate name, *mons offensionis,* which is here translated as 'Mount of Scandal', clearly follows the Hebrew version of the text.

4 The Latin *offensio* is here translated as 'scandal'. When Bede claims that *offensio* is often used in Scripture to designate idols, he is thinking, for example, of passages like Ezek. 20:7, which in translation from the Latin Vulgate reads: 'Let every one cast away the scandals (*offensiones*) from his eyes, and do not pollute yourselves with the idols (*idolis*) of Egypt.' This passage provides an example of what Bede, following Cassian, called *schesis onomaton*, or synonymous parallelism, whereby phrases alike in meaning but different in wording are juxtaposed (*De sch. et trop.* 2, 1, 10, *CCSL* 123A: 148, 103-7). In this particular passage, the parallelism demands that 'scandals' (*offensiones*) and 'idols' (*idolis*) be understood as synonyms. Other passages in which Bede may have seen *offensio* as referring to an idol include Ecclus. 31:7, and Ezek: 5:11 and 11:18.

5 Cf. Luke 3:8

that served as a stumbling block for the simple-minded. Scripture is mindful of this place, saying earlier, *On the mountain facing Jerusalem Solomon then built a temple for Chemosh the idol of Moab and for Molech the idol of the sons of Ammon.*[1] It should not seem strange that the mountain on which these idols were made is here said to be *facing Jerusalem* since it doubtless lay so near the city that it seemed a part of it, even contaminating the city with the sordid things heaped up there.[2]

30

(2 Kgs. 24:14)

AND HE TOOK ALL JERUSALEM AND ALL ITS RULERS, ETC.

When Scripture reported that Nebuchadnezzar took **into captivity all Jerusalem, all the princes, and all the army's valiant men, to the number of ten thousand,** it added: **and every artisan and smith.** When the Philistines had earlier held sway over the people Israel, they were said to have done the same thing: *Now no iron smith was to be found in all Israel; the Philistines had taken this precaution to keep the Hebrews from making sword or spear.*[3] For just as the Philistines then took care so that the Hebrews should have no iron-smiths, and so might not make arms with which to rebel, so later did the Chaldeans[4]—with Jerusalem destroyed and the entire promised land laid waste—take pains to insure that no artisan or smith remain there who could build up the city's damaged ramparts or repair what had been destroyed. What is more, the Chaldeans took back to Babylon every skill that they had found among that exiled nation so that such skills might be of no further use, or else serve the needs of Babylon. Because the allegory of so lamentable a history fits so well with the negligence of our own time, it must not—I believe—be passed over in

1 1 Kgs. 11:7

2 Bede seems concerned in this last sentence to identify Jerusalem's 'Mount of Scandal', mentioned in 2 Kgs. 23:13, with the 'mountain facing Jerusalem', mentioned in 1 Kgs. 11:7 as the place where Solomon erected his temple to idols. Whereas 2 Kgs. 23:13 refers to the Mount of Scandal as a place within Jerusalem itself, 1 Kgs. 11:7 seems to refer to a mountain just outside Jerusalem. Aware of this apparent discrepancy, Bede is nevertheless convinced these two verses are referring to one and the same mountain.

3 1 Sam. 13:19. The Philistines exercised hegemony over Israel sometime after 1050 BCE, just prior to Saul's elevation to the kingship. Some 460 years later, in 587, Nebuchadnezzar destroyed Jerusalem and deported its leading citizens to Babylon.

4 The term 'Chaldeans' is a synonym for Babylonians, the Mesopotamian people over whom Nebuchadnezzar ruled.

silence.[1] For it is clear that Jerusalem and the land of Israel here stand for the city of Christ—which is the Holy Church—and that Babylon and the Chaldeans (and also the Philistines) stand for the city of the devil—which [321] is the whole multitude of evil humans and angels—and that Israel serves the Philistines or Chaldeans whenever any of the faithful who stand nominally inside the Church but are deceived by unclean spirits or humans bow the necks of their conscience to greed, self-indulgence, or any other sin. But Nebuchadnezzar leads Jerusalem, all its princes, and its army's ten thousand valiant men into captivity when the world's temptations, or its calamities, suddenly overwhelm even the people's teachers and those who have been seen to serve the Lord with invincible spirit and to keep the Ten Commandments faithfully in love of God and neighbour. And so, they either defile themselves with wicked deeds or, by turning away toward heresy, incur the mark of open apostasy. Indeed, apart from Scripture's utterances, are there any other arms with which we who oppose the devil may defend the liberty given us by God? For there we learn from the examples of the Lord himself and his saints—more clearly than from a light—by what tactics the wars against vices ought to be won.[2] But the Philistines deprive Israel's sons of their armsmakers when evil spirits hinder the minds of the faithful from meditation on sacred reading by so preoccupying them with worldly affairs that the faithful may neither gain the confidence to resist vices, which comes by training in this [meditation], nor arouse by exhortation and reproof [those] others to do so who perhaps cannot read.[3] They carry off armsmakers when [evil spirits] mire Holy Scripture's students so deeply in sins that they grow utterly ashamed to declare the good things that they have learned. They deport every artisan and smith from Jerusalem to Babylonia

1 For a fuller and more direct expression of Bede's concern over church corruption in his own day, see his *Letter to Egbert* (ed. Plummer, 1: 405-23).

2 Note Bede's consistent and somewhat artistic use of military language to allegorize things spiritual: the arms in which church leaders must trust are Scripture's utterances; their war is against vices; the battle ranks within which they must fight are those of the Lord and his saints, and not those of faithless leaders and teachers, of whom the deported citizens of Jerusalem serve as the prototype.

3 Bede saw meditation upon sacred reading, especially Scripture, as an essential part of any ecclesiastical vocation, but especially the monastic one. Unlike our modern understanding of meditation, the ancient and medieval concept of *meditatio* involved bodily as well as cognitive activity. One must not simply think about Scripture, or read it silently. *Meditatio* requires the voicing of Scripture's words with the mouth, hearing them with the ear, and eventually knowing them by heart. Moreover, its effect was intended to be not merely intellectual, but existential: it always aimed at conversion and amendment of life. The centrality of such prayerful reading to the monastic life of Bede's time is amply attested in *Reg. Ben.* 48 (ed. Fry, 248-52). For more on monastic *meditatio*, see Fry (1981), 446-7 and Leclercq (1982), 13-30.

when [evil spirits] turn from their purpose those who once were accustomed to benefit many by the manifold activity of their virtues and to fortify the city of God against temptation's assaults, and when they compel these same ones to waste their ability—which they should have used to build up the Holy Church—to gratify instead the whim of vice's king.[1] But if we want to understand here a smith not of doors or walls, but of gold and gems, the spiritual exposition would yet yield one and the same result. Indeed, it is said that wisdom *is gold and a multitude of jewels*.[2] Because of this we can understand that the smiths of these are really none other than those teachers who, so long as they live and teach rightly, strenuously use their art and industry to adorn the holy city. But if they happen to fall into error, what is that if not captives being deported to Babylonia by the Chaldean king? And, inasmuch as artisan and smith were deported from Jerusalem to Babylonia, this denotes the burial in the ground of the talent of the Word that one has received from heaven.[3] It is to press spiritual knowledge into the service of the deeds of sinners.

[322] If I have said anything of use to you in these little explanations, I implore you, dear reader, to praise God who gave it; and if not, to excuse my ignorance or audacity so that, in every way that you can, you will continue to meditate frequently upon, attend unceasingly to, and preach regularly the Divine Scriptures. And let us strive by our common toil so that we may be found to be faithful merchants of the Lord's riches, artisans and smiths of spiritual gems or ramparts, defenders of the holy city, and makers of heavenly arms, so that when our Most High Lord has returned from the wedding, he might think it fit to say to us, *Because you have been faithful over a few things, I will place you over many. Enter into the joy of your Lord.*[4] Amen.[5]

1 I.e., the devil

2 Prov. 20.15

3 Matt. 25:24-5

4 Matt. 25:21 and 23; cf. Matt. 13:45. Bede here alters the Vulgate's wording by substituting his own plural 'you' for Scripture's singular. He thus paraphrases this passage so that it is addressed not to the faithful steward in Matthew's gospel, but to Nothhelm and other monastic readers as faithful latter-day stewards of God's Word. Cf. Bede *Ep. Ecg.* 2 (ed. Plummer, 1: 406).

5 In an article to appear in *Filologia mediolatina* 4 (1997) Michael Gorman raises the possibility that this final paragraph, or epilogue, was not included in the original work that Bede sent to Nothhelm, but was added later when Bede decided to 'publish' the work.

THIRTY QUESTIONS ON THE BOOK OF KINGS: APPENDICES

Note: In the keys that accompany the following drawings, references are to the question number and line number in the *CCSL* edition e.g., Q. 12, 10 = Question 12, line 10. The number in parentheses following Josephus references designates the sentence number in the Loeb edition.

APPENDIX I: THE TEMPLE OF SOLOMON

(side view from the east front)
as described in *Thirty Questions on the Book of Kings* 11-13

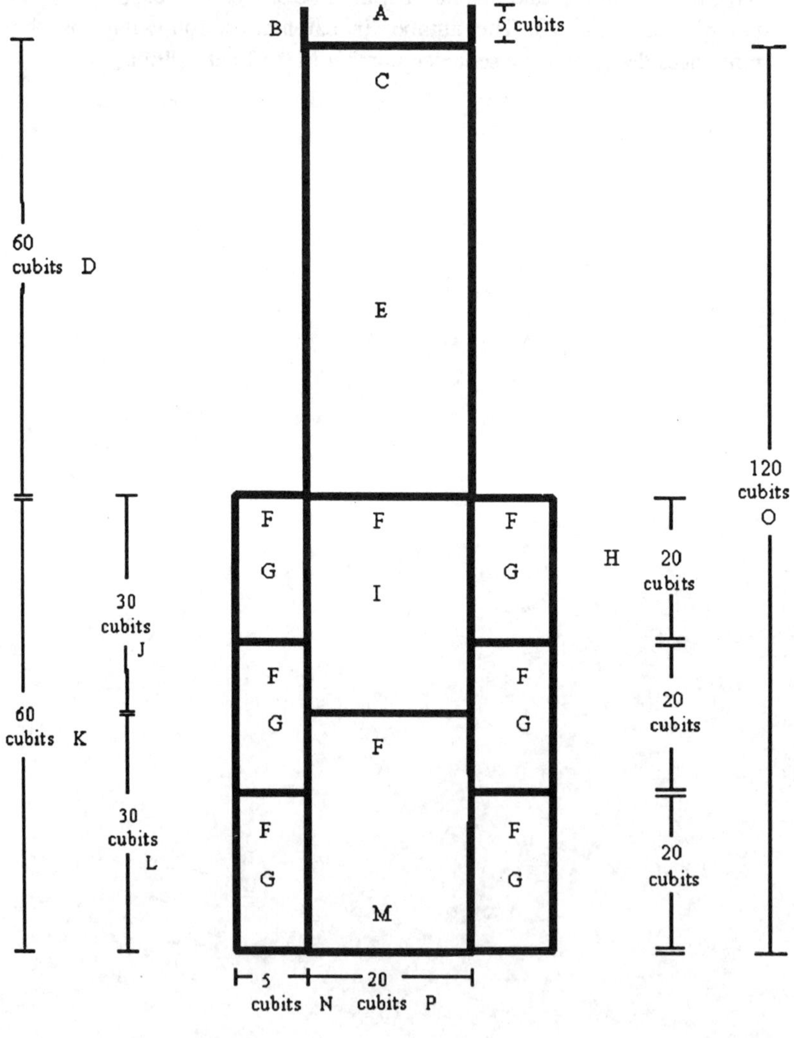

KEY TO THE TEMPLE DRAWING
in Bede's *Thirty Questions on the Book of Kings* 11-13

A boarded floor [*tabulatum*, pl. *tabulata*]—Q. 1, 39-42. Source: 1 Kgs. 6:10b

B boarded barrier [*tabulatum*]—Q. 13, 27-38. Source: 1 Kgs. 6:10a

Here Bede uses *tabulatum* not to mean 'boarded floor', as for example the Douai-Rheims translation does, but 'boarded barrier'. He indicates this by designating *tabulatum*'s synonyms as 'wall' [*murus*], 'railings' [*cancelli*], and 'parapet' [*luricula* or *loricula*].

C panelled ceiling [*laquear*, pl. *laquearia*]—Q. 13, 7-8. Source: 1 Kgs. 6:9b

D height of the upper half of the Temple (Q. 11, 9-10). Source: Josephus *Ant. Jud.* 8, 3, 2 (64)

E third house [*tertia domus*] (Q. 12, 12) = third storey [*tertium caenaculum*] (Q. 11, 7; 11, 16; and 11, 23-4) = uppermost storey [*supremum caenaculum*] (Q. 12, 31). Source: 1 Kgs. 6:8

F panelled ceiling [*laquear*] (Q. 13, 17-19)

G side chamber [*porticus*] (Q. 11, 7-9; Q. 13, 6; Q. 13, 16-17; Q 13, 19-26). The Vulgate refers to these side chambers as *latera* (1 Kgs. 6:5; Ezek. 41:5-11). It never designates them as *porticus*, the term that Bede employs exclusively for them. Whenever Bede refers to the side chambers he always employs the plural form, perhaps to distinguish them from the front porch at the Temple's east entrance, for which he employs the singular form. Bede calculates that there are ninety side chambers in all, thirty on each of three storeys. Each storey of side chambers is twenty cubits high. Thus, the roof over the third and highest storey of the side chambers is sixty cubits high, and is thus even with the ceiling panels of the middle storey. Sources: 1 Kgs. 6:5, Josephus *Ant. Jud.* 8, 3, 2 (65-6)

H height of the side chambers (Q. 13, 17-19 and 23-4). Source: Josephus *Ant. Jud.* 8, 3, 2 (66)

I middle storey [*medium caenaculum*] (Q. 11, 6, Q. 12, 16 and 23) = upper house [*superior domus*] (Q. 12, 11-12 and 28-9). Source: 1 Kgs. 6:8

J height of the second storey (Q. 11, 6-7). Bede here deduces the height of the second storey by assuming that the Temple's lower house, which was sixty feet in height, contained two storeys of equal height.

K height of the lower half of the Temple (Q. 11, 9). Source: Josephus *Ant. Jud.* 8, 3, 2 (64)

L height of the first storey (Q. 11, 5-6). See note J. Source 1 Kgs. 6:2

M ground floor [*pavimentum*] (Q. 11, 5-6)

N breadth of side chambers (Q. 13, 22-3). Source: Josephus *Ant. Jud.* 8, 3, 2 (66)

O height of the entire Temple (Q. 11, 10-11).
Source: 2 Chr. 3:4 and Josephus *Ant. Jud.* 8, 3, 2 (65)

P breadth of Temple. Although Bede does not discuss the Temple's breadth, we can safely assume that he put it at twenty cubits, since all three of his main sources unambiguously did so (1 Kgs. 6:2, 2 Chr. 3:3, and Josephus *Ant. Jud.* 8, 3, 2 (64)).

APPENDIX II: THE TEMPLE COMPLEX in Bede's *Thirty Questions on the Book of Kings* 18

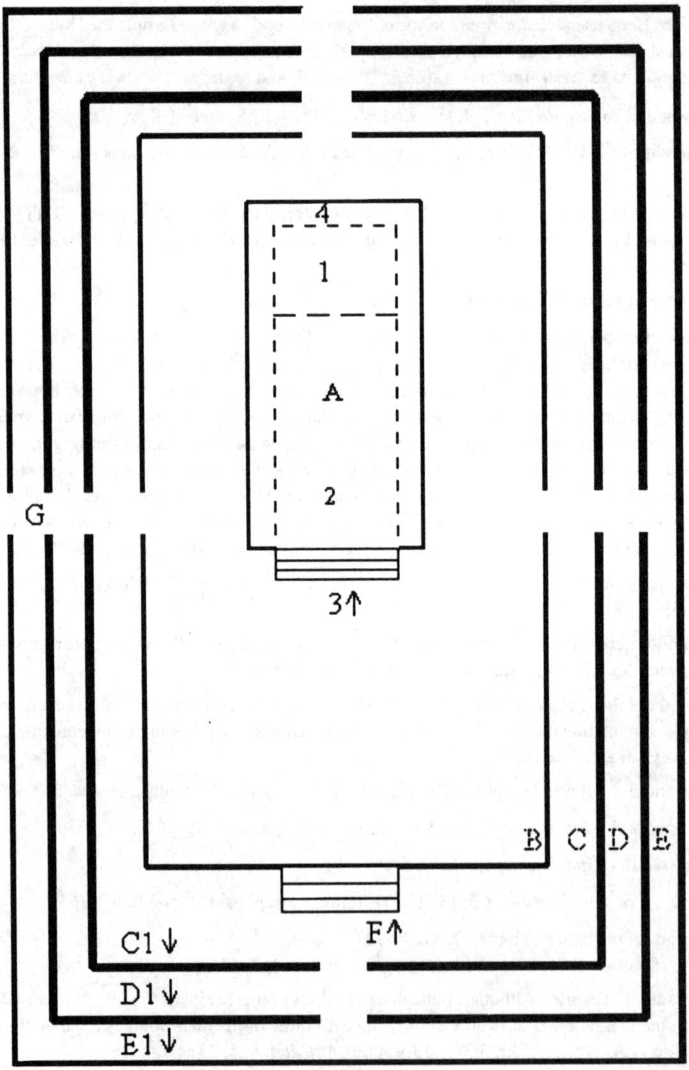

KEY TO THE TEMPLE COMPLEX
in Bede's *Thirty Questions on the Book of Kings* 18

A. Temple

1. Holy of holies
2. Sanctuary
3. Porch
4. Surrounding porticos (*porticus*), or side chambers

B. Court of the Priests [*atrium sacerdotum*] = the inner court [*atrium interius*]—Q. 18, 15-33 and 63. Sources: 1 Kgs. 6:36, 2 Chr. 4:9; Josephus *Ant. Jud.* 8, 3, 9 (95). Cf. Bede *De templo* 2 (*CCSL* 119A: 192, 1-27). Bede uses the term *atrium* in a twofold way: (1) to designate the 3-cubit high structure which enclosed the area where the priests and levites congregated (e.g., Q. 18, 15-6) and to designate the enclosed area itself (e.g., Q. 18, 63).

C. Court of the Israelites—Q. 18, 63-6. Source: Josephus *Ant. Jud.* 8, 3, 9 (96). Cf. Bede *De templo* 2 (*CCSL* 119A: 193, 43-6).

C1. very long rectangular building [*longe aedis permaxima in quadrum*]—Q. 18, 33-40. Sources: Josephus *Ant. Jud.* 8, 3, 9 (96). Cf. Bede *De templo* 2 (*CCSL* 119A: 192, 30-2).

D. Court of the Women—Q. 18, 66-8. Source: Josephus *Ant. Jud.* 8, 3, 9 (97); *Bel. Jud.* 5, 5, 2. Cf. Bede *De templo* 2 (*CCSL* 119A: 193, 46).

D1. another (building) [*altera (aedis)*]—Q. 18, 40-1. Source: Josephus *Ant. Jud.* 8, 3, 9 (98). Cf. Bede *De templo* 2 (*CCSL* 119A: 192, 32-3).

E. Court of the Gentiles—Q. 18, 69-72. Cf. Bede *De templo* 2 (*CCSL* 119A: 193, 46-8).

E1. a third (building) [*tertia (aedis)*]—Q. 18, 41-2. Cf. Bede *De templo* 2 (*CCSL* 119A: 192, 33-4).

F. staired entrance to the Court of the Priests [*introitus per gradum*]—Q. 18, 27.

G. doors [*ostia*]: Q. 18, 42-5 and 74-6.

ON EIGHT QUESTIONS: INTRODUCTION

Bede did not include a work entitled *De octo quaestionibus* in the catalogue of his works at the end of the *Ecclesiastical History*. In some manuscripts, and in Migne's *Patrologia latina*, the eight questions translated here are followed by expositions of seven more questions which are clearly not by Bede. As a result, this work has often been listed as 'doubtful' or 'spurious'. However, in 1919 Paul Lehmann published an article in which he argued that both the content and form of the first several questions were compatible with Bedan authorship; he also showed that some of the first eight questions were quoted by several Carolingian writers who attributed them to Bede.[1] Some years later, in 1943, M. L. W. Laistner noted that three continental manuscripts from the twelfth and thirteenth centuries identify this work as *De octo quaestionibus* and indicate that it was, like the *Thirty Questions on the Book of Kings* to which it is usually attached in the manuscripts, addressed to Nothhelm, who was a priest of London before his election as archbishop of Canterbury in 735.[2] Since the work of Lehmann and Laistner, the authenticity of *On Eight Questions* has generally been accepted by scholars.[3]

The date of the work cannot be determined with precision. Since there is a mention in Question 2 of one Cuthwine who was bishop of the East Angles some time between 716 and 731, Bede must have composed his answer to that question, at least, after 716. Laistner supposed that *On Eight Questions* might be identified with the treatise on 'names and words that can be explained more easily and briefly' which Bede indicated that he was sending to Nothhelm along with the *Thirty Questions*, but Paul Meyvaert has pointed out that Bede's language implies that all Nothhelm's questions dealt with the Books of Kings.[4] Charles Jones reckoned that *On Eight*

1 Lehmann (1919)

2 Laistner and King (1943), 155-8. It was suggested by Henderson (1980), 6, that Nothhelm's devotion to St. Paul as patron of the cathedral he served in London may account for the Pauline material discussed in Questions 2 and 3.

3 For a full account of modern scholarship on this text, see Gorman (forthcoming).

4 *XXX Quaest.*, Prol. (*CCSL* 119: 293, 7-8); Laistner and King (1943), 156; Meyvaert (1997)

Questions does not appear in Bede's catalogue of his works because it was composed after 731, and can therefore be said to contain 'some of Bede's mature thought'[1]—but this must be classified as mere conjecture, since Bede neglected to list a number of other works certainly completed before 731. More probable are Meyvaert's suggestions that *On Eight Questions* was a compilation of Bedan material put together by others at Wearmouth-Jarrow, probably after Bede's death, and that Questions 2-7 represent replies to questions by Nothhelm while Question 8 is part of a commentary on 2 Samuel.[2]

The questions addressed by Bede in this work treat both Old Testament and New Testament themes—a fact which inspired Paul Lehmann to suggest that this may be the 'questions of Bede on both testaments' for which Abbot Lupus of Ferrières sent to Abbot Altsig of York in the mid-ninth century.[3] The first question deals with the star of Bethlehem and the gifts of the Magi in Matthew's account of the Nativity, while the next four interpret particular verses in the writings of the Apostle Paul. The last three questions concern passages from the Old Testament: David's lament for Saul and Jonathan in 2 Samuel 1:19-27, a verse from Psalm 119, and the account of David bringing the ark into Jerusalem given in 2 Samuel 6:1-23.

Bede's answers to the first two questions remain on the literal or historical level of interpretation. In Question 3, he appends a 'mystical' interpretation to his discussion of a problem of literal meaning, and in Questions 4 and 5 he provides a moral or tropological interpretation of certain Pauline exhortations.[4] Questions 6 and 7 explain and defend the propriety of particular allegorical associations, while Question 8 is the kind of complex allegorical exposition more commonly found in Bede's verse-by-verse commentaries.

On Eight Questions has attracted the attention of modern scholars chiefly for three reasons. First, it contains explicit statements of two important principles for biblical interpretation: in Question 5, Bede says that willing obedience to the norm of orthodoxy is justified by the assurance that God will provide faithful teachers to instruct the faithful and correct them when

1 Jones (1969-70), 147

2 Meyvaert (1997)

3 Lehmann (1919), 21, n. 2, citing *Ep.* 62 in *MGH Epp.* 6:1

4 For Bede's understanding of 'tropology' as a figure of speech which may be either 'plain' (straightforward ethical injunction) or 'figurative' (moral teaching implicit in symbols), see *De tab.* 1 (*CCSL* 119A: 25, 794-801).

necessary, and in Question 6 he follows Gregory the Great in explaining how it is sometimes possible for Scripture to signify the good by the bad, and vice versa. Second, references to manuscript illumination in Question 2, and to wall painting in Question 6, provide precious information about the relationship between biblical exegesis and the visual arts in early Anglo-Saxon England. Third, in Question 3, Bede cites a gloss which he had heard attributed to Theodore of Tarsus, thereby giving us a tantalizing glimpse of the teaching offered at the famous seventh-century school at Canterbury.

The nine extant manuscripts containing *On Eight Questions* are dated from the twelfth to the fourteenth century.[1] This work was first published by John Heerwagen in the Basel edition of Bede's works in 1563. The present translation was originally made from this text as reprinted by Migne in *PL* 93: 455-62, but thanks to the generosity of Michael Gorman it has been possible to incorporate a number of corrected readings from his new critical edition of the text prepared for publication in a forthcoming volume of the *Revue Bénédictine*. The chapter headings given here as titles of the eight questions are found in the index that appears in five of the extant manuscripts, and Gorman supposes that they may well be attributed to Bede himself.

1 Gorman (forthcoming)

ON EIGHT QUESTIONS

QUESTION 1: ON THE WISE MEN WHO ADORED THE LORD AT HIS BIRTH, AND ON THE STAR [455]

Some think that the wise men who came from the East to the Lord when he was born in the flesh and who adored him by offering gifts[1] did by no means understand in those same gifts the noblest mysteries that Holy Church now sublimely understands—namely: in gold, a king; in incense, a God; in myrrh, a human being who would in due course die and be buried[2]—but that they were bringing mysteries greater than they knew, and each simply offered as gift to him whom they had come to adore as king the most valued product of his country. But if we diligently ponder their own words we ascertain it to have been far otherwise; for this is what they said when they were coming into Jerusalem: **Where is he who has been born king of the Jews? For we observed his star in the East, and have come to adore him.**[3] Surely it is apparent that they understood him to be a human being, because they say: **Where is he who has been born?** And it is apparent [that they also understood him to be] a king, because they declare it in the same saying. And it is apparent that they also believed him to be God, whence they add afterwards: **And we have come to adore him.** For such learned men would not have come so far to worship one whom they believed to be merely a human being and a king, and not God as well. They also had this lofty and noble[4] perception about him: namely, that although he was king of the Jews, he was also able to save the Gentiles who were willing to believe in him and to come to him. They proved this especially by their own coming, and by their action.

But as for the star, some who consider Scripture less diligently say that it appeared to them as a guide for their journey from the East right up to the

1 Matt. 2:1-12

2 Augustine *Sermo* 202, 2 (*PL* 38:1034); Gregory the Great *Hom. in euang.* 10, 6 (*PL* 76: 1112D)

3 Matt. 2:2

4 Gorman: *sublimissime ac nobilissime*

vicinity of Bethlehem, leading the way on the road, but that when they had left the road to Bethlehem and turned their eyes toward the way to Jerusalem, the star which was leading them disappeared, until they again returned on foot from Jerusalem to Bethlehem. But the very truth of the gospel, once examined, shows that it by no means happened in this way; rather, it was only in the East that they had seen the star, and they had immediately understood that it signified the rising of a king born in Judea, concerning whom Balaam had predicted: *A star shall come forth out of Jacob, and a rod shall rise from Israel, and it shall smite the leaders of Moab.*[1] For because they were astrologers, they had also diligently committed to memory the things which had been spoken so marvellously[2] concerning the star. And so, as soon as they saw it they came at once to Judea, in which they had known that the king was to be born, and specifically to the royal city, so that they might find the place where, in their estimation, his birth would be more precisely known. And because they had learned from the prophetic testimonies that he was to be born in Bethlehem, as soon as they were making their way there they merited to have the star which they had seen in the East as their guide. For thus you have in the gospel the first thing the wise men themselves said: **Where is he who is born king of the Jews? For we have seen his star in the East.** For they did not say, 'It led us from the East right to these places by going before [us].' Accordingly, the evangelist also testifies concerning them: **When they had heard the king, they departed; and behold! the star that they had seen in the East went before them.**[3] For he certainly did not write that they had seen the star from anywhere other than the East, until having heard the king they directed [their] way to Bethlehem.

[456] Concerning this star, we should note that those who were coming to Bethlehem by no means saw it in the highest altitude of heaven among the rest of the stars, but near the earth. For when the evangelist says, **It went before them until it stood still when it came above the place where the child was,**[4] he is openly suggesting that it had stood still when it was near the house in which the child was. For surely stars that are located in the

1 Num. 24:17. Bede's argument here assumes that the wise men were somewhere east of the Holy Land when they saw the star in the western sky and (on the basis of Balaam's prediction) set out for Judea. Bede implies that the star then disappeared from their sight while they travelled to Herod's court, and only reappeared to guide them on the way from Jerusalem to Bethlehem.

2 Gorman: *tam mirabiliter*

3 Matt. 2:9

4 Matt. 2:9

highest heaven, when they reach the center of the sky, appear to stand still over the top of every house, however large the city.

QUESTION 2: *FIVE TIMES I HAVE RECEIVED FROM THE JEWS THE FORTY MINUS ONE.*[1]

What the Apostle says, **Five times I have received from the Jews the forty minus one,** signifies that he had been whipped by them five times, in such a way, however, that he was never beaten with forty lashes, but always with one less, or thirty-nine. For it was a precept of the law that when the judges flogged a wrongdoer they must temper the measure of the punishment in such a way that the number of lashes should by no means go beyond forty in number, *lest,* it says, *your brother should lie lacerated and degraded before you.*[2] That it is to be understood in this way and was understood in this way by the ancients is also attested by the picture of the Apostle in the book which the most reverend and most learned Cuthwine, bishop of the East Angles, brought with him when he came from Rome to Britain, for in that book all of his sufferings and labours were fully depicted in relation to the appropriate passages.[3] This passage was there depicted in such a way that it was as if the Apostle were lying naked, lacerated by whips and drenched with tears. Now above him there was standing a torturer having in his hand a whip divided into four parts, but one of the strings is retained in his hand, and only the remaining three are left loose for beating. Wherein the intention of the painter is easily apparent, that the reason he was prepared to scourge him with three strings was so that he might complete the number of thirty-nine lashes.[4] For if he were to strike with four cords, striking ten times would make forty lashes; but if he were to beat [him] thirteen times with three, how would he complete forty lashes? And so it was certainly lawful for the Jews to strike a sinner forty times, but they were striking the Apostle thirty-nine times so that they might leave

1 2 Cor. 11:24. Note that the Vulgate does not specifically identify the 'forty minus one' that the Apostle received five times, so it might not have been immediately obvious to the reader that Paul in this verse is describing a series of whippings.

2 Deut. 25:3

3 Cuthwine was bishop of Dunwich some time between 716 and 731; the book he brought from Rome may have been an illustrated copy of Arator's *De actibus apostolorum*. Since Bede is not known to have visited East Anglia, the volume might have been sent to Northumbria on loan. See Levison (1946), 133; Whitelock (1960), 5-6; Mayr-Harting (1972), 191-2; Henderson (1980), 7. Note the comment in reference to this passage in Whitelock (1976), 23: 'This shows that Bede was willing to regard ancient illustrators as authoritative in their interpretation of the scriptures.'

4 Gorman: *undequadragenarium plagarum numerum*

the forsaken person something of his own [dignity] and show some mercy.[1] Now the fact that the same Apostle says 'forty' (in the feminine gender) surely signifies that he had received [that number of] lashes,[2] which he endured five times with the forty minus one. In the Greek, in place of this phrase it simply says τεσσαράκοντα παρὰ μίαν, that is, 'one before forty'.[3]

QUESTION 3: *FOR A NIGHT AND A DAY I WAS IN THE DEPTH OF THE SEA.*[4]

Concerning what the same Apostle says, **For a night and a day I was in the depth of the sea,** I have heard certain people asserting that Theodore of blessed memory, that most learned man who was formerly archbishop of the English people,[5] explained it in this way: there was in Cizico[6] a certain exceedingly deep pit prepared for torturing criminals, which on account of its immense deepness used to be called 'the depth of the sea'. It was the filth and darkness of this which Paul endured, among innumerable other
[457] things, for Christ's sake.

But if we consult the venerable writings of the fathers, it is assuredly plain that they were not accustomed to understand in these words anything other than what it says, which is that when the Apostle came to some misfortune in the depth of the sea and was enveloped by the waves for a day and also a night, after these things he returned by God's guidance to

1 'thirty-nine times' = *undequadragies* (Gorman). Bede's explanation of the reason why Paul was whipped thirty-nine times instead of forty differs from that of modern commentators, who indicate that the lashes were given one stroke at a time and that it was customary to administer only thirty-nine lashes in order make it less likely for a miscount to put the total over the maximum number prescribed; see Furnish (1964), 515-16.

2 *plagas*, a feminine plural noun in the accusative case

3 Bede points out that the Greek text of 2 Cor. 11:24 expresses the number thirty-nine as 'one before forty', while the Vulgate uses a term meaning 'forty minus one'. On Bede's knowledge of Greek, see Dionisotti (1982), Lynch (1983) and Martin (1984).

4 2 Cor. 11:26

5 Theodore, a native of Tarsus in Asia Minor who was accomplished in both Greek and Latin, was the archbishop of Canterbury (669-90) of whom Bede wrote that 'the English Churches made more spiritual progress while he was archbishop than ever before'— *Hist. eccl.* 5, 8 (ed. and transl. Colgrave and Mynors, 474-5); on this important figure see Lapidge (1995). The school established at Canterbury by Theodore and Hadrian (the Italian monk who accompanied him to England and became abbot of Canterbury) was renowned for its high standard of learning and distinguished by its propensity for literal exegesis drawing on Theodore's firsthand knowledge of Near Eastern traditions; see Bischoff and Lapidge (1994).

6 Gorman: *Cizico,* which has been identified as Cyzicus (modern day Erdek), a city in Asia Minor on the south coast of the Sea of Marmara about seventy-five miles from Constantinople. See Mayr-Harting (1972), 207; Henderson (1980), 7; Bischoff and Lapidge (1994), 41-2.

the air and open land. Hence they also reckon it among the divine miracles that a man who had been held under the waves for some time was able to avoid being suffocated by the surrounding waters or devoured by the monsters of the sea. Accordingly, they proclaimed that it was no more amazing that Peter walked upon the waves and did not sink than that Paul was held under the waves and did not drown.[1]

Now if we wish to understand something mystical in such dissimilar miracles of the two apostles, it is easy [to see] that Paul, who was not only shipwrecked three times[2] but was also cast into the depth of the sea for a night and a day and was everywhere protected and delivered by the Lord, signifies the righteous who are to be rescued by the Lord from all perils. Not only are they to be saved externally from assailing trials, but even if they seem to be sinking into the very whirlpool of death, and hidden from things human, they will nevertheless be recalled to life by the power of their Creator. On the other hand, Peter, who walked with unimpeded steps over the waves which were stirred up by the wind but was raised up by Christ's right hand when on account of fear he began to sink, signifies that with invincible faith those same elect overcome and regard as nothing all the efforts of the impious and the persecutions thrown at them at the devil's instigation. So they cannot be submerged by the waves of the world at all, since they are encircled by the ever-present aid of their Maker. If they ever begin to falter[3]—as they are [only] human—they are immediately rescued by the one whom they are accustomed to call upon without ceasing, saying: *And lead us not into temptation, but deliver us from evil.*[4]

QUESTION 4: *'VENGEANCE IS MINE, AND I WILL REPAY,' SAYS THE LORD.*[5]

What the Apostle says, **'Vengeance is mine, and I will repay,' says the Lord,** has this sense: What use is it for you to set out to avenge your own

1 McCready (1994), 63-4, observes that the weight of patristic commentary on 2 Cor. 11:25 actually inclines against Bede's view that Paul was literally submerged beneath the water for a night and a day, and that this was no less a miracle than Peter's walking over the waves, as recorded in Matt. 14:28-31. While Bede's preferred interpretation was advanced by Sulpicius Severus *Ep.* 1, 6 (*SC* 133: 318-20) and Pseudo-Augustine *Sermo* 203, 3 (*PL* 39: 2123), it was opposed by John Chrysostom *Hom. in 2 Cor.* 25, 1 (*PG* 61: 570-1), and even by Bede's favourite mentor, Gregory the Great, in *Dial.* 1, 12, 4-5 (*SC* 260: 116).

2 2 Cor. 11:25

3 Gorman: *titubare*

4 Matt. 6:13

5 Rom. 12:19; cf. Deut. 32:35 and Heb. 10:30

injuries—you who are able neither to know the hearts of humans nor to know and judge their wickednesses with a calm mind? But rather, whatever sin is committed against you, forgive from your heart, as though to brothers and neighbours, so that God may also forgive you your sins: for you know that if they are willing to be corrected you will have them as companions in blessings; if not, they will be condemned more justly by divine judgement—which cannot err just as it cannot be angry—than by yours: 'Acknowledge that **vengeance is mine,** (it says) **and I will repay.'** For we are obliged not only to endure patiently the evils of the unjust but also to expend freely for them our goods through which they, having been vanquished, may return to our love. Marvelling at the virtue of our clemency and patience, they may also begin to imitate them, and forsaking their vices[1] they may be converted to works of virtue. For this reason he added by way of admonition: *If your enemy is hungry, feed him; if he is thirsty, give him something to drink; for by doing this you will heap coals of fire on his head.*[2] For he is saying that [the enemy's] head is his mind, which holds the chief place and presidency, as it were, among all our deeds and thoughts. And the flame of love he calls 'coals of fire', concerning which the Lord says in the gospel: *I have come to bring fire to the earth, and what do I wish, except that it might be kindled?*[3]

For let us not believe that the Apostle, or Solomon, from whose Proverbs the saying above was taken, wished to teach us that we should do temporal good things[4] to our adversaries with the purpose and intention that those who persist ungrateful for these things might perpetually suffer the torments of greater fires. But they rather desire that by doing mercy to enemies who are in need we might mollify the swollenness and hardness of their minds[5] with the poultices of kindnesses, and strive to employ the fire of love to incite them to love us in the Lord in return.

[458] QUESTION 5: *LET EACH ONE ABOUND IN HIS OWN SENSE.*[6]

Some think that what the Apostle says, **Let each one abound in his own sense,** was said in such a way as if he meant to say: 'It suffices unto righteousness for each one to do those things that appear best to himself.'

1 Gorman: *relictisque vitiis*
2 Rom. 12:20; cf. Prov. 25:21-2
3 Luke 12:49
4 Gorman: *bona faciamus temporalia*
5 Gorman: *mentis*
6 Rom. 14:5

But it is by no means to be understood in this way. For what if there is a heretic who thinks himself to be catholic, or if there is someone living wickedly who supposes that he is in walking in the right way of truth? Will labour or faith[1] of that sort suffice for him as a work of righteousness through which he may come to salvation, especially since the Apostle does not say in the indicative mood, 'He abounds' but in the imperative, **Let each one abound in his own sense**? Therefore, he was commanding that if we cannot grasp the more sublime secrets of the divine mysteries,[2] we should nevertheless humbly and devoutly serve the Lord in those things that we understand and perceive are to be truly believed and confessed. In this way, what he commanded will be fulfilled—that each one should abound in his own sense—when we take care to persevere abundantly by good works in those things which we have learned from the great teachers ought to be believed or done, in order that by performing those things that we have come to understand, we may also merit to apprehend sublimer things that we have not yet come to understand. Hence he properly adds: *If you discern something otherwise, this also God will reveal to you,*[3] that is: 'If through charity you put into operation the good things that you know, then should you discern something in a way that is other than seemly, divine grace will eventually grant you a right[4] understanding of this as well.' Clearly, this is just what happened to blessed Cyprian, who along with his fellow bishops who were in Africa determined, contrary to the Church's custom, that heretics must be rebaptized.[5] But because he was zealous to abound in good works in his own sense, which seemed right to him, he soon merited to be corrected and to be led back to the universal norm of Holy Church through the instruction of spiritual men.[6]

---

1 Gorman: *uel fides*

2 'mysteries' = *sacramentorum*, a term Bede often uses to refer to the mysteries of faith, including those found in the Bible as well as those enacted in the liturgy.

3 Phil. 3:15

4 Gorman: *recte*

5 Cyprian (*ca.* 200-58), bishop of Carthage in North Africa during the persecution of Decius, opposed the Roman bishop Stephen I by denying the validity of baptisms performed by heretics and schismatics.

6 In actuality, Cyprian was martyred in 258 without having revised his position on rebaptism. Perhaps Bede was confused by his reading of Rufinus' translation of Eusebius of Caesarea's *Historia ecclesiastica* 7, 3-9 (*GCS* 9.2: 637-49), in which a brief mention of Cyprian's disagreement with Stephen immediately precedes the transcription of several letters from Bishop Dionysius of Alexandria (d. 264/5) which relate that prelate's opposition to rebaptism.

QUESTION 6: THAT DAVID CURSED THE MOUNTAINS OF GILBOA.[1]

You have asked about the words with which David was lamenting that Saul and his son Jonathan had been killed, where he seems to curse even the mountains of Gilboa in which they had been killed, wondering how [these words] might be consistent with the time or the mystery of the Lord's passion, in such a way that (as you write) in the responsories on Holy Sabbath before Easter they are spoken throughout all the churches as if in memory of the same passion;[2] for how can an impious king, who was destroyed by enemies on account of his own wickedness, [pre]figure the innocent death[3] of Christ the King, *who committed no sin, and no deceit was found in his mouth?*[4] You must understand, then, that Saul, who deserved to be killed by enemies after having been anointed with the sacred chrism on account of which he too was called 'the Lord's christ', actually does point to the death that the true Christ deigned to undergo [although he was] without fault.[5] The mountains of Gilboa upon which he perished suggest the lofty designs with which the Jewish people rebelled against the Author of life.[6] For this reason Gilboa is properly interpreted as 'wallowing' or 'descent'.[7] For [the Jews who put Christ to death] were wallowing in the squalour of sins, in accordance with that [saying] of Proverbs, *The sow is washed to wallow in the mire.*[8] Straying from the rectitude of the salutary way, they had already been descending to things below—that is, to this world's base[9] pleasures, on account of which they did not hesitate to betray the King of heaven and earth unto death. Because of this, it was justly

---

1 2 Sam. 1:19-27

2 The reference is to the pseudo-Gregorian responsories for the first nocturn in the liturgy of Holy Saturday (*PL* 78: 768A); see Jones (1969-70), 149, n. 114; Frank (1974); and Henderson (1980), 29, n. 48.

3 Gorman: *mortem*

4 1 Pet. 2:22; cf. Isa. 53:9

5 *christus*; literally, 'anointed one'. 2 Sam. 1:21 (Vulg.) refers to the shield of Saul having been cast away on the mountains of Gilboa 'as though he had not been anointed (*unctus*) with oil.' Bede also interpreted Saul's death as a type of the death of Christ in *In Sam.* 2 (*CCSL* 119: 92, 1001-6), where he identified his authority as Gregory the Great *Moral.* 4, Praef., 4 (*CCSL* 143: 161, 117-18). Much of what follows in Bede's exposition of Question 6 is also reminiscent of that passage in Gregory's work.

6 Gorman's edition provides this sentence, omitted in *PL*.

7 Jerome *Nom.*, 1 Reg. G (*CCSL* 72: 104, 27)

8 2 Pet. 2:22. Bede indicates that Proverbs is the source of this saying, but only the first half of this verse (about the dog returning to its vomit) actually comes from Prov. 26:11.

9 Gorman: *infima*

wished for them that they should receive neither dew nor rain from heaven,[1] which today we see fulfilled in actual fact, inasmuch as the heavenly grace which has deserted them has been transferred to the people of the Gentiles. Isaiah also warned that this would happen when on the Lord's behalf he spoke of them under the figure of the vineyard: *And I will command the clouds that they should rain no rain upon it.*[2] Which is to say openly: 'I will command all the apostles and apostolic men that they should preach the word of life to them no more, but leave them—unworthy as they are of the watering of the heavenly word which they have stubbornly rejected—to be empty in their own barrenness and fit to be burned in perpetual fire.'

Nor should it seem absurd to you that the bad actions of the reprobate should signify something good, or on the other hand that the good works of the righteous should bear a contrary signification. For you should read the *Morals* [written by] the saintly Pope Gregory, in which he explained [459]
how blessed Job uttered a curse against his own day, saying: *Let the day perish in which I was born,* and so forth,[3] and you will see that it is very common in the Scriptures both that the deeds of bad persons should be taken in signification of good things, and the deeds of good persons in signification of bad things.[4] Accordingly, in the case of Uriah, the most faithful soldier of King David, [Gregory] interpreted his most pious and innocent works and sayings in a bad signification, and on the contrary David himself in his greatest crime in a good signification.[5] Otherwise, if good could not be signified by bad things, nor bad by the good, it would never be permissible to write with black ink, and it would always be necessary to write in shining gold that *God is light and in him there is no darkness;*[6] nor could the names of Absalom and Doeg, those reprobate persons, be written in red in the titles of the Psalms,[7] but only in black ink.

---

1 2 Sam. 1:21

2 Isa. 5:6

3 Job 3:3. Commenting on this verse, Gregory the Great compares it with other curses found in Scripture, including the curse against the mountains of Gilboa in 2 Sam. 1:19-27, which he interprets as a condemnation of the arrogance of the Jews who killed Christ; see *Moral.* 4, Praef., 4 (*CCSL* 143: 161, 104-29).

4 Gregory the Great *Hom. in euang.* 7, 4 (*PL* 76: 1102C); cf. Bede *In Gen.* 4 (*CCSL* 118A: 236, 1515-16); *In Sam.* 2, 10, 25 (*CCSL* 119: 92, 995-8); *In Tob.* (*CCSL* 119B: 5, 3-5)

5 Gregory the Great *Moral.* 3, 28, 55 (*CCSL* 143: 148, 7 - 150, 66); cf. Bede *In Gen.* 4 (*CCSL* 118A: 236, 1519-20)

6 1 John 1:5; cf. Bede *In Sam.* 2 (*CCSL* 119: 92, 98-1001); *In Tob.* (*CCSL* 119B: 5, 5-6)

7 Absalom, the treacherous son of David whose rebellion against his father is recounted in 2 Sam. 15-18, is mentioned in the opening ascription to Pss. 3 (Vulg. 3:1) and 143 (Vulg. 142:1); Doeg, the Edomite who betrayed David to Saul in 1 Sam. 22:9-10, appears in the opening ascription to Ps. 52 (Vulg. 51:1). It was customary in early medieval manuscripts to rubricate the titles of the Psalms, so that the names of Absalom and Doeg would often have been inscribed with red ink.

Therefore, just as in the pages of books we can figure both bad things and good things with any colour we please without any censure, so also in the case of significations can good things and bad things be most rightly expressed by means of any human actions. However, it happens much more often, and is much sweeter to hear, that good things are figured by good things and bad things by bad. But just as it is not permitted in a wall painting[1] to depict a dark Ethiopian with white colouring, or a Saxon's white body or hair with black,[2] so in the recompense of merits each one will receive according to that one's own work, and however one is in deed, that is also how one will appear in countenance at the judgement; it will not matter at all what someone might have [pre]figured, but what that person will have done.

QUESTION 7: *YOUR SPEECH IS VEHEMENTLY FIRED.*[3]

Meanwhile, you have asked about what is in the psalm: **Your speech is vehemently fired.** This saying is also placed in Proverbs: *Every word of God is fiery.*[4] Therefore, learn that this saying ought to be taken far otherwise than it appears to sound. For surely it is customary to say that something is 'fired' when it is completely imbued and filled with fire; as iron and bronze, for example, are liquefied in the presence of fire, or perhaps I should say they are most full of fire. With this figure [of speech] it was said of Joseph: *The speech of the Lord fired him,*[5] that is, he was filled with the ardour and flame of divine virtue in such a way that he was totally enkindled by the Spirit of God and seemed as if he had been imbued with fire. Of this sort are those who were saying: *Were not our hearts burning within us while he was talking to us on the road and opening the Scriptures to us?*[6]

---

1 Meyvaert (1979), 70-4, explains that the wall paintings known to Bede, such as those at Wearmouth and Jarrow which he described in *Hist. abb.* 6 and 9 (ed. Plummer, 1: 369-70 and 373), were actually painted on panels which were then affixed to the walls of church buildings.

2 A full discussion of the classical and patristic background of this example is given in Henderson (1980), 9-13, where it is suggested that Bede was thinking of a wall painting in which dark Ethiopian and fair Saxon appeared together as representatives of diverse races paying homage to Christ at the time of the Last Judgement. Cf. Bede *In Sam.* 2 (*CCSL* 119: 93, 1044-9).

3 Ps. 119:140 (118:140); 'speech' = *eloquium*

4 Prov. 30:5; much of what follows here also appears in Bede's discussion of this verse in his commentary *In Prou.* 3 (*CCSL* 119B: 142, 43-64).

5 Ps. 105:19 (104:19)

6 Luke 24:32

But that the Lord's speech was declared to be 'fired', or the word of God 'fiery', ought not[1] to be taken as though it were being tried by fire in the same way that gold or any other metal is melted down by fire so that it wills not contain in itself any alien and useless impurity, and all that remains in it is made true and perfect, purged from every contagion of vices. For the speeches of the Lord contain in themselves the assurance of eternal blessings, since all of them are true and comprise nothing idle or useless. Hence the Lord says: *Not one iota, not one stroke will pass away from the law until all things are accomplished,*[2] lest it should be surmised that there is something there that is not perfected and permanent. That is how you must understand 'fired' as meaning 'tried by fire' or 'purged by fire'. Therefore, the same [word] in Greek—that is, πεπυρωμένον—was translated two [different ways] in Latin, as both 'fired' and 'tried by fire', according to the choice of the translators. For also where it is said, *The speeches of the Lord are tried by fire,*[3] in Greek the same single word is used, πεπυρωμένα.[4] From this word there was also derived [the verse], *You have tried us by fire,* for which some say: 'You have fired us.'[5] Now every word of God is fired, or tried by fire, because it is upheld by genuine and firm truth through the illumination of the Holy Spirit.

QUESTION 8: THAT DAVID RECOVERED THE ARK FROM THE HOUSE OF ABINADAB.[6]

And David again gathered all the elect of Israel, thirty thousand, and so forth.[7] In the history of the blessed king and prophet David where it is *[460]*
narrated that he recovered the ark of God, humility is shown to be approved,

1 Gorman: *non.* Bede is explaining here how the word of God can be described as having been tried by fire even though it never contained any impurity to begin with. Cf. the similar discussion in his *In cant.* 3 (*CCSL* 119B: 286, 604-6.

2 Matt. 5:18

3 Ps. 18:30 (17:31)

4 It is not clear how Bede would have known that this Greek word was used in the LXX, as that fact does not seem to have been provided by Augustine or Jerome, who were his usual sources for this sort of information.

5 Ps. 66:10 (65:10). Bede probably knew this variant in the Latin text of the psalm from his reading of Augustine, *Enarr. in ps.* 65, 16 (*CCSL* 39: 850, 7-10).

6 The biblical text under consideration here is 2 Sam. 6:1-23 (cf. 1 Chr. 15-16), an account of events during and immediately following David's triumphal installation of the ark of the covenant in his own royal city of Jerusalem. The ark was a portable wooden chest above which the Lord was considered to be invisibly enthroned (Exod. 25:10-22). It was captured by the Philistines in the time of Samuel and remained in enemy hands for seven months, after which it was returned to Israel and lodged for twenty years at the house of Abinadab (1 Sam. 4:11-7:2).

7 2 Sam. 6:1

pride condemned, and rashness punished. For David himself, who was not ashamed to dance humbly before the ark of the Lord,[1] soon afterwards deserved to receive the promise that the Son of God would be born from his own lineage.[2] And the consort who despised his act of humility did not merit to be fertilized with his seed, but suffered the penalties of perpetual sterility.[3] And the priest who touched the ark of God with ill-advised rashness was to make expiation for the guilt of his audacity with an untimely death[4]—which should cause us to consider that while any offender who approaches the body of the Lord is guilty of transgression,[5] if that person has undertaken vows as a priest he will be punished with death for having taken hold of that ark (namely, the figure of the Lord's body) with less reverence than it deserves.

But according to the allegory, David signifies Christ and the ark signifies the Church. Now David sought to bring the ark into his own city, but when something happened to prevent this he diverted it elsewhere for a while, and afterwards achieved what he had so greatly desired.[6] For when the Lord appeared in the flesh he preached the gospel to the children of Israel (that is, to his own people), but *blindness fell upon part of Israel, until the fullness of the Gentiles should come in, and so all Israel should be saved.*[7] But so that we might see these things more plainly one by one, **David gathered all the chosen ones of Israel, thirty thousand,**[8] because it was out of Israel that the Lord established the primitive Church—not out of all Israel, to be sure, but by associating the elect to himself. *For not all who are of Israel are Israelites, but the children of the promise are counted among the seed.*[9]

Those who are referred to as the 'thirty thousand' are those who are perfect in firmness of faith, work, and hope. For the number three pertains to faith on account of the confession of the Holy Trinity; ten to work, on account of the Decalogue of the law; and a thousand, on account of its perfection, to the hope of eternal life—to which there is nothing superior, just as there is no number greater than a thousand.[10] For if you say 'ten

1 2 Sam. 6:5
2 2 Sam. 7:11-16
3 2 Sam. 6:16, 20-3
4 2 Sam. 6:6-7
5 1 Cor. 11:27
6 2 Sam. 6:9-12
7 Rom. 11:25-6
8 2 Sam. 6:1
9 Rom. 9:6, 8; 'are counted' = *deputantur* (Old Latin); cf. Vulg. *aestimatur*
10 The largest number that can be written in Roman numerals with a single letter is one thousand, represented by 'M'.

thousand' or 'thirty thousand' or even 'a thousand thousand', you will not go beyond a thousand in enumerating it, but in your calculation you are multiplying it either by itself or (more frequently) by lesser numbers. Therefore, you must multiply three by ten, lest *faith without works* should be *dead*,[1] and you must multiply thirty again by a thousand, so that *faith which works through love*[2] may hope for its reward nowhere else than in heaven. Let the elect of Israel, then, suggest the people who believe, work, and hope rightly; and let the men of Judah who were with David[3] indicate those very apostles and teachers who cleave to Christ's side, as it were, more intimately. Accompanied by both of these hosts,[4] the Lord rejoices to bring the ark forward (that is, to extend the Church) and to introduce it into the hearts of those who had not believed. Now the ark is laid on a new cart[5] so that [the Church] might be immersed in the grace of the New Testament when the minds [of the faithful] are renewed in baptism, and so that it might be commanded to preserve *new wine in new wineskins*.[6] Surely the ark was previously in **the house of Abinadab who lived in Gabaa**[7] because the same faith of the Church which is now preached was also flourishing before the time of the Lord's incarnation among those who imitated the devotion of the patriarchs and prophets. For Abinadab, whose name is interpreted as 'my willing father',[8] signifies either Abraham the father of the faith or Moses the lawgiver, both of whom keep the ark in Gabaa[9] because they fortify the hearts of believers with sublime examples of virtue. For this reason,[10] Gabaa (which is a place in the city of Kiriath-jearim[11]) is also interpreted as 'hill'.[12] As they bore the ark outdoors, therefore, David and all Israel played before the Lord on various kinds of musical instruments,[13] because as soon as the new grace begins to be proclaimed, the Lord invites everyone to show forth praises of humility to God the Father by saying,

1 James 2:26

2 Gal. 5:6; 'love' = *dilectionem* (Old Latin); cf. Vulg. *caritatem*

3 2 Sam. 6:2, Vulg.

4 'both of these hosts' = *utroque stipatus exercitu*, which echoes 2 Sam. 6:2, in which David invokes the name of the Lord 'of hosts' (*exercituum*)

5 2 Sam. 6:3. Bede's allegorical interpretation emphasizes the cart's newness, but he also seems to have in mind its utility for transporting objects across water, and for hauling goods.

6 Matt. 9:17

7 2 Sam. 6:3

8 Jerome *Nom.* 1 Reg. A (*CCSL* 72: 102, 11-12)

9 2 Sam. 6:4

10 I.e., because of the 'sublime' examples of virtue

11 Kiriath-jearim is identified as the location of Abinadab's house in 1 Sam. 6:21-7:2.

12 Jerome *Nom.* 1 Reg. G (*CCSL* 72: 104, 24)

13 2 Sam. 6:5

Whoever serves me must follow me,[1] and by giving *to one through the Spirit the utterance of wisdom, to another the utterance of knowledge, to another [various] kinds of tongues, to another the gift of healing,* and so forth.[2]

But as the ark was going forward with these and other such kinds of gifts (that is, as the primitive Church was increasing), it came to the threshing floor of Nacon[3]—that is, to the threshing floor which had been prepared, namely, the Church of the Gentiles which was to be consecrated in the true faith, and concerning which John [the Baptist] says, *And he will thoroughly cleanse his threshing floor.*[4] It was here that the priest who recklessly
[461] touched the ark as if to straighten it was soon afterwards killed by a blow from the Lord.[5] For as long as the Jewish people detest the Gentiles, they deprive themselves of the gift of salvation; as long as they want to mingle the law with the gospel, they forfeit the grace of them both. It says: **And he took hold of it, for the oxen shook it.**[6] Surely the kicking of the oxen is to be interpreted spiritually as the preachers of the gospel acting quite freely in faith, and not proceeding according to the custom of the law, but giving spiritual interpretation to its sabbaths, new moons, circumcision, and sacrifices. The ones who took hold of them to correct them as if they were wavering were those *who came down from Judea and were teaching the brothers, 'Unless you are circumcised according to the custom of Moses, you cannot be saved,'*[7] and those of whom James says to Paul: *You see, brother, how many thousands there are among the Jews who have believed, and they are all zealous for the law.*[8]

Because the priest had been killed, **David did not want to take the ark of the Lord to his own home in the city of David, but he took it into the house of Obed-edom the Gittite.**[9] The reason for this was that when the Jews rejected the word, the apostles were taken away from them and sent to the Gentiles who needed to be instructed, in order that the preaching might not do further injury to those who heard it and did not receive it. For the same reason, the place of Nacon's threshing floor, which shows the Gentiles' faith being prepared for the Lord's grace, is called **the striking**

1 John 12:26

2 1 Cor. 12:8-10; 'healings' = *curationum* (Old Latin); cf. Vulg. *sanitatum*. Bede omits several items in Paul's catalogue of spiritual gifts.

3 2 Sam. 6:6

4 Matt. 3:12; cf. Jerome *Loc.*'N' Reg. (*PL* 23: 914A)

5 2 Sam. 6:6-8

6 2 Sam. 6:6

7 Acts 15:1

8 Acts 21:20; Gorman: *in Judaeis* ('among the Jews'), rather than *PL*: *in Judaea* ('in Judea')

9 2 Sam. 6:10

of Uzzah,[1] evidently because it is through the transgression of those [Jews] that salvation has come to the Gentiles. For Obed-edom, whose name is interpreted as 'serving man',[2] is surely that one of whom the Lord says to the Father: *You will make me the head of the Gentiles; a people whom I have not known has served me.*[3] In the same place, he also anticipates the casting off of the Jews as if it were the death of Uzzah, when he says: *You will deliver me from the contradictions of the people.*[4] And the name of [Obed-edom's] city is appropriate, for Gath is interpreted as 'winepress', signifying the cross on which the *true vine* deigned[5] to be trampled upon and squeezed out.[6] Accordingly, the whole people of the Gentiles can rightly be called residents of Gath, for it says: *But may I never glory, except in the cross of our Lord Jesus Christ.*[7]

Now the three months during which the ark tarried in [Gath][8] are faith, hope, and charity.[9] For just as a month is filled with days, so does each one of the virtues come to its perfection step by step. These months do not end until *the fullness of the Gentiles* comes in.[10]

At last, David returns to bring the ark into the city of David,[11] because the Lord will turn the hearts of the parents to the children through the preaching of Enoch and Elijah.[12] And he offers oxen and rams[13]—that is,

1 2 Sam. 6:8

2 Jerome *Nom.* 2 Reg. O (*CCSL* 72: 108, 21)

3 Ps. 18:43 (17:44-5)

4 Ps. 18:43 (17:44)

5 Gorman: *dignata*

6 Obed-edom 'the Gittite' was a citizen of the city of Gath. For the interpretation of Gath as 'winepress', see Jerome *Nom.* Ios. G (*CCSL* 72: 94, 25). For Jesus as 'true vine', see John 15:5. The interpretation of the winepress of Isa. 63:3 as a figural way of speaking of the cross of Christ is traditional; see, e.g., Jerome *In Es.* 17 (*CCSL* 73A: 723, 26-50).

7 Gal. 6:14

8 2 Sam. 6:11

9 1 Cor. 13:13

10 Rom. 11:25

11 2 Sam. 6:12

12 Mal. 4:5-6; 'the hearts of the parents to the children' = *corda patrum in filios* (Old Latin); cf. Vulg. *cor patrum ad filios* = 'the heart of the parents toward the children'. This biblical text indicates that it is the prophet Elijah who will turn the hearts of parents and children toward one another before the coming day of the Lord, and early Christian tradition identifed him as one of the 'two witnesses' of Rev. 11:3-6. The author of that book probably had in mind Elijah and Moses, but Christian apocryphal literature and many patristic authors often identified the other witness as Enoch, who like Elijah was thought to have been assumed bodily into heaven without suffering death (Gen. 5:24 and Heb. 11:5; 2 Kgs. 2:11, Ecclus. 48:9-13, and 1 Macc. 2:58). On this traditional identification of the 'two witnesses', see Black (1978) and Bauckham (1985). For its clear expression in an author well known to Bede, see Cassiodorus, *Exp. in pss.* 51, 11 and 103, 11 (*CCSL* 97: 477, 230-3; 98: 930, 275-8).

13 2 Sam. 6:13

he crowns with the blood of martyrdom those who tread the Lord's threshing floor and those who exercise leadership among his sheep, and he openly manifests both himself and the example of his incarnation and passion, in which the Jews have not yet believed.

And this is what it signifies that **David was girded with a linen ephod:**[1] linen, because it comes from the earth and through much labour is made white and fashioned into clothing,[2] shows the truth of human flesh which is triumphant amidst scourgings.

But among those who are bringing in the ark, only **Michal the daughter of Saul** is missing from all those who are rejoicing and resounding with songs at the entrance of the heavenly ark.[3] Indeed, she even looks down upon David's humility from on high, because at the end of the world when the Jews believe, there will be many people who will follow Christ in profession, but Antichrist in deed. This accords well with the fact that the same Michal—whose name is interpreted as 'all water'[4] since she must [pre]figure the instability of those who are carnal—is called not 'the wife of David' but 'the daughter of Saul', because those who serve Christ in name only will never be crowned in his kingdom but will rather be damned with the same anathema as were his persecutors whom they have imitated.

But although the perverse are enraged and despise the humility of the Church, the ark of the Lord nevertheless proceeds to its place and is set **in the midst of the tabernacle that David had pitched for it**[5]—that is, the faith of the Church is preached, makes progress, and is introduced into the hearts of all those whom the Lord has preordained *to life eternal.*[6] David offers burnt offerings and peace-offerings before the Lord: Christ, *who is at the right hand of the Father, and who intercedes for us,*[7] commends the faith and devotion of the Church to the Father. Following David's example, he blesses those who are faithful and humble and feeds them with the food of the saving mystery.[8] He distributes **to each of them the one cake of that bread** *which comes down from heaven and gives life to* this *world;*[9] **and a**
[462] **piece of roasted meat** from that fatted calf which was slaughtered and

1 2 Sam. 6:14
2 Isidore *Etymol.* 19, 27, 1 (ed. Lindsay, vol. 2); Pliny *Nat. hist.* 19, 1, 5 (*LCL* 5: 422)
3 2 Sam. 6:16
4 Jerome *Nom.* 1 Reg. M (*CCSL* 72: 104, 8-9)
5 2 Sam. 6:17
6 Acts 13:48
7 Rom. 8:34; 'who is...and who' = *qui...qui et* (Old Latin); cf. Vulg.: *qui et...qui etiam*
8 2 Sam. 6:18-19
9 John 6:33

roasted in the fire of suffering for the younger son upon his return to the father,[1] saying, *My strength is dried up like a potsherd;*[2] **and fine flour fried with oil**, namely, the cleanest flesh free from the stain of sin, but baked on the frying-pan of the cross on account of his abounding desire to save humankind. And rightly was there given one cake of bread and one piece of roasted meat, because there is *one Lord, one faith, one baptism, one God and Father of all.*[3] Otherwise, the faithful receive these gifts when in Christ *we, though many, are one bread, one body,*[4] and when, by punishing the lasciviousness of the flesh and subjecting it to servitude,[5] they cook it in the fire of the Holy Spirit and through love of neighbor actually make fervid the fruits of good works enriched by the oil of mercy.

By contrast, the daughter of Saul who goes into the bedchamber of the king in vain does not produce fruit by conceiving any offspring,[6] because those who receive the word of God only with the ear and without the progeny of good works await the day of perpetual death.

1 Luke 15:23-4
2 Ps. 22:15 (21:16)
3 Eph. 4:5-6
4 1 Cor. 10:17
5 1 Cor. 9:27
6 2 Sam. 6:23

SELECT BIBLIOGRAPHY

PRIMARY SOURCES

Adamnan, *De locis sanctis*, ed. L. Bieler, *CCSL* 175 (Turnhout, 1965); transl. D. Meehan, in *De locis sanctis (Scriptores Latini Hiberniae* 3; Dublin, 1958; reprinted 1983).

________, *Vita sancti Columbae*, ed. and transl. A. O. Anderson and M. O. Anderson, *Oxford Medieval Texts* (Oxford, 1991); also transl. R. Sharpe (London, 1995).

Alcuin, *Epistola sanctissimis in Sancti Petri ecclesia fratribus*, ed. A. W. Haddan and W. Stubbs, *Councils and Ecclesiastical Documents Relating to Great Britain and Ireland* 3 (Oxford, 1871).

Aldhelm, *Epistulae*, ed. R. Ehwald, *MGH AA* 15 (Berlin, 1919); transl. M. Lapidge and M. Herren, in *Aldhelm: The Prose Works* (Cambridge and Totowa, N.J., 1979).

Ambrose, *De Abraham*, ed. in *PL* 14.

________, *De excessu fratris Satyri*, ed. O. Faller, *CSEL* 63 (Vienna, 1955).

________, *De Tobia*, ed. L. M. Zucker (*Catholic University of America Patristic Studies* 35; Washington, D. C., 1933).

________, *Expositio Psalmi CXVIII*, ed. M. Petschenig, *CSEL* 62 (Vienna, 1913).

________, *In Lucam*, ed. M. Adriaen, *CCSL* 14 (Turnhout, 1957).

Pseudo-Ambrose, *De XLII mansionibus filiorum Israel*, ed. in *PL* 17.

Augustine, *De ciuitate Dei*, ed. B. Dombart and A. Kalb, *CCSL* 47-8 (Turnhout, 1955); transl. H. Bettenson (*Penguin Classics*; Harmondsworth, 1972).

________, *De doctrina christiana*, ed. and transl. R. P. H. Green, *Oxford Early Christian Texts* (Oxford, 1995).

________, *De sermone domini in monte*, ed. A. Mutzenbecher, *CCSL* 35 (Turnhout, 1967); transl. D. J. Kavanagh, *FOTC* 11 (New York, 1951).

________, *Enchiridion ad Laurentium de fide et spe et caritate*, ed. E. Evans, *CCSL* 46 (Turnhout, 1966); transl. L. A. Arand (*ACW* 3; New York, 1947).

________, *Enarrationes in psalmos*, ed. D. E. Dekkers and J. Fraipont, *CCSL* 38-40 (Turnhout, 1956); transl. A. C. Coxe, *NPNF*, 1st ser., 8 (New York, 1888; reprinted Grand Rapids, 1950).

________, *Sermones*, ed. in *PL* 38; transl. E. Hill (New Rochelle, N.Y., 1990-).

________, *Quaestiones euangeliorum*, ed. A. Mutzenbecher, *CCSL* 44B (Turnhout, 1980).

Pseudo-Augustine, *Sermo* 203, ed. in *PL* 39.

Bede, *De arte metrica*, ed. C. B. Kendall and M. H. King, *CCSL* 123A (Turnhout, 1975); also ed. and transl. C. B. Kendall (*Bibliotheca Germanica*, ser. nova, 2; Dudweiler, 1991).

________, *De eo quod ait Isaias*, ed. in *PL* 94.

________, *De locis sanctis*, ed. J. Fraipont, *CCSL* 175 (Turnhout, 1965); ed. and transl. J. A. Giles, in *The Complete Works of Venerable Bede*, vol. 4 (London, 1843-4).

________, *De mansionibus filiorum Israel*, ed. in *PL* 94.

________, *De natura rerum*, ed. C. W. Jones, *CCSL* 123A (Turnhout, 1975).

________, *De octo quaestionibus*, ed. in *PL* 93.

________, *De schematibus et tropis*, ed. C. B. Kendall, *CCSL* 123A (Turnhout, 1975); transl. G. H. Tanenhaus, in *Quarterly Journal of Speech* 48 (1962), 237-53; reprinted in *Readings in Medieval Rhetoric*, ed. J. M. Miller et al. (Bloomington, 1973); also ed. and transl. C. B. Kendall (*Bibliotheca Germanica*, ser. nova, 2; Dudweiler, 1991).

________, *De tabernaculo*, ed. D. Hurst, *CCSL* 119A (Turnhout, 1969); transl. A. G. Holder (*TTH* 18; Liverpool, 1994).

________, *De templo*, ed. D. Hurst, *CCSL* 119A (Turnhout, 1969); transl. S. Connolly (*TTH* 21; Liverpool, 1995).

________, *De temporibus*, ed. C. W. Jones and T. Mommsen, *CCSL* 123C (Turnhout, 1980).

________, *De temporum ratione*, ed. C. W. Jones and T. Mommsen, *CCSL* 123B (Turnhout, 1977).

________, *Epistola ad Albinum*, ed. C. Plummer, in *Venerabilis Baedae opera historica*, 1 (Oxford, 1896; reprinted 1946, 1956).

________, *Epistola ad Ecgbertum Episcopum*, ed. C. Plummer, in *Venerabilis Baedae opera historica*, 1 (Oxford, 1896; reprinted 1946, 1956); transl. D. H. Farmer, in *Ecclesiastical History of the English People, with Bede's Letter to Egbert and Cuthbert's Letter on the Death of Bede* (*Penguin Classics*; London, 1990); also transl. J. McClure and R. Collins, in *Bede: The Ecclesiastical History of the English People* (*The World's Classics*; Oxford, 1994).

________, *Epistola ad Helmuualdum*, ed. C. W. Jones, *CCSL* 123C (Turnhout, 1980).

________, *Epistola ad Pleguinam*, ed. C. W. Jones, *CCSL* 123C (Turnhout, 1980).

________, *Epistola ad VVicthedum*, ed. C. W. Jones, *CCSL* 123C (Turnhout, 1980).

________, *Expositio Actuum Apostolorum*, ed. M. L. W. Laistner, *CCSL* 121 (Turnhout, 1983); transl. L. T. Martin (*Cistercian Studies Series* 117; Kalamazoo, 1989).

________, *Historia abbatum*, ed. C. Plummer, in *Venerabilis Baedae opera historica*, 1 (Oxford, 1896; reprinted 1946, 1956); transl. D. H. Farmer, in *The Age of Bede* (*Penguin Classics*; Harmondsworth, 1983); also ed. and transl. J. E. King, *LCL* 2 (Cambridge, Mass. and London, 1930).

________, *Historia ecclesiastica gentis Anglorum*, ed. and transl. B. Colgrave and R. A. B. Mynors (Oxford, 1969; reprinted with corrections, 1991); also transl. L. Sherley-Price, revised by R. E. Latham (*Penguin Classics*; Harmondsworth, 1968; reprinted London, 1990).

________, *Homiliae euangelii*, ed. D. Hurst, *CCSL* 122 (Turnhout, 1965); transl. L. T. Martin and D. Hurst, 2 vols. (*Cistercian Studies Series* 110-11; Kalamazoo, 1991).

________, *In Apocalypsin*, ed. in *PL* 93; transl. E. Marshall (Oxford, 1878).

________, *In Cantica Canticorum*, ed. D. Hurst, *CCSL* 119B (Turnhout, 1983).

________, *In Esram et Neemiam*, ed. D. Hurst, *CCSL* 119A (Turnhout, 1969).

________, *In Habacuc*, ed. J. E. Hudson, *CCSL* 119B (Turnhout, 1983); transl. S. Connolly (Dublin, 1997).

________, *In Lucam*, ed. D. Hurst, *CCSL* 120 (Turnhout, 1960).

________, *In primam partem Samuhelis*, ed. D. Hurst, *CCSL* 119 (Turnhout, 1962).

________, *In principium Genesim*, ed. C. W. Jones, *CCSL* 118A (Turnhout, 1967).

________, *In Regum librum XXX quaestiones*, ed. D. Hurst, *CCSL* 119 (Turnhout, 1962).

________, *In Tobiam*, ed. D. Hurst, *CCSL* 119B (Turnhout, 1983); transl. S. Connolly (Dublin, 1997).

________, *Nomina regionum atque locorum*, ed. M. L. W. Laistner, *CCSL* 121 (Turnhout, 1983).

________, *Retractatio in Actus Apostolorum*, ed. M. L. W. Laistner, *CCSL* 121 (Turnhout, 1983).

________, *Vita sancti Cuthberti metrica,* ed. W. Jaager, *Palestra* 198 (Leipzig, 1935).

________, *Vita sancti Cuthberti prosaica*, ed. and transl. B. Colgrave (Cambridge, 1940); also transl. J. F. Webb, in *The Age of Bede* (*Penguin Classics*; Harmondsworth, 1983).

Biblia Sacra iuxta uulgatam uersionem, ed. R. Weber, 2 vols. (Stuttgart, 1969; 2nd ed., 1975).

Cassiodorus, *Expositio in Psalmorum*, ed. M. Adriaen, *CCSL* 97-8 (Turnhout, 1958); transl. P. G. Walsh, *ACW* 51-3 (New York, 1990-1).

Cuthbert, *Epistola de obitu Bedae*, ed. and transl. B. Colgrave and R. Mynors, in *Bede's Ecclesiastical History of the English People* (*Oxford Medieval Texts*; Oxford, 1969).

Egeria, *Itinerarium ad loca sancta*, ed. A. Franceschini and R. Weber, *CCSL* 175 (Turnhout, 1965); transl. J. Wilkinson (London, 1973).

Pseudo-Eucherius, *De situ Hierusolimae*, ed. J. Fraipont, *CCSL* 175 (Turnhout, 1965).

Gelasian Sacramentary, ed. L. C. Mohlberg, L. Eizenhofer, and P. Siffrin, *Liber sacramentorum Romanae Aeclesiae ordinis anni circuli* (*Rerum Ecclesiasticarum documenta—Series maior: Fontes* 4; Rome, 1960); baptismal rites transl. E. C. Whitaker, in *Documents of the Baptismal Liturgy*, 2nd ed., *Alcuin Club Collections* 42 (London, 1970).

Gregory of Tours, *Historia Francorum*, ed. W. Arndt, *MGH SRM* 1 (Hannover, 1885); transl. Lewis Thorpe (Harmondsworth, 1974).

Gregory the Great, *Dialogorum libri quatuor de miraculis patrum italicorum*, ed. A. de Vogüé, *SC* 251, 260, 265 (Paris, 1978-80), transl. O. Z. Zimmerman (*FOTC* 39; New York, 1959).

________, *Homiliae in euangelia*, ed. in *PL* 76; transl. D. Hurst (*Cistercian Studies Series* 123; Kalamazoo, 1990).

________, *Homiliae in Ezechielem*, ed. M. Adriaen, *CCSL* 142 (Turnhout, 1971); also ed. (with French transl.) C. Morel, *SC* 327, 352, 360 (Paris, 1986-90); transl. T. Gray (Etna, Calif., 1990).

________, *In librum I Regum*, ed. P. Verbraken, *CCSL* 144 (Turnhout, 1963).

________, *Moralia in Iob*, ed. M. Adriaen, *CCSL* 143, 143A, 143B (Turnhout, 1979-85); to date only Books 1-16 have appeared in a new ed. (with French transl.) by R. Gillet, *SC* 32, 212, 221 (Paris, 1952-1975; 2nd ed. of vol. 32, 1975); transl. in *Library of Fathers of the Holy Catholic Church* 18, 21, 23, 31 (Oxford, 1844-50).

________, *Regulae pastoralis liber*, ed. F. Rommel with French transl. C. Morel, *SC* 381-2 (Paris, 1992); transl. H. Davis, *ACW* 11 (Westminster, Md., 1950).

Pseudo-Gregory the Great, *Liber responsalis*, ed. in *PL* 78.

Hegesippus, *Historia*, ed. V. Ussani, *CSEL* 66 (Vienna, 1932).

Herodotus, *Historiae*, Greek text ed. and transl. A. D. Godley, *LCL*, 4 vols. (Cambridge, Mass. and London, 1960).

Hilary of Poitiers, *In Matthaeum*, ed. (with French transl.) J. Doignon, *SC* 254, 258 (Paris, 1978-9).

Isidore, *De ecclesiasticis officiis*, ed. C. M. Lawson, CCSL 113 (Turnhout, 1989).

________, *Etymologiae*, ed. W. M. Lindsay, 2 vols., (*Scriptorum classicorum bibliotheca Oxoniensis*; Oxford, 1911).

________, *Quaestiones in Vetus Testamentum*, ed. in *PL* 83.

Jacobus de Voragine, *Legenda Aurea*, ed. T. Graesse, 2 vols. (Osnabrück, 1965; reprint from 3rd ed., 1890); transl. W. G. Ryan, 2 vols. (Princeton, 1991).

Jerome, *De nominibus hebraicis*, ed. P. de Lagarde, *CCSL* 72 (Turnhout, 1959).

________, *Epistulae*, ed. I. Hilberg, *CSEL* 54-6 (Vienna, 1910-18); also ed. (with French transl.) J. Labourt (Paris, 1949-63).

________, *In Danielem*, ed. F. Glorie, *CCSL* 75A (Turnhout, 1964).

________, *In Esaiam*, ed. M. Adriaen, *CCSL* 73 and 73A (Turnhout, 1963).

________, *In Hieremiam*, ed. S. Reiter, *CCSL* 74 (Turnhout, 1960).

________, *In Sophoniam*, ed. M. Adriaen, *CCSL* 76A (Turnhout, 1970).

________, *Liber locorum*, ed. in *PL* 23.

________, *Prologus in libro Regum*, in *Biblia Sacra* (1975).

________, *Hebraicae quaestiones in libro Geneseos*, ed. P. de Lagarde, *CCSL* 72 (Turnhout, 1959).

John Chrysostom, *Homiliae in Epistolam secundam ad Corinthios*, ed. in *PG* 61; transl. J. Ashworth in *Library of the Fathers of the Holy Catholic Church* 27 (Oxford, 1848); reprinted with revisions in *NPNF*, 1st ser., 12 (New York, 1889).

Josephus, *Antiquitates Judaicae*, Latin version ed. J. Froben in *Opera omnia* (Basel, 1524); Latin version of Books 1-5 ed. F. Blatt in *The Latin Josephus* (*Acta Jutlandica* 30; Copenhagen, 1958); Greek text ed. and transl. H. St. J. Thackeray, *LCL*, 6 vols. (London and New York, 1926).

________, *Bellum Judaicum*, Greek text ed. and transl. H. St. J. Thackeray, *LCL*, 2 vols. (London and New York, 1926).

________, *Vita*, Greek text ed. and transl. H. St. J. Thackeray, *LCL* (London and New York, 1926).

Juvencus, *Euangeliorum libri quattuor*, ed. J. Huemer, *CSEL* 24 (Vienna, 1891).

Lactantius, *De mortibus persecutorum*, ed. and transl. J. L. Creed (Oxford, 1984).

Letter of Aristeas, ed. H. St. J. Thackeray, in H. B. Swete, *An Introduction to the Old Testament in Greek* (2nd ed.; Cambridge, 1914); transl. R. J. H. Shutt, in J. H. Charlesworth, *The Old Testament Pseudepigrapha*, vol. 2 (Garden City, N.Y., 1985).

Lupus of Ferrières, *Epistolae*, ed. E. Dümmler, *MGH Epp.* 6:1 (Berlin, 1902).

Origen, *De principiis*, ed. (with French transl.) H. Crouzel and M. Simonetti, *SC* 268 (Paris, 1980); transl. G. W. Butterworth (London, 1936; reprinted London and Gloucester, Mass., 1973).

________, *Homiliae in Numeros*, ed. W. A. Baehrens, *GCS* 30 (Leipzig, 1921).

Philo, *De congressu eruditionis gratia*, ed. and transl. F. H. Colson and G. H. Whitaker, *LCL* 4 (New York and London, 1932).

Pliny, *Naturalis historia*, ed. and transl. H. Rackham, W. H. S. Jones, and D. E. Eichholz, *LCL*, 10 vols. (Cambridge, Mass. and London, 1938-52).

Regula sancti Benedici, ed. T. Fry, O.S.B., in *RB 1980: The Rule of St. Benedict in Latin and English with Notes* (Collegeville, Minnesota: 1981).

Rufinus, *Historia ecclesiastica Eusebii*, ed. T. Mommsen, *GCS* 9 (1 vol. in 3 pts.; Leipzig, 1903-9).

Sedulius, *Carmen Paschale*, ed. J. Huemer, *CSEL* 10 (Vienna, 1885); Book 1, transl. R. A. Swanson, in *The Classical Journal* 52 (1957), 290-7.

Sulpicius Severus, *Epistulae*, ed. J. Fontaine, *SC* 133 (Paris: 1967).

Victorinus (Ps. Cyprianus), *De Pascha*, ed. W. Hartel, *CSEL* 3, pt. 3 (Vienna, 1871).

Vita Ceolfridi, ed. C. Plummer as *Historia abbatum auctore anonymo*, in *Venerabilis Baedae opera historica*, 1 (Oxford, 1896; reprinted 1946, 1956); transl. D. S. Boutflower (Sunderland, 1912); also transl. D. Whitelock, in *English Historical Documents*, 1 (London and New York, 1955; 2nd ed., 1979).

SECONDARY WORKS

R. J. Bauckham, 'Enoch and Elijah in the Coptic Apocalypse of Elijah', *Studia Patristica* 16 (1985), 69-76.

Bede and His World: The Jarrow Lectures, 2 vols. (Aldershot, 1994).

A. E. Bernstein, *The Formation of Hell: Death and Retribution in the Ancient and Early Christian Worlds* (Ithaca, 1993).

W. Berschin, '*Opus deliberatum ac perfectum*: Why Did the Venerable Bede Write a Second Prose Life of St. Cuthbert?', in Bonner et al. (1989), 95-102.

L. Bieler, 'Adamnan und Hegesipp', *Wiener Studien* 69 (1956), 344-9.

________, 'Ireland's Contribution to Northumbrian Culture', in Bonner (1976), 21-6.

B. Bischoff and M. Lapidge, *Biblical Commentaries from the Canterbury School of Theodore and Hadrian* (*Cambridge Studies in Anglo-Saxon England* 10; Cambridge, 1994).

M. Black, 'The 'Two Witnesses' of Rev. 11:3f in Jewish and Christian Apocalyptic Tradition', in *Donum Gentilicum: New Testament Studies in Honour of David Daube*, ed. E. Bammel, C. K. Barrett, and W. D. Davies (Oxford, 1978), 227-37.

A. Blaise, *Dictionnaire latin-français des auteurs chrétiens* (Turnhout, 1967).

G. Bonner, 'Bede and Medieval Civilization', *Anglo-Saxon England* 2 (1973), 71-90.

________, (ed.), *Famulus Christi: Essays in Commemoration of the Thirteenth Centenary of the Birth of the Venerable Bede* (London, 1976).

________, *Saint Bede in the Tradition of Western Apocalyptic Commentary* (Jarrow Lecture, 1966); reprinted in *Bede and His World* (1994).

G. Bonner, D. Rollason, C. Stancliffe (eds.), *St. Cuthbert: His Cult and His Community to A.D. 1200* (Woodbridge, Suffolk, 1989).

A. E. Brooke, N. McLean, and H. St. John Thackeray (eds.), *The Old Testament in Greek*, Vol. 3, Pt. 1 (Cambridge, 1940).

F. Brown, S. Driver, and C. Briggs, *A Hebrew and English Lexicon of the Old Testament* (Oxford, 1972).

G. H. Brown, *Bede the Venerable* (*Twayne's English Authors Series* 443; Boston, 1987).

R. L. S. Bruce-Mitford, *The Art of the Codex Amiatinus* (Jarrow Lecture, 1967); reprinted in *Journal of the Royal Archaeological Association* 32 (1969), 1-25; reprinted in *Bede and His World* (1994).

F. Cabrol and H. Leclercq, *Dictionnaire d'archéologie chrétienne et de liturgie*, 15 vols (Paris, 1907-53).

D. Capelle, 'Le rôle théologique de Bède le Vénérable', *Studia Anselmiana* 6 (1936), 1-40.

M. T. A. Carroll, *The Venerable Bede: His Spiritual Teachings* (*Catholic University of America Studies in Mediaeval History*, n. s. 9; Washington, D.C., 1946).

E. A. Clark, *The Origenist Controversy: The Cultural Construction of an Early Christian Debate* (Princeton, 1992).

J. Davidse, 'The Sense of History in the Works of the Venerable Bede', *Studi Medievali* 23 (1982): 647-95.

H. de Lubac, *Exégèse médiévale: les quatre sens de l'Écriture*, 2 vols. in 4 pts. (Paris, 1959-64).

M. Deanesly, *The Pre-Conquest Church in England* (London, 1961).

A. C. Dionisotti, 'On Bede, Grammars, and Greek', *Revue Bénédictine* 92 (1982), 111-41.

R. K. Emmerson and B. McGinn (eds.), *The Apocalypse in the Middle Ages* (Ithaca and London, 1992).

T. M. Finn, *Early Christian Baptism and the Catechumenate: Italy, North Africa, and Egypt* (*Message of the Fathers of the Church* 6; Collegeville, Minn., 1992).

B. Fischer, *Lateinische Bibelhandschriften im frühen Mittelalter* (*Vetus Latina: Aus der Geschichte der lateinischen Bibel* 11; Freiburg, 1985).

H. Frank, 'Die Bezeugung eines Karsamstagsresponsoriums durch Beda Venerabilis', *Archiv für Liturgiewissenschaft* 16 (1974), 150-3.

K. Froehlich, *Biblical Interpretation in the Early Church (Sources of Early Christian Thought*; Philadelphia, 1984).

V. P. Furnish, *II Corinthians* (*The Anchor Bible* 32A; Garden City, N.Y., 1964).

T. Fry, O.S.B. et al., *RB 1980: The Rule of St. Benedict in Latin and English with Notes* (Collegeville, Minnesota, 1981).

K. Furrer, '*Adamnanus. Abt von Jona* (P. Geyer)', *Theologische Literaturzeitung* 18 (1896): 472-3.

S. Gelen (ed.), *Opera d. Joannis Chrysostomi . . .*, 5 vols. (Basel, 1547).

M. M. Gorman, 'Bede's *VIII Quaestiones* and Carolingian Biblical Scholarship', *Revue Bénédictine* (forthcoming).

J. Gray, *I & II Kings: A Commentary*, 2nd ed. (*The Old Testament Library*; London, 1970).

A. Heisenberg, *Grabeskirche und Apostelkirche, zwei Basiliken Konstantins*, 2 vols. (Leipzig, 1908).

G. Henderson, *Bede and the Visual Arts* (Jarrow Lecture, 1980); reprinted in *Bede and His World* (1994).

A. G. Holder, 'Allegory and History in Bede's Interpretation of Sacred Architecture', *American Benedictine Review* 40 (1989), 115-31.

________, 'Bede and the Tradition of Patristic Exegesis', *Anglican Theological Review* 72 (1990), 399-411.

P. Hunter Blair, *The World of Bede* (Cambridge, 1970; reprinted New York, 1971 and London, 1990).

C. W. Jones, 'Some Introductory Remarks on Bede's Commentary on Genesis', *Sacris Erudiri* 19 (1969-70), 115-98.

J. N. D. Kelly, *Jerome: His Life, Writings, and Controversies* (London, 1975).

M. L. W. Laistner, 'Introduction', in Bede, *Expositio Actuum Apostolorum et Retractatio*, ed. M. L. W. Laistner (Cambridge, Mass., 1939), xi-xlv.

________, 'The Library of the Venerable Bede', in Thompson (1935), 237-66; reprinted in *Intellectual Heritage of the Early Middle Ages*, ed. C. G. Starr (Ithaca, 1957), 93-116.

________, 'Source-Marks in Bede Manuscripts', *Journal of Theological Studies* 34 (1933): 350-4.

M. L. W. Laistner and H. H. King, *A Hand-List of Bede Manuscripts* (Ithaca, 1943).

R. Landes, 'Lest the Millennium Be Fulfilled: Apocalyptic Expectations and the Pattern of Western Chronography 100-800 CE', in *The Use and Abuse of Eschatology in the Middle Ages*, ed. W. Verbeke, D. Verhelst, and A. Welkenhuysen (Leuven, 1988), 137-211.

M. Lapidge (ed.), *Archbishop Theodore: Commemorative Studies on his Life and Influence* (*Cambridge Studies in Anglo-Saxon England* 11; Cambridge, 1995).

J. Leclercq, *The Love of Learning and the Desire for God*, transl. C. Misrahi, 3rd. ed. (New York, 1982).

P. Lehmann, 'Wert und Echtheit einer Beda abgesprochenen Schrift', *Sitzungsberichte der Bayerischen Akademie der Wissenschaften* 4 (1919), 3-21.

R. E. Lerner, 'The Medieval Return to the Thousand-Year Sabbath', in Emmerson and McGinn (1992), 51-71.

________, 'Refreshment of the Saints: The Time after Antichrist as a Station for Earthly Progress in Medieval Thought', *Traditio* 32 (1976), 97-144.

W. Levison, *England and the Continent in the Eighth Century* (Oxford, 1946).

B. Leyerle, 'Landscape as Cartography in Early Christian Pilgrim Narratives', *Journal of the American Academy of Religion* 64 (1996): 119-38.

E. A. Lowe, *English Uncial* (London, 1960).

K. M. Lynch, 'The Venerable Bede's Knowledge of Greek', *Traditio* 39 (1983), 432-9.

P. K. McCarter, Jr., *I Samuel* (*The Anchor Bible* 8; Garden City, N.Y., 1980).

________, *II Samuel*. (*The Anchor Bible* 9; Garden City, N.Y., 1984).

W. D. McCready, 'Bede and the Isidorian Legacy', *Mediaeval Studies* 57 (1995), 41-73.

________, *Miracles and the Venerable Bede* (*Studies and Texts* 118; Toronto, 1994).

B. McGinn, *Antichrist: Two Thousand Years of the Human Fascination with Evil* (San Francisco, 1994).

R. Marsden, 'The Survival of Ceolfrith's *Tobit* in a Tenth-Century Insular Manuscript', *The Journal of Theological Studies* 45 (1994), 1-23.

________, *The Text of the Old Testament in Anglo-Saxon England* (Cambridge, 1995).

L. T. Martin, 'Bede as a Linguistic Scholar', *American Benedictine Review* 35 (1984), 204-17.

________, 'Introduction', in Bede, *Homilies on the Gospels*, transl. L. T. Martin and D. Hurst, 2 vols. (*Cistercian Studies Series* 110; Kalamazoo, 1991), 1: xi-xxiii.

E. A. Matter, 'The Apocalypse in Early Medieval Exegesis', in Emmerson and McGinn (1992), 38-50.

H. Mayr-Harting, *The Coming of Christianity to Anglo-Saxon England* (London, 1972; 2nd ed., 1977; 3rd ed., 1991).

________, 'The Venerable Bede, the Rule of St. Benedict, and Social Class', (Jarrow Lecture, 1976); reprinted in *Bede and His World* (1994).

D. Meehan, *Adamnan's 'De Locis Sanctis' (Scriptores Latini Hiberniae* 3; Dublin, 1958; reprinted 1983).

P. Meyvaert, 'Bede and the Church Paintings at Wearmouth-Jarrow', *Anglo-Saxon England* 8 (1979), 63-77; reprinted in his *Benedict, Gregory, Bede and Others* (London, 1977).

________, 'Bede, Cassiodorus, and the Codex Amiatinus', *Speculum* 71 (1996), 827-83.

________, 'Bede the Scholar', in Bonner (1976), 40-69.

________, 'The Date of Bede's *Thirty Questions on the Books of Kings* to Nothelm', in *The Limits of Ancient Christianity: Essays in Late Antique Thought and Culture in Honor of R. A. Markus*, ed. M. Vessey and W. Klingshirn (Ann Arbor, 1997).

C. Moore, 'Tobit, Book of', in *Anchor Bible Dictionary*, ed. D. N. Freedman (New York, 1992), 6: 585-94.

R. P. Multhauf, *Neptune's Gift: A History of Common Salt* (*Johns Hopkins Studies in the History of Technology*; Baltimore, 1978).

J. M. Myers, *I and II Esdras* (*The Anchor Bible* 42; Garden City, N.Y., 1974).

T. O'Loughlin, 'The Exegetical Purpose of Adomnán's *De Locis Sanctis*', *Cambridge Medieval Celtic Studies* 24 (1992), 37-53.

J. O'Reilly, 'Introduction', in *Bede: On the Temple*, transl. S. Connolly, (*TTH* 21; Liverpool, 1995), xvii-lv.

A. Palmer, S. Brock, and R. Hoyland, *The Seventh Century in the West-Syrian Chronicles* (*TTH* 15; Liverpool, 1993).

M. B. Parkes, *The Scriptorium of Wearmouth-Jarrow* (Jarrow Lecture, 1982); reprinted in *Bede and His World* (1994).

R. Pfeiffer, *History of Classical Scholarship from the Beginnings to the End of the Hellenistic Age* (Oxford, 1968).

C. Plummer, *Venerabilis Baedae opera historica*, 2 vols. (Oxford, 1896; reprinted 1946, 1956).

J. Quasten and A. di Berardino, *Patrology*, 4 vols. (Westminster, Md., 1983-6).

R. Ray, 'Bede, the Exegete, as Historian', in Bonner (1976), 125-40.

J. Richards, *Consul of God: The Life and Times of Gregory the Great* (London, 1980).

B. P. Robinson, 'The Venerable Bede as Exegete', *Downside Review* 388 (1994), 201-26.

H. Savon, 'L'antéchrist dans l'oeuvre de Grégoire le Grand', in *Grégoire le Grand*, ed. J. Fontaine, R. Gillet, and S. Pelistrandi (Paris, 1986), 389-405.

J. A. Scott, 'A Note on Herodotus i.66', *Classical Philology* 8 (1913), 481.

D. R. Seely, 'Zin, Wilderness of', in *Anchor Bible Dictionary*, ed. D. N. Freedman (New York, 1992), 6: 1095-6.

P. Siniscalco, 'Le età del mondo in Beda', *Romanobarbarica* 3 (1978), 297-332.

P. Verbraken, 'Le commentaire de St. Grégoire sur the premier livre des Rois', *Revue Bénédictine* 66 (1956), 159-217.

A. de Vogüé, 'L'auteur du Commentaire des Rois attribué à saint Grégoire: un moine de Cava?', *Revue Bénédictine* 106 (1996): 319-31.

B. Ward, *The Venerable Bede* (*Outstanding Christian Thinkers Series*; London, 1990).

________, 'Preface', in Bede, *Homilies on the Gospels*, transl. L. T. Martin and D. Hurst, 2 vols. (*Cistercian Studies Series* 110; Kalamazoo, 1991), 1: iii-ix.

D. Whitelock, *After Bede* (Jarrow Lecture, 1960); reprinted in *Bede and His World* (1994).

________, 'Bede and His Teachers and Friends', in Bonner (1976), 19-40.

A. Wilmart, 'La collection des 38 homélies latines de Saint Jean Chrysostome', *Journal of Theological Studies* 19 (1917-18), 305-27.

P. Wormald, 'Bede and Benedict Biscop', in Bonner (1976), 141-70.

G.E. Wright and F. V. Filson, *The Westminster Historical Atlas to the Bible*, (rev. ed.; Philadelphia, 1956).

INDEX OF BIBLICAL QUOTATIONS AND ALLUSIONS

INDEX OF PATRISTIC AND CLASSICAL SOURCES